Leadership
Team
Coaching

'Never doubt that a small group of thoughtful committed citizens could change the world. Indeed, it's the only thing that ever has.'
(Attributed to Margaret Mead; source unknown.)

'Not finance. Not Strategy. Not Technology. It is teamwork that remains the ultimate competitive advantage, both because it is so powerful and so rare.'
Patrick Lencioni (2002: vii)

'Teams outperform individuals acting alone or in large organizational groupings, especially when performance requires multiple skills, judgements and experiences.'
Katzenbach and Smith (1993b: 9)

Leadership Team Coaching

Developing collective transformational leadership

Peter Hawkins

KoganPage

LONDON   PHILADELPHIA   NEW DELHI

First published in Great Britain and the United States in 2011 by Kogan Page Limited.

Reprinted 2011 (twice)

Apart from any fair dealing for the purposes of research or private study, or criticism or review, as permitted under the Copyright, Designs and Patents Act 1988, this publication may only be reproduced, stored or transmitted, in any form or by any means, with the prior permission in writing of the publishers, or in the case of reprographic reproduction in accordance with the terms and licences issued by the CLA. Enquiries concerning reproduction outside these terms should be sent to the publishers at the undermentioned addresses:

120 Pentonville Road	1518 Walnut Street, Suite 1100	4737/23 Ansari Road
London N1 9JN	Philadelphia PA 19102	Daryaganj
United Kingdom	USA	New Delhi 110002
www.koganpage.com		India

© Peter Hawkins, 2011

The right of Peter Hawkins to be identified as the author of this work has been asserted by him in accordance with the Copyright, Designs and Patents Act 1988.

ISBN   978 0 7494 5883 6
E-ISBN   978 0 7494 5884 3

British Library Cataloguing-in-Publication Data

A CIP record for this book is available from the British Library.

Library of Congress Cataloging-in-Publication Data

Hawkins, Peter, 1950-
  Leadership team coaching : developing collective transformational leadership / Peter Hawkins.
      p. cm.
  Includes bibliographical references and index.
  ISBN 978-0-7494-5883-6 – ISBN 978-0-7494-5884-3 1. Teams in the workplace–Management. 2. Leadership. 3. Employees–Coaching of. 4. Executive coaching. I. Title.
  HD66.H3855 2011
  658.4'092–dc22

                                                    2010040544

Typeset by Saxon Graphics Ltd, Derby
Print production managed by Jellyfish
Printed and bound in the United States of America

To all those engaged in leading and coaching the teams who face the great challenges of our time.

CONTENTS

Preface xi
Acknowledgements xiii

Introduction 1

PART ONE High-performing teams 5

01 Why the world needs more high-performing leadership teams 7

The changing challenge for teams 9
Are leadership teams ready to respond? 14
The challenge to the leadership development and coaching industry 16
Conclusion 18

02 The high-performing team and the transformational leadership team 21

Introduction 21
Do you need to be a team? 22
Effective teams 24
High-performing teams 26
High-performing transformational leadership teams 27
Conclusion 31

03 The five disciplines of successful team practice 33

Introduction 33
The five disciplines 35
Connecting the disciplines 38
Conclusion 43

PART TWO   Team coaching 45

04   What is team coaching? 47

Introduction 47
History of team coaching 48
Limiting assumptions concerning team coaching 52
Defining team coaching 52
The extended team coaching continuum 61
The who of team coaching 61
Conclusion 63

05   The team coaching process 65

Introduction 65
The role of the team coach 66
The CID-CLEAR relationship process 67
The CLEAR way of structuring an individual event 81
The team leader as team coach 81
Conclusion 82

06   Coaching the five disciplines: systemic team coaching 83

Introduction 83
Discipline 1: Commissioning and re-commissioning 86
Discipline 2: Clarifying 87
Discipline 3: Co-creation 89
Discipline 4: Connecting 93
Discipline 5: The core learning 95
Coaching the interconnections between the disciplines 98
Conclusion 99

PART THREE Coaching different types of teams 101

07 **Many types of teams: coaching the virtual, dispersed, international, project and account team** 103

Introduction 103
Types of teams 103
Management teams 104
Project teams 106
Virtual teams 111
International teams 112
Client or customer account teams 116
Conclusion 120

08 **Coaching the board** 121

Introduction 121
The growing challenges for boards 122
Coaching the board 122
Clarifying the role of the board: Disciplines 1 and 2 124
The dynamics of the board: Discipline 3 132
Coaching the board on how it connects: Discipline 4 133
Coaching the board on how it learns and develops:
    Discipline 5 135
Conclusion 136

PART FOUR Selecting, developing and supervising team coaches 139

09 **How to find, select and work with a good team coach** 141

Introduction 142
An approach to finding, selecting and working effectively with a
    quality team coach 143
Conclusion 149

10   Developing as a team coach 151

Introduction 151
The transition 152
Stepping into the role – the necessary demeanour 154
The core capabilities 155
Team coach dilemmas 166
Conclusion 168

11   Supervising team coaching 169

Introduction 169
What is supervision? 170
Different contexts for supervising team coaching 171
The six-step team coaching supervision model 173
Reflections on the six-step supervision process 178
Conclusion 182

12   Team coaching methods, tools and techniques 183

Introduction and principles for using tools and methods 183
1. Psychometric instruments 184
2. Team appraisal questionnaires and instruments 189
3. Experiential methods for exploring team dynamics and functioning 196
Team culture review 202
When to use which tools and methods 203
Conclusion 203

13   Conclusion 207

Introduction 207
Who or what does team coaching serve? Overcoming the Parsifal trap 208
An agenda for moving forward 211

Glossary 213
Recommended reading 215
Resources for finding team coaches and team coach training 216
Bibliography 219
Index 225

PREFACE

> *At heart of effective team coaching is the generative relationship between the team and their coach, in which all members of the relationship should be constantly learning.*

T eam coaching, outside the world of sport, is a relatively new kid on the block. So recent, indeed, that a simple search through the websites of organizations offering team coaching services is bewildering in its lack of consensus. It seems that team coaching is being used to describe a wide variety of interventions that include facilitation, consultancy, team-building, and group counselling. Team coaching is presented in some cases as a process involving all the team at the same time; in others, as the sum of individual coaching of each of the members. The team leader is sometimes seen as an essential member of the team; sometimes as an external influencer. Of the various claims made for these interventions, perhaps the most signal common feature in the majority of cases is the lack of credible evidence.

Fortunately, we are now beginning to see the growth of two essential processes for bringing order to this chaos. One is the gradual emergence of empirical research – evidence-based studies that explore the practical dynamics of coaching interventions in a team setting. The second is the appearance of books, such as this, in which experienced team coaches define their role and present a theoretical underpinning for the team coaching process – which in turn can provide the fuel for future empirical research.

In *Leadership Team Coaching*, Peter Hawkins has distilled a great deal of practical wisdom. In particular, he has expanded the scope of team coaching to embrace a systemic perspective, which recognizes that the team's ability to implement change and radically improve performance is influenced as much by external as internal factors. He presents a series of robust yet simple models that enable both practitioners and corporate purchasers to address more coherently the two critical questions of:

- What should an effective team coach do?
- How do you tell if they are right for the needs of *this* team?

The book also provides a valuable perspective on supervision. It is a sad state of affairs that the majority of coaches do not have supervision; and that those who do, gain less from supervision than they should, because they lack insight into how to be supervised. The issue is even more serious, in the context of team coaching, because the potential to miss signs is so much greater, and the consequences of doing so are so much higher. The effective team coach is also 'systemically aware' – conscious that what happens in the room is only part of a much larger picture of interactions, allegiances, encouragements and discouragements, collaborations and conflicts between the team and other stakeholders.

In my observation, the role of the team coach varies greatly, according to the circumstances and needs of the individual team. Some of the most vital roles, however, include:

1 Helping the team discover its identity.

2 Helping the team clarify what it wants to achieve and why.

3 Helping the team come to terms with what it can't or shouldn't do, as well as understand its 'potential to achieve'.

4 Helping the team understand its critical processes. I am often shocked by how little insight top teams have into how they make decisions; or how they communicate collectively with others. Team coaches challenge this complacency and amateurishness and help the team develop more functional processes that sustain collective performance.

5 Helping the team access its suppressed creativity.

6 Helping the team develop collective resilience. Team coaches can help teams to improve how they manage their collective emotional well-being and learn how to moderate their responses to success and set-backs.

7 Helping the team monitor its own progress. Teams benefit from measuring not just task outputs, but learning and process quality – how the team works together – from the perspective of various stakeholders. Again, the team coach helps the team work out 'how do we know how we are doing?' Additionally, the team coach can help create processes that enable the team to be aware of and challenge its own myopia – the tendency to ignore or downgrade feedback that is too uncomfortable or which does not reinforce the team self-image.

Leadership Team Coaching addresses all these issues and will be an invaluable resource for both practitioners and users of this emergent discipline.

Professor David Clutterbuck
Joint Founder of the European Mentoring and Coaching Council (EMCC)
Visiting Professor in Coaching at the University of Sheffield Hallam and
the University of Oxford Brookes

ACKNOWLEDGEMENTS

This book is a product of a team and although it is my name on the cover I would like to thank all the other members of the team who have made it possible.

I would like first to thank all those who have coached, mentored and supervised me in my work as a team leader, team coach and team coach supervisor.

Much of the material on which this book is based has been developed over the last 30 years or more in work in and with teams and in the training courses I have been developing with Bath Consultancy Group and the Academy of Executive Coaching in Team Coaching and the courses in coaching supervision through Bath Consultancy Group in partnership with the Centre for Supervision and Team Development. I would like to thank all those I have coached, mentored, consulted to, supervised and trained. They have been my best and constant teachers in continuing to develop the craft, and continue to provide me with fresh challenges and challenging and encouraging feedback.

The thinking in this book builds crucially on the work pioneered and written with my colleagues at Bath Consultancy Group (**www.bathconsultancygroup.com**) over the last 25 years. My colleagues in BCG have brought great quality of challenge and support to our thinking, writing and practice in the team coaching craft. Especially I would like to thank those who have developed some of the thinking including John Bristow (particularly on the chapter on boards); Gil Schwenk (on supervision); Robin Coates, Nick Smith (for co-writing with me *Coaching, Mentoring, and Organizational Consultancy: Supervision and development,* and letting me draw liberally from it in this book); Chris Smith and Fiona Ellis (for their contributions to the team models and questionnaires and Fiona for her contribution on appreciative inquiry); and John Leary Joyce of the Academy of Executive Coaching, who has been a great colleague in devising together the first ever UK certificate programme in team coaching. They also commented on parts of the text, as did Marianne Tracy in New York and Kirsty Leishman of Lettoch Associates in Scotland, and Peter Binns in Brighton. Also thanks to my new colleagues at Henley Business School for furthering the exploration of collective leadership.

My dear friend Michaela von Britzke brought loving attention to making the book more readable.

Malcolm Parlett and Judy Ryde have been great friends and colleagues on writing weeks, and my other colleagues at the Western Academy (Peter Reason, John Crook and Peter Tatham) and Centre for Supervision and

Team Development (Robin Shohet and Joan Wilmot) continue to challenge, support and inspire me.

In preparing the text we have had enormous support from the administrative staff at Bath Consultancy Group, especially Fiona Benton.

Finally I would once more like to thank my wife and partner Judy Ryde for her love, patience, colleagueship, support and her many important contributions to the writing of this book.

Peter Hawkins
Professor of Leadership, Henley Business School
Emeritus Chairman, Bath Consultancy Group
Chairman, Renewal Associates

Introduction

This book is written for all those who are excited by the challenges of leading or coaching teams that can provide effective collective leadership. Never has this task been more urgent or more demanding. In Chapter 1 I will show how the world has moved beyond the time when the major challenges could be met by the great individual leader, or the complexities of transformation in companies could be solved by the heroic CEO. Human beings have created a world of such complexity, global interdependence, of continuous and fast moving change, that leadership is beyond the scope of the individual and requires more effective collective leadership and high performing teams.

Traditionally, leadership development has been about cognitively educating individuals through theories and case examples. Over the last 40 years there has been a move to much more experiential, real-time action learning, on the job facing real challenges, which has focused on affect as well as cognition. But the emphasis has still been on leader development, not collective leadership. The field of individual coaching has expanded exponentially over the last 30 years, with hundreds of new books, courses, accreditations, etc; but the field of coaching leadership teams has been relatively neglected.

The team development that has been carried out has often been time-limited pieces of facilitation, over-focused on the team members relating better to each other, or on team structure, selection and processes. There has been a lack of an integrated approach that brings together the best of coaching, consultancy and team development approaches, providing an extended relationship over time that helps the team work, relate and learn better together.

What limited research there has been on efforts to help teams (Clutterbuck, 2007; Wageman *et al*, 2008), shows that team-bonding and team-building exercises do not deliver sustainable and lasting improvement to team performance, but that a sustained coaching approach, whether delivered from within the team by the team leader or by an external coach, can create sustained performance improvement.

Teams need to know what high performance looks like in order to plan and commit to their own journey to raise their team performance. In Chapters 2 and 3 I outline the key elements of a high-performing team. In Chapter 3 I present the 'Five disciplines of team performance' which comprise:

1 *Commissioning* – being clear about the commissioning of the team.

2 *Clarifying* – the team clarifying and committing to their own mission, purpose, strategic aims, values, goals, roles and processes.

3 *Co-creating* – the team being more effective in how they collectively work together to co-create generative thinking and action, which is greater than the sum of their individual efforts.

4 *Connecting* – engaging with the staff the team leads, the customers and investors it serves, the suppliers, partners, regulators and local communities it relies upon to do its work. Leadership lies in the ability to transform relationships and inspire, motivate and align those wider parts of the system necessary to transform the contribution of the team.

5 *Core learning* – unless the team is learning and unlearning at a rate equal to or greater than the rate at which the environment is changing around it, it cannot thrive, so the last and central discipline is the team's commitment, not only to core learning but learning how to learn more effectively.

In Chapter 4 I outline and define the new craft of Team Coaching, which – although it has historical roots in the fields of organizational development, consulting, team facilitation, coaching and sports psychology – is distinct from all of these.

In Chapter 6 I illustrate ways of coaching each of these five disciplines and how they each require a different focus and skill set from the team coach or team leader. In Chapter 5 I show how the relationship between the coach and the team he or she is working with needs to develop through a number of key stages. I use the CID-CLEAR model to illustrate each of these stages.

In Chapters 7 and 8 the book broadens out from leadership teams to consider a variety of other sorts of teams:

- management;
- project – for which I supply a new stage model of development;
- virtual;
- international;
- customer or client account teams;
- the board.

The final section of the book begins in Chapter 9 with guidance for team leaders and those resourcing team coaching in their organizations, on finding, selecting, assessing and working with team coaches. Then there is a series of chapters focused on the training, development and supervision of team coaches:

- the key capabilities and capacities and how to develop them (Chapter 10);
- supervision approaches for supervising team coaching (Chapter 11);
- key additional models, tools and methods for team coaching (Chapter 12; others are scattered through the rest of the book and Table 12.2 on page 204 shows where they are located).

In the final chapter, I offer an agenda for the field of team coaching, and how it might develop to better meet the growing needs of teams and team leaders throughout the world.

PART ONE
High-performing Teams

Why the world needs more high-performing leadership teams

01

> *Never doubt that a small group of thoughtful committed citizens could change the world. Indeed, it's the only thing that ever has.*
>
> **(ATTRIBUTED TO MARGARET MEAD – SOURCE UNKNOWN)**

W hen Katsuaki Watanabe was asked by *Time Magazine*, 'Why is Toyota more profitable than America's Big Three carmakers combined and why has it been so much more successful?' he replied: 'In Toyota everybody works as a team. We even call our suppliers our partners, and we make things that everybody thinks we should make.' (**http://www.time.com/time/magazine/article/0,9171,1086192,00.**)

I was working with the senior executive team of a leading financial company. After an exploratory round of individual meetings, I was struck by how much of the views of the team were focused on what was wrong with their chief executive. I was aware that they had a number of chairmen and chief executives who had quite short tenures and there had been competition before the latest (internal) appointment. After my first few months of working alongside them in their meetings and facilitating a team off-site, I was still being lobbied in the corridor about the CEO's weaknesses. At the next meeting I said to the team: 'I am fed up with you all telling me what is wrong with your chief executive.' The chief executive who was sitting next to me, turned and looked at me with shock and anger, and the team members all looked down at their papers! I continued, somewhat in trepidation: 'I think you are all delegating leadership upwards, and playing the game of "waiting for the perfect chief executive". Well I have some bad news for you. In all my years working with a great variety of organizations, I have never met a perfect chief executive. So the question for you as senior team members is: "How are you as a team going to take responsibility for his weaknesses?"' The team coaching had begun.

The myth of the perfect CEO or perfect leader is prevalent in many companies, organizations, sports teams and indeed even in the politics of nations. We expect more and more from our leaders and invest such hope in their miraculous powers to turn things round, and then are quick to criticize and blame them when they do not live up to our unrealistic expectations. Warren Bennis, who has spent a lifetime studying leadership, writes:

> Our mythology refuses to catch up with us. And so we cling to the myth of the Lone Ranger, the romantic idea that great things are usually accomplished by a larger-than-life individual working alone. Despite evidence to the contrary – including the fact that Michelangelo worked with a group of 16 to paint the Sistine Chapel – we still tend to think of achievement in terms of the Great Man or the Great Woman, instead of the great Group.
>
> (Bennis, 1997)

Since Bennis wrote this, the challenges of the world have continued to grow exponentially in terms of complexity, interconnection, speed of change and the major threats now facing us as a species, and there is more to come. 'The next 30 years will be the most exciting time to be alive, in the whole history of human beings on this planet.' So said Tim Smit, the inspirational founder of the Lost Gardens of Heligan and the Eden Project, 'for in that period we will discover whether Homo is really Sapiens or whether we are going to join the fossil records of extinct species'. The ecologist Paul Hawken echoed these statements when he addressed the Class of 2009 at the University of Portland:

> Let's begin with the starting point. Class of 2009: you are going to have to figure out what it means to be a human being on earth at a time when every living system is declining, and the rate of decline is accelerating … Basically, civilization needs a new operating system, you are the programmers, and we need it within a few decades.

The challenge is greater now than it has ever been, for when we wake up in the morning and look in the mirror we see staring back at us one of the many endangered species on this planet.

The challenge would be great if we were just facing global warming or population explosion or technological interconnectedness or the exhaustion of accessible oil supplies or the extinction of species at a rate 1,000 times greater than ever before; but we are not. We are facing a world where all of these challenges and many more are happening in a systemically complex web of interconnecting forces, at an exponentially accelerating rate so that no expert can possibly understand the whole pattern, let alone know how to address it.

The challenge, so positively drawn by Tim Smit and Paul Hawken, cannot be addressed satisfactorily by individual expert scientists, or by teams of scientists drawn from the same discipline, not even by multidisciplinary teams of scientists drawn from the finest institutions in the world. It certainly cannot be solved by politicians, even with a greater level of cross border cooperation than has ever existed, nor by pressure groups focusing on one aspect of the complex pattern. The current world challenges task us as a species to find a way of working together, across disciplines and borders, beyond local and self interest in a way that has never been attained before. In working together we need to generate new ways of thinking, for as Einstein so memorably pointed out, you cannot solve a problem with the same thinking that created it.

While writing this book I became fascinated with listening to the UK Iraq Inquiry, which is setting out to discover what contributed to the UK's political decision to engage with the United States and other allies in a very costly war in terms of human lives, economic cost and creation of further conflict with many Islamic cultures. The testimony of cabinet ministers starts to give pointers to how, at a time when quality, critical, challenging dialogue was most needed, the pressures both within the cabinet and without were driving a dangerous 'groupthink'. Tony Blair had tried to avoid the failing of the later cabinets of Margaret Thatcher, one of his predecessors as British prime minister, by having different perspectives in his cabinet, which at the time of the Iraq war decisions included Robin Cook and Claire Short. However, when their challenging voice was most needed, they became isolated, and their contributions were marginalized and disparaged as a dangerous collective mindset developed. This episode contrasts with what we read of the cabinet of Abraham Lincoln at the time of the American Civil War. Historian Doris Kearns Goodwin (2005) refers to his 'political genius' in including in his cabinet his chief political rivals, people who would passionately and vocally disagree with his own arguments and beliefs, and encourage depth of critical debate. This is an approach that the current US President Obama is trying to emulate.

The changing challenge for teams

So how do these global challenges manifest in the world of leadership teams? Here are some of the key themes that are experienced by nearly all the leadership teams we have worked with or seen reported in the major research studies. These challenges are requiring all the members of leadership teams and those who coach and support them to raise their game.

1. *Managing expectations of all the different stakeholders*

A CEO of a successful financial company told me how everyone saw him as having enormous freedom, power and choice as CEO, but his experience was that he had less freedom, power and choice now than when he was a front-line team leader. He explained how his diary was fixed for him and driven by the corporate calendar; how he was constantly at the beck and call of regulators, board members, shareholders, key customers and partner organizations; and every division and function expected a personal visit at least once a year. There were more meetings he was expected to attend than hours in the day and at every meeting he was being lobbied from different perspectives and interest groups. He told me how he felt like the intersection of all the conflicting demands within and around the company.

I have spoken to permanent secretaries of government departments and CEOs of local government and health bodies who tell similar stories. It is no surprise that the average time most CEOs stay in post is becoming shorter and shorter.

Our expectations and demands on leaders are greater than ever before. In 2000 Hooper and Potter wrote:

> The key issue facing future leaders is unlocking the enormous human potential by winning people's emotional support ... our leaders of the future will have to be more competent, more articulate, more creative, more inspirational and more credible if they are going to win the hearts and minds of their followers.

Since then all the research on generation Y suggests that future generations will have even greater expectations and less automatic respect for titles and roles and will demand that leaders earn their respect.

2. *Leadership teams have to run and transform the business in parallel*

Team coaching can also focus on the senior team or board running their business, and not recognize fully enough that most senior teams, in parallel to running the business have to focus on transforming the business and its wider system. These two activities require different approaches from the team and hence different forms of team coaching. Philip Sadler (2002) in *Building Tomorrow's Company*, defined 'transformational leadership' as: 'The process of engaging the commitment of employees to radical change in the context of shared values and a shared vision.'

This, I would argue, is too narrow as it focuses on only one of the major stakeholder groups, namely the employees. I would suggest that 'transformational leadership' is the process of collectively engaging the commitment and participation of all major stakeholder groups to radical change in the context of shared endeavour, values and vision. The stakeholder groups at a minimum include employees, customers or service users, suppliers or partners, investors or voters, regulators, the communities in which the enterprise takes place and the natural environment.

This is not an activity that can be done by an individual or by a group of individuals acting in parallel. Often senior teams that are under pressure and being overloaded will allocate responsibility for each stakeholder group to an individual director or senior executive. The financial director or corporate affairs director will look after the investors; the HR director the employees; the sales director the customers; the compliance director the regulators, etc. This can lead to systemic and stakeholder conflict in the leadership team, between these various leaders, with a need to create integration through effective collective transformational leadership.

3. *Teams need to increase their capacity for working through systemic conflict*

This process of teams re-enacting stakeholder conflict is also prevalent in boards. One of the most important and difficult relationships in many organizations is the one between the chairman and the chief executive. Often this can become personalized or be seen as a power battle, when a stakeholder conflict that has not been articulated or worked through is played out with the chairman carrying the needs of the investors or regulators and the CEO carrying the needs of the employees or customers.

A senior team can have too much conflict to be effective, but it can also have too little. My proposition is that the level of conflict in a team should be no greater or no less than the conflict in the system they are leading and operating within. This being so, there is a need to help teams (and boards) expand their collective capacity to manage systemic conflict.

4. *Human beings learning to live with multiple memberships and belonging*

Another increasing challenge for team members is that the world is becoming more interconnected and organizations are becoming more matrixed. Rarely do senior leaders or managers now belong to just one team. A chief executive may be a member of the board, lead the senior executive team, and chair some of the subsidiary business boards, as well as sit on industry committees, joint ventures and working groups. This can be replicated throughout the senior levels of an organization. Yet psychologically most leaders and managers struggle with multiple membership and belonging. Sociologists and anthropologists tell us that as a species we have learnt how to create loyalty to our family group or tribe, which leads to wanting to protect it from other groupings that can easily be seen as a threat.

I remember as a very young manager being the leader of a key division of the organization I worked for, which meant I was automatically a member of the national management team. As soon as I was appointed, my team members in the division would ask, 'Whose side are you on? Are you part of our team or part of the central management?' I very quickly had to learn to say I am 100 per cent a committed member of both teams. However, saying it was one thing, being able to practise it was another, particularly when I would experience each team telling me, sometimes quite vehemently, what was wrong with the other team. Under this pressure it is very easy to fall into a representational delegate role, where rather than act as a full team member you are only there to represent the views of the other team you come from and only speak when their interests are threatened or need promoting. Then one returns to the other team to represent the views of the senior management. One becomes what Barry Oshry (1995) so neatly describes as a 'torn middle' – a postman, envoy or arbitrator between one team and another and belonging nowhere.

5. *The world is becoming more complex and interconnected*

A coaching colleague of mine recounted to me the story of a senior executive who spoke of how the only place he felt free was on long-haul flights, where he found he could think more widely about the bigger challenges facing his business and reflect in a less cluttered way on the dynamics of the system in which he was required to give leadership. The long-haul flight provided the sealed container in which he could acquire a helicopter view of what he was normally immersed within.

He returned several years later, in a state of being overwhelmed by all the issues that were constantly flooding his desk, his laptop and his consciousness. My colleague asked him how the long-haul flights were helping him get some perspective. He looked surprised: 'I have forgotten all about that blissful state,' he began, 'for now I carry the organizational entanglement with me. I continue to have the demands and dynamics of my business flow into my phone and e-mail, wherever I am travelling in the world, and the plane is the only time I catch up on the backlog of unread e-mails!'

We live in a world where it is harder and harder to escape or get the distance necessary to stand back, reflect and see the bigger picture, which is probably one of the major factors why more and more senior leaders turn to coaches who can provide some of that protected space and outsider perspective.

6. *The growth of virtual working*

Jessica Lipnack, who has spent many years studying virtual teams, reports that in the United States in 2006, 68 per cent of the workforce worked virtually and this would rise to 73 per cent by 2011. In Asia in 2006, 480 million people worked virtually and this would grow to 671 million by 2011. Human beings are having to rapidly develop to ways of working for which there is no blueprint. The working day is now 24/7 as the enterprise follows the sun, its activity moving to different parts of the globe as the day progresses. Team work is often electronic, rather than face-to-face – e-mail, telephone, video conferencing – all of which require not just new communication skills but also new ways of developing and sustaining trust. Throughout human history teams have relied on informal socializing, often involving colleagues, families and sharing of interests from beyond work, to both build and sustain trust between colleagues. How to replace this vital ingredient in the virtual team is still an open question.

7. *The major leadership challenges lie not in the parts but in the interconnections*

As we explored above, the challenges in the world are becoming more complex and involve greater interconnection. No longer do the main challenges in organizations lie in the people or in the parts but in the interfaces and relationships between people, teams, functions and different stakeholder needs. Yet we know far more about how to address issues in people, in teams, in functions and in stakeholder groups than between them. One coach said to me: 'I was trained as a coach to believe that my job was to help change what lay between the ears of my coaching client. Now I realize that I need to change what lies between the noses!'

Yet we know more about how to enable personal change than we do about how to enable change in relationships. What we do know about coaching relationships also tends to be in the domain of enabling dialogue or resolving conflict between individuals, or helping the team to relate better interpersonally. For effective team coaching there are at least four levels of relationships that have to be attended to, often simultaneously:

1 The relationship between the coach and the client team including how they relate to all the different individuals within the team and the team as an entity.

2 How the team members relate to each other.

3 How the team as a whole relates to and engages all its critical stakeholders that include the employees, the customers, the suppliers and partners, the investors and regulators and the communities in which it operates.

4 How the leadership team enables all these stakeholders to engage differently with their stakeholders. No longer is it sufficient for a company to be customer-focused; to make a valuable contribution they need to focus on their customer's customer – enabling their customers in turn to make a difference for their customers. The same

is paralleled in the focus on the staff's staff, the investor's investors, the supplier's suppliers and the regulator's constituency.

I remember being called in as a team coach by a sales team in an electronics company. They told me that their biggest problem was that they had been highly successful at reaching their sales targets, but were being let down by the production department, which was not keeping up with delivering the right products at the right quality and the right time. How frustrating, I felt, as I listened to them, and we worked on how they might be clearer in communicating their demands to the production people.

Only later did I talk to the colleague who was working with the production department, who told me that its biggest problem was the sales department. 'How come?' I asked, noticing I was already tightening up ready to defend my team! 'Because they are motivated by quarterly sales targets and bonuses and at the end of every quarter, work hard at selling to customers what they know my team cannot deliver. This means we get more disgruntled customers who are harder to sell too, which mean the sales department make even more unachievable promises!' The only way such cyclical patterns can be resolved is if those leading the departments act as a joined-up leadership team that thinks systemically and do not just represent the interests of their function.

In the public sector the challenges can be even greater, with many issues lying not in the jurisdiction of one organization, but having to be addressed across many participating organizational bodies. When working with a major government department I interviewed the relevant Secretary of State. He ended by saying that he thought that the inability to make enough progress in joined-up government had been the biggest failure of the UK Labour government through its three terms of office.

Are leadership teams ready to respond?

No single leader can any longer meet the demands placed on them and there is a growing recognition of the need for highly effective leadership teams.

Teams have so much more potential than individuals to rise to the growing, current and future challenges that face all organizations, countries and our species, and this is being increasingly recognized in many areas. Here are just a few instances that I quoted in an earlier book (Hawkins and Smith, 2006):

'We know that about a third of local government performance is attributable to the collective leadership capability of the local authority, both members and chief officers, but we have no way of assessing that capability' and 'We know how to assess individual leaders, but not collective leadership groups.'

(Member of the Audit commission)

'In the three companies where I have been a senior executive the biggest development challenge has been how to develop the top team, when people are constantly leaving and joining.'

(FTSE 100 chief executive)

'We have done a lot to develop individual leaders, but in many departments the top team functions at less than the sum of its parts.'

(Senior member of the civil service, Cabinet Office)

'The quality of the executive team is one of the three most important factors in a growing business being successful.'

(Venture capitalist)

But are leadership teams ready to respond? Peter Senge said: 'It is amazing how often you come across teams with an average intelligence of over 120, but the team functions at a collective intelligence of about 60' (personal communication).

James Surowiecki in his fascinating book *The Wisdom of Crowds* (2005) gives some examples of how individual experts are less accurate than the averaged scores of a diverse group. From numerous studies he concludes:

Ask a hundred people to answer a question or solve a problem, and the average answer will often be at least as good as the answer of the smartest member ... With most things the average is mediocrity. With decision-making, it's often excellence. You could say it's as if we've been programmed to be collectively smart. (p 11)

If you can assemble a diverse group of people who possess varying degrees of knowledge and insight, you are better off trusting it with major decisions rather than leaving them in the hands of one or two people, no matter how smart the people are. (p 31)

However, he also explores at length studies of 'groupthink' and social conformity and how teams can become foolish through consensus thinking. He wants to discover the conditions necessary for a team or crowd to be wise rather than foolish, and arrives at four basic conditions. There need to be:

1 *diversity of opinion* (each person should have some private information, even if it is an eccentric interpretation of the known facts);

2 *independence* (people's opinions are not determined by the opinions of those around them);

3 *decentralization* (people are able to specialize and draw upon local knowledge);

4 *aggregation* (some mechanism for turning private judgements into a collective decision).

We will explore how you can build processes that support these enabling conditions later in the book.

In Hawkins and Smith (2006) I looked at some of the prevailing conditions in leadership teams that drive the team to greater 'groupthink'. These included:

- Organizations and teams tend to recruit and promote people who are most like existing members, which increasingly diminishes diversity.

- Organizational culture, which we sometimes define as 'what you stop noticing when you have worked somewhere for three months', has as one of its functions to 'create social cohesion', but in so doing further lessens the amount of independence and diversity. Collective assumptions and beliefs develop and create limiting mindsets that constrain the thinking and creativity of the team.

- Teams are keen to bond and many team-building events are geared to increase the 'togetherness of the team'. Norms and unwritten rules develop about how to behave and what can be said and not said.

- Other teams have members who are very anxious to please the top leader since he or she is the person who will influence their bonus and future promotion. Fear of being judged, criticized, isolated or indeed removed from the team can make many team members hold back.

- Teams often arrive at decisions by collective discussion that – while building consensus – also develops 'groupthink', with no mechanism for aggregating independent and decentralized thinking. We have discovered in recruitment that if the panel initially discusses the candidate together, the group will quickly cohere around a dominant reaction. If, on the other hand, they score the candidate against set criteria in private and then tabulate the results, a much richer picture of the candidate emerges.

In this book I will explore how high-performing teams rise to the challenge of performing at more, rather than less, than the sum of their parts but will argue that they need the right sort of development, learning and support to do so and generally this has been missing.

The challenge to the leadership development and coaching industry

So if the world needs more highly effective leadership teams, and the challenges and hurdles they have to overcome are getting even greater, we need to explore what can be done to support the development of such teams, as well as their leaders and their team members.

Yet even here, I would contend, the tide has been flowing against the direction that is needed because so much of the literature and leadership training is based on seeing and developing leadership within individuals. The industry of leadership development, including coaching, which is a worldwide multi-billion dollar business, has failed to move fast enough to address the changing challenges and needs. For example, more money than ever before was spent in the UK by the Labour government of 1997–2010 and yet every capability review of government departments has highlighted the need for better collective leadership from the senior team.

Many people use the term 'leadership development' when what they are actually talking about is 'leader development'. Leadership does not reside in individuals, for leadership is always a relational phenomenon which at a minimum requires a leader, followers and a shared endeavour. Many leaders have IQs (intelligence quotients) many times greater than their EQs (emotional quotients) and are, by nature, overly individualistic and less skilled at collaboration. Many leadership development programmes take these leaders away from their current context and challenges and provide them with individual and cognitive based learning.

In a series of research projects into best practice in leadership development we found it was best when it was:

- *Real time* – based on the real challenges that were current for the leaders and which they had a hunger to resolve.
- *Behaviourally transformative* – not just leading to new insights and good intentions, but new actions and relating, live in the workshop, coaching session, etc.
- *Relational* – leaders learning together with colleagues, where attention is given not only to the individuals changing but also changing the relationships between them.
- *Involving real stakeholder perspectives* – including the challenges from employees, customers, partners, commissioners and regulators in live interaction.
- *Including unlearning* – addressing limiting assumptions, mindsets, habitual patterns that have been successful in the past and previous roles but need to be unlearnt for leadership to progress.

Coaching has been the fastest growing component of leadership development in the last 10 years. However, if we judge it against the aspects of the most effective leadership development quoted above, we find a lot of leadership coaching does not match up. Nearly all coaching is of individuals, focusing on the personal development of the leader.

In the wide experience we have had in training and supervising coaches and consulting to organizations on their coaching strategy (Hawkins, 2011), we have found that many individual coaches over-focus on the individual client and under-serve the organizational client.

The small percentage of coaching that has been focused on teams has also been constrained by its name, approach, methodology and assumptions. Literature and practice have often referred to team building, team facilitation, team away-days or process consulting. Team building implies a focus only on the beginning life of a team, whereas most senior teams are in constant change of both membership and focus. Team facilitation and process consulting imply a focus on process divorced from the task and performance of the team and how that is changing. Team away-days are only one of the ways of working alongside and with a team, and by themselves can generate a lot more insight and good intention than is sustained back in the midst of every-day demands. We will explore these various teamwork definitions in Chapter 4.

Even the team coaching that does focus not just on the process of the team but also its task and performance, tends to centre on the team relating to itself, with an implicit belief that a good team is one that has efficient meetings and where everyone gets on well together.

Many team coaches have focused on such activities as:

- the team understanding each other's Myers-Briggs personality types,
- exploring the Belbin team role preferences, and
- exercises for team bonding.

While these can all be useful activities, they keep the focus on the personal and interpersonal layers of the team, which is often where issues appear and are addressed, but not where the issues are rooted or can best be attended to.

As Barry Oshry (1995) so simply but powerfully puts it: 'the first law of Organizations is that Stuff Happens'. The second law is 95 per cent of what we experience as personal is not personal. Team coaching can further accentuate the tendency to over-focus on the personal and interpersonal and under-focus on the team raising its collective performance, both internally and externally. How to do this will be a major focus of this book.

Conclusion

A senior official from the United Nations quoted by Peter Senge and colleagues (Senge *et al*, 2005) said:

> I have dealt with many different problems around the world, and I have concluded that there is only one real problem: over the past hundred years, the power that technology has given us has grown beyond anyone's wildest imagination, but our wisdom has not. If the gap between our power and our wisdom is not redressed soon, I do not have much hope for our prospects.

For the human species to survive, and for Homo to become truly Sapiens, we are going to need to adapt and evolve our ways of being in the world and with each other, more dramatically than ever before. Our technical ingenuity has allowed us to:

- expand the human population from 1 billion in 1830 to well over 6 billion today and is predicted to reach 9 billion by 2050;
- devise modes of communication that connect us instantaneously with all parts of the globe;
- make more knowledge available at a click on our personal computers than was ever held in the largest libraries in the world;
- massively raise expectations of health, longevity, affluence, travel, lifestyle choices and diet; and
- create levels of complexity in the management, financing, ownership and regulation of organizations.

But as the quote above suggests, our wisdom has not kept pace and we look to leaders to show us how to manage the complexity we have collectively created. The challenges are beyond the individual leaders we continue to invest so much hope in and then blame for our disappointment.

Global companies have been major players in developing and spreading the benefits of the technological revolution and they need to be part of addressing the enormous challenges those benefits have brought in their wake and the growing 'technological ingenuity versus wisdom gap'. Indra Nooyi, President of PepsiCo, said at the Davos World Economic Forum in 2008: 'It is critically important that we use corporations as a productive player in addressing some of the big issues facing the world.'

But if corporations and organizations of all shapes and sizes, local and global, commercial and not-for-profit, are going to rise to the challenge of making a contribution, they will need to become the laboratories in which we discover new forms of collective leadership. The Chinese symbol for crisis combines danger and opportunity, and in my doctoral thesis on organizational learning I wrote: 'Crisis creates the heat in which new learning is forged' (Hawkins, 1986).

In the next two chapters I will show what has so far been discovered about collective leadership teams in the highly pressurized laboratories of top teams, before showing, in the following section, how team coaches can make a significant difference through their support and development of such teams. The final section will look at the skills and capacities that such team coaches need to develop, and what sort of development, supervision and coaching resources can support their efforts.

The high-performing team and the transformational leadership team

02

> *Not finance. Not Strategy. Not Technology. It is teamwork that remains the ultimate competitive advantage, both because it is so powerful and so rare.* **(PATRICK LENCIONI, 2002: VII)**

Teams outperform individuals acting alone or in large organizational groupings, especially when performance requires multiple skills, judgements and experiences. **(KATZENBACH AND SMITH, 1993B: 9)**

Introduction

In the previous chapter I showed how the world needs more high-performing teams and in this chapter we will explore what a high-performing team is. First we will look at the research on what makes for an effective team, then explore the common patterns that can hinder a team in being effective. After this we will look at the nature of collective transformational leadership and what a high-performing transformational leadership team is.

Do you need to be a team?

Although the world needs many more high-performing teams, they are not the panacea for all the problems of the world and they do need time and emotional investment, so it is important to begin by being clear whether you want and need such a team and are prepared to commit the investment it will require.

It is important to distinguish a real team from other sorts of working groups, to know when each is needed and for all members to have a shared clarity about the nature of the group one is in. I believe it is useful to distinguish teams from:

- *Consultative advisory groups* – where a leader has created a group drawn from either inside the organization or an external advisory board that he or she uses to inform and check out their decisions.

- *A reporting and information sharing group* – where divisional and functional heads report on what is happening in their part of the organization and share useful information with colleagues.

- *A decision-making body where the work is carried out by others* – this would include some boards and committees, but not all.

- *A task-focused work group* – where a group is brought together to deliver a specific task that requires separate activity and low degrees of interdependency.

In my early days as a team development consultant I would find myself with so-called teams who wanted to spend much of our time together debating whether they were a team or not. I rarely found that this led to any progress in their collective clarity or performance, so I explored with colleagues how I could better facilitate such situations, and I developed some useful inquiry questions:

A What can we do together that we cannot do apart?

B What do we need or want to achieve that requires us to be more than the sum of our parts?

C What is the nature of our interdependency?

If the answer to A was predominately, 'We are only there to advise the boss,' then they were clearly a consultative group. If the answer was to share information or make decisions, then I would help them look at how to be an effective information-sharing or decision-making group. Only if the group could identify real tasks that the team had to collectively achieve did I move on to helping them decide where they needed to be on the continuum between being a task-focused group and a high-performing team. At the task-focused end of the continuum is a group that needs to coordinate its varied activities for collective success, but most of the work is done independently. At the other end of the continuum is a team that, to be successful, needs high levels of interdependency and mutual accountability, where the team members are committed to and can represent the collective enterprise, not just their part of it.

Building on the work of other researchers in the field of teams (Katzenbach and Smith, 1993a; Wageman *et al*, 2008), we distinguish this continuum in Table 2.1, which represents the two ends of the spectrum. Team members can place their view of where their own team needs to be in order to be effective on a 1–5 scale between each of the items. Only if there is a collective average score of more than 4 would we believe that it is worth investing in becoming a high-performing team.

TABLE 2.1

Working Group	Score 1,2,3,4,5	Team
Strong clearly focused leadership		Shared leadership roles
Individual accountability		Individual and mutual accountability
The group's purpose is the same as the broader organizational mission		Team purposes are different from both the organizational mission and the sum of individual team member's objectives
Individual work products		Collective work products
Runs efficient agenda-based meetings		Creates generative dialogue, with open discussion and active problem solving
Measures its effectiveness indirectly by its influence on others (eg financial performance of the business)		Measures performance directly by assessing collective work products
Discusses, decides and delegates		Discusses, decides and does real work together
Members are only part of the group when they are together		Members are still part of the team when they are not together
The group is task focused		The team is task, process and learning focused

Effective teams

There has been much more research on effective teams in the last 50 years than there has on either leading teams or coaching them. Some of the early research was done in the field of organizational development by writers like Douglas McGregor (1960), Rensis Likert (1967) and Bill Dyer (1977) in the USA, and John Adair (1986) and Meredith Belbin (2004) in the UK. Some of the most influential research on effective teams was carried out by Katzenbach and Smith (1993b). They define a team as:

a small number of people with complementary skills who are committed to a common purpose, set of performance goals, and shared approach for which they hold themselves mutually accountable.

At Bath Consultancy Group we built on this work with our own research into effective teams and our work in developing systemic team coaching. Our research suggested that there were four major dimensions that needed to be added to the Katzenbach and Smith definition for a group to not only be a team but an effective team. These were:

1 The team's ability to have effective meetings and internal communication.
2 The team's ability to work individually and collectively in representing the team to all the team's major stakeholders in a way that successfully engages the stakeholders and has impact.
3 The team as a 'learning system' that can serve to increase the capacity and capability of each of its team members, as well as continually develop its own performance and collective capacity and capability.
4 The emotional work of the team. An effective team also acts as an emotional container that addresses and resolves conflict; aligns the work of all members; provides emotional support across the team; and increases morale and commitment.

So we have enlarged Katzenbach and Smith's definition to read:

a small number of people with complementary skills who are committed to a common purpose, set of performance goals and shared approach for which they hold themselves mutually accountable. The common approach needs to include ways of effectively meeting and communicating that raise morale and alignment, effectively engaging with all the team's key stakeholder groups and ways that individuals and the team can continually learn and develop.

Within this short definition are ten aspects of an effective team:

1 *a small number* – keep the team to a manageable size. There is not a definitive upper number, but there is a point when team members can no longer relate to every other member as an individual and start to

sub-group them, and where some team members become bystanders. This can start to happen once you get more than 10 members; some teams can function very effectively with up to 20 members, but this needs working at.

2 *with complementary skills* – recruit for difference. There is a human tendency to recruit people who are like oneself and for teams to become less diverse as they recruit more people with the same background, personality type or bias. Teams have to work consciously to recruit difference and they often need to be helped to make good use of the complementary skills. Complementary skills come in many forms and include: different technical and functional expertise, different team skills including problem solving and decision-making capabilities; and different interpersonal styles. (See also the section in Belbin, 2004, ch. 12, on team roles.)

3 *who are committed* – do not confuse commitment with 'agreement' or 'willing to go along with'. Commitment is active embodied engagement that cares about the collective endeavour.

4 *to a common purpose* – a team can only exist if it has a collective endeavour that cannot be achieved by the group of individuals acting separately. Yet very few teams can articulate their common purpose and joint endeavour in a clear and motivating way.

5 *set of performance goals* – regularly translate the common purpose into outcome performance goals that are specific, measurable and actionable. Without such outcome goals by which the team can measure itself the purpose can remain as a lofty aspiration supported only by good intent. These goals need to be more than the sum of the individual performance goals of the individual team members: they need to be goals that can only be achieved by the team working together.

6 *shared approach* – agree how you are going to best work together to fulfil the common purpose and achieve the performance goals. These need to include the principles, processes and protocols the team will adopt for its joint working and how they will monitor and review them.

7 *for which they hold themselves mutually accountable* – ensure that the responsibility for the team is not left just with the nominal team leader, but is collectively held and all team members are actively held accountable by all their colleagues.

8 *ways of effectively meeting and communicating that raise morale and alignment* – the team meetings not only align team activities through information sharing, discussion and making effective decisions, but the team acts as an emotional container and energy source, raising the morale and energy of the team members.

9 *effectively engaging with all the team's key stakeholder groups* – all members can represent the team in ways that engage the team's varied stakeholders and in a manner that transforms performance through others.

10 *continually learn and develop* – one of the key outputs from high-performing teams is that they provide individual learning and development to all team members as well as attending to increasing their own collective capacity.

High-performing teams

Katzenbach and Smith (1993b) developed their original work to look at how effective teams can develop into high-performing teams. Their model, in Figure 2.1, shows how for a work group to decide to become a team, they have to invest time and energy in making it happen and also be willing to see performance potentially dip as the group makes the transition into being a team.

They describe the journey from being a potential team, to a real team, to a high-performing team. A real team fulfils all the criteria outlined in their earlier definition quoted above. They defined a high-performing team as: 'a group that meets all the conditions of real teams and are also deeply committed to one another's personal growth and success' (1993b: 92). Their research went on to indicate that in addition to this commitment to each other's growth and success, high-performing teams had a number of distinguishing characteristics:

- Exceptional performance – 'outperform all reasonable expectations of the group, including those of the team members themselves' (p 107).
- High levels of enthusiasm and energy.
- Personal commitment that is willing to go the extra mile.
- Great stories of 'galvanizing events' – turning points in their history where they overcame the odds.
- More fun and humour than ordinary teams.

Finally, in their epilogue they simply define a high-performing team as: 'A small group of people so committed to something larger than themselves that they will not be denied' (p 259). This simple but powerful statement provides a provocative challenge to all those who want to lead or coach high-performing teams: how to help the team discover its compelling purpose which will engender the passion and commitment to fulfil it?

FIGURE 2.1 The team performance curve

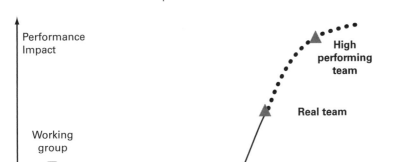

SOURCE Taken from page 84 of Katzenbach and Smith (1993b)

High-performing transformational leadership teams

There has been a great deal written about transformational leaders, but much less about transformational leadership. Tichy and Devanna (1986) give seven characteristics of the transformational leader:

1 They clearly see themselves as change agents.
2 They are courageous.
3 They believe in people.
4 They are driven by a strong set of values.
5 They are lifelong learners.
6 They can cope with complexity, uncertainty and ambiguity.
7 They are visionaries.

I would contend that the transformational leadership team needs all of these in both its members and in its collective ways of engaging, both internally and externally.

In 1993 Senge and Kofman wrote: 'Leadership is both deeply personal and inherently collective. At its essence it concerns the capacity of a human community to shape its destiny and in particular to bring forth new realities in line with peoples' deepest aspirations.' Thus the transformational leadership team needs to have effective meetings but does its most important work when it is out transforming its wider community of stakeholders and being transformed by that community.

Here I will explore the characteristics of a high-performing transformational leadership team by first looking at the extensive research carried out on such teams. In the next chapter I will present my own model of the five disciplines that such leadership teams need to constantly attend to, which later in this book will provide the foundation for looking at how team coaches can coach each of the five disciplines and the connections between them.

Some of the most useful research on highly effective leadership teams is that of Wageman *et al* (2008). Since 1998 they have studied 120 senior leadership teams from around the world, ranging from small businesses to large conglomerates, including high-profile companies such as IBM, Shell, Philips Electronics and Unilever. In reviewing this large sample they worked with 12 experienced top team consultants and coaches to rate the teams against three key criteria:

1 Whether the performance of the team met or exceeded the standards of the people both inside and outside the organization who were most affected by the team's work.

2 How well members worked together to enhance – rather than undermine – their capability to work together in the future. Did they build shared commitment collective skills and smart work strategies, become adept at detecting and correcting errors early and noticing and exploiting emerging opportunities?

3 Whether the group experience contributed positively to the learning and personal development of individual team members.

They found that 'teams that excel on all three of these dimensions are rare – but they exist. More common are leadership teams that fall short on at least one of these three criteria. Sadly some fail them all. Most common are teams that are modestly successful' (Wageman *et al*: 11).

After identifying the outstanding, mediocre and poor teams, they then explored what had led to these differences in outcomes. This was done through a mixture of in-depth interviews with CEOs and those they identified as being in their leadership team with the same people completing a written assessment of various aspects of the team's purpose, structure, composition, resources and coaching support. From this extensive work they developed a model of three essential and three enabling conditions that seem to foster leadership team effectiveness; see Figure 2.2.

From the research they concluded that, 'if it is not possible to establish the essential conditions for a senior leadership team it is better not to form one at all' (Wageman *et al*: 15) but if you want to have a high-performing leadership team you need to invest in the three enabling conditions. Now we look at each of their six conditions:

FIGURE 2.2 Six conditions for senior leadership team effectiveness

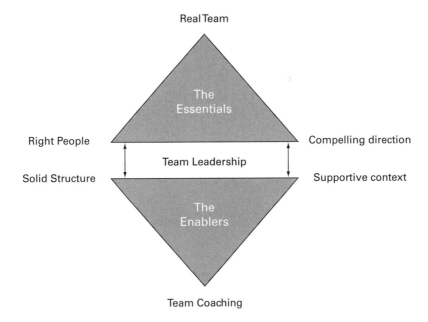

SOURCE (Wageman *et al*, 2008)

1. A real team

Their starting place is similar to Katzenbach and Smith's distinction between a team and a working group. For Wageman *et al*, a real leadership team requires:

- *interdependency* – this means it has collective work to do that requires members of the team to work together. They also stress: 'that sense of interdependence does not fade when the meeting ends. The leader and the members continue working together, seeking one another's advice and support and holding one another accountable' (p 51).
- *boundedness* – it needs to be clear who is in the team and who is not. Surprisingly Wageman and her fellow researchers found that only 7 per cent of their teams agreed when asked who was on their team (p 47).
- *a degree of stability* – 'Groups of people cannot become teams without stable membership for a reasonable period' (p 49). However, they also recognize that in today's world leadership teams and indeed their CEOs are constantly changing, so ways of managing the leadership team's inherent instability are critical.

2. A compelling direction

'The team's purpose is not merely the sum of the individual member's contributions, nor is it the purpose of the organization' (p 17) and they suggest that every leadership team should ask itself the question: 'What is the team for that no other entity in the organization could accomplish?'

3. The right people

In highly effective leadership teams the CEO does not just include all his or her direct reports, but selects team members who are committed to the compelling direction and contributing to a collective leadership team that takes enterprise-wide responsibility. They also need to have the right capabilities and capacities such as:

- the necessary skills and experience;
- an executive leader self-image;
- conceptual thinking;
- empathy and integrity;
- team players.

Selecting such people is only the first step: being clear with them about what is expected in terms of contribution and behaviour, and how their particular characteristics can best be used to take the team forward is essential, and then following through with regular feedback to all team members including the CEO.

4. A solid team structure

This includes being the right size (they recommend not more than eight or nine members); having a few clear team tasks that are strategic, mission critical and which cannot be delegated; clear norms and protocols about how the team should behave both in meetings and beyond; and a sense of collective responsibility.

5. A supportive organizational context

To be highly effective the team needs to have the information, education and material resources necessary to do its job, and a performance management and reward structure that recognizes joint accountability and team contribution above and beyond individual and divisional performance.

6. Competent team coaching

'The best teams are continually being coached' (p 20). Their research showed that all the CEOs of the companies studied had a strong external focus, but that the CEOs of the highest performing teams had an equally strong internal focus on the development of their team both collectively and individually. In the best teams coaching was not only done by the CEO but increasingly by peer members, and external coaches would be used to help take the team to the next level. Such teams have developed a coaching culture (see Hawkins, 2011).

Conclusion

The journey from being an effective team to being a high-performing transformational leadership team is challenging and demanding. A carefully selected and well supported team have far more chance of being successful in leading today's complex organizations than a heroic leader. We must beware of replacing the myth of the super-hero leader with the myth of the super-team that will do it all themselves and try and shoulder all our expectations and projections. A successful team needs to attend to practising the five key disciplines of transformational leadership, which we will explore in the next chapter. They also need constant learning and development and quality team coaching. We will explore quality team coaching in the next section of the book.

The five disciplines of successful team practice

03

" *If you could get all the people in an organization rowing in the same direction, you could dominate any industry, in any market, against any competition at any time.*

(A SUCCESSFUL BUSINESS FOUNDER QUOTED IN LENCIONI, 2002: VII)

Introduction

In Chapter 2 we explored what constitutes a team as opposed to various types of work groups, the key ingredients of an effective team, and the additional elements needed to be a high-performing leadership team.

You may be a team leader or a team member who is asking, 'How do I set about helping my team become high performing?' In this chapter I will present my own model of the five major disciplines that I have found are essential for a high-performing team. This model has been developed over the last 30 years of working with and in a wide variety of teams, but particularly leadership teams.

I began my life in teams, believing that if one recruited the right people, did some team building to ensure the team members understood each other, related well together and were motivated about the task, the team would perform well. As I became a team coach I found that this was a common assumption. I was brought in to facilitate team activities and team away-days, enable better feedback and understanding of each other's personality types and team role preferences, resolve team conflict, provide process consultancy and a great number of other team facilitation processes. But too often the focus was on the team dynamic, when the fundamentals of what the team had been set up to achieve, its purpose, goals and roles, were far from clear, so no end of team process facilitation would remove team conflict that originated from task confusion.

I also gradually came to realize that the performance of a team is not transformed just by the team relating well internally, for the team performance is fundamentally dependent on how the team collectively engages with all its stakeholders. Internal functioning is necessary but not sufficient for high performance and most teams were far too internally focused. This led me to experiment with helping teams to shift their focus from 'inside-out', starting with themselves and only then looking at their stakeholders; to focusing 'outside-in', starting with who the team is there to serve and what those people need and want from the team. Only then could we explore how the team needed to function differently to meet those ends.

In the 1990s my colleagues and I had the privilege of working with every team in a major international financial company as part of a significant culture change programme for the whole organization. Each team was target-driven and often saw their goal as out-performing the 'internal competition'. The organizational transformation had to shift the focus to outperforming the *external* competition by being the best in their sector, through every team being clear and focused on their key internal and external customers, investors, sponsors, senior leaders, and partners/ suppliers/support functions.

Every team started their journey by being asked to map their critical stakeholders. Then the team collectively prioritized them and arranged for team members, either individually or in pairs, to interview representatives of those with the highest priority. The team members brought their findings to an off-site team workshop ready to make a presentation. We explained that we wanted them to role-play the stakeholders they interviewed, while the rest of the team role-played themselves, inviting the stakeholder into a team meeting to give feedback. This role-played feedback provided much richer data than they had prepared in the notes they thought they were going to present.

At the end of the feedback session the team were expecting to thank the role-played stakeholder for their feedback before they left the room. But at this point we moved towards the surprise second part of the process. We asked the stakeholders while still in role to say what they would be saying in the corridor, supposedly out of earshot, about the meeting they had just taken part in. Then we asked the team playing themselves to do the same. This enactment provided second-order feedback on the dynamic relationship between the two parties. Those role-playing the stakeholders made comments such as:

- They were being polite but they are not really going to do anything about what we said.
- Did you notice how defensive they were?
- I felt they were coming from different places.
- That was a waste of time; they were not really listening.

The team role-playing themselves would catch some of what Argyris and Schön (1978) call 'defensive routines' with comments like:

- Well, they would say things like that.
- They clearly talked to a disgruntled client; I am sure that the others are not like that.
- We should note the name of that staff member. They are clearly a trouble maker.

Through this process the team would be able to collect the key messages from the feedback and the key dynamics they noticed in the interaction. Doing this for all the different stakeholders provides the team with a rich field of data to explore as well as a better understanding of what they need to do differently.

The five disciplines

To hold the dynamic interrelationships of a) internal and external focus, and b) the focus on task and on process, I first developed a four-box model that connected these two dimensions, which was used to help teams explore each of the four domains: external task, internal task, internal process and external process. Gradually I realized that high-performing teams also focused on the dynamic interconnections between the domains, and developed a collective capacity to 'helicopter up' and see the wider systemic picture that connected all four domains. This capacity was critical to their ability to constantly learn and develop to ever increasing levels of both functioning and performance, so at the heart of the model I added a fifth core domain; that of core learning (see Figure 3.1). As I used this model with a wide variety of leadership teams, I realized that each domain required a distinctive team discipline and I found teams that were strong in one or even two of the disciplines, but were unaware of, or were undeveloped in, the other disciplines.

1. Commissioning

For a team to be successful it needs a clear commission from those who bring it into being. This includes a clear purpose and defined success criteria by which the performance of the team will be assessed. Once there is a clear commission, the role of the board (in the case of a leadership team, or more senior management in the case of other teams) is to appoint the right team leader that they believe can deliver this mission. The team leader then has to select the right team members, who will have the right chemistry and diversity to work well together so the team will perform at more than the sum of their parts. Jim Collins (2001) describes this process as 'getting the right people on the bus'.

FIGURE 3.1 The five disciplines of high-performing teams

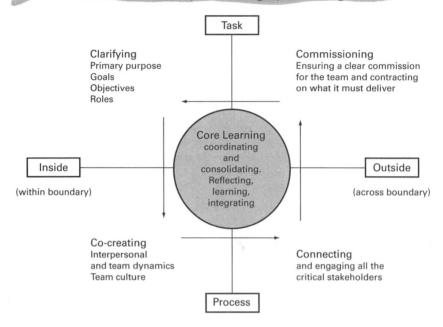

2. Clarifying

Having ascertained its commission from outside itself and assembled the team, one of the first tasks is for the new team to internally clarify and develop its own mission. As we will see below the process of creating this mission together leads to higher levels of ownership and clarity for the whole team. This mission includes the team's:

- purpose;
- strategic goals and objectives;
- core values;
- protocols and ways of working;
- roles and expectations;
- compelling vision for success.

3. Co-creating

Having a clear purpose, strategy, process and vision that everyone has signed up to is one thing; living it is a completely different challenge. If the mission is not going to just stay as a well-constructed group of words, but have a beneficial influence on performance, the team needs to constantly attend to how they creatively and generatively work together. This involves the team appreciatively noticing when they are functioning well at more than the sum of their parts and to also notice and interrupt their own negative patterns, self-limiting beliefs and assumptions.

4. Connecting

Being well commissioned, clear about what you are doing and co-creative in how you work together is necessary but not sufficient. The team only makes a difference through how they collectively and individually connect and engage with all their critical stakeholders. It is through how the team engage in new ways, to transform the stakeholder relationships that they drive improvement in their own and the organization's performance.

5. Core learning

This fifth discipline sits in the middle and above the other four, and is the place where the team stand back, reflect on their own performance and multiple processes and consolidate their learning ready for the next cycles of engagement. This discipline is also concerned with supporting and developing the performance and learning of every team member. Collective team learning and all the individual team member's learning go hand in hand and all high-performing teams have a high commitment to both processes.

The high-performing leadership team needs to be effective in all five of these disciplines. Although there is clearly an implied progression for moving through these disciplines, they are a continuous cycle. As the context in which the team work changes, the team and particularly its leader have to engage in *re-commissioning* with those that provide their legitimacy to operate. Politicians have to seek a new mandate from their electorate; leadership teams have to achieve backing from their board and shareholders for their next transformational change, etc. This then requires *re-clarifying* their internal mission as a team and *co-creating* new ways of working effectively together to deliver the new agenda, while *re-connecting* with their stakeholders who need to be aligned and brought into the change.

The model is cyclical rather than linear and requires internal flows that move it beyond the sequential. To illustrate this we can look at the four double-loop flows that make the connections between the domains dialogical and interactive (for more explanation of double-loop flow processes see Argyris and Schön (1974, 1978), Garratt (1987, 1995, 2003), and Hawkins (1991, 2004)).

Connecting the disciplines

Connecting disciplines 1 and 2: the commission – mission dialogue

Rarely does a leadership team receive a clear charter from their board or investors, or a government or local government organization receive a clear commission from the elected politicians from which they can clarify their own mission.

I remember the first time I was appointed a leader of a therapeutic community, which was the model training house for a large international mental health charity. I quickly learnt that the charismatic head of the organization was unable to answer my repeated questions about what she wanted from me, my team and the enterprise. She, like many entrepreneurially instinctive leaders, was very good at pointing out when things did not match her sense of what should be happening, but poor at being able to describe what good looked like in advance. I then discovered the process of what I later termed 'managing upwards by inviting red ink'. I would send the chief executive my draft of what I believed the commission to be and how I planned to carry it out, and ask her to correct what I had failed to understand or got wrong. Having received the red ink corrections, I would redraft and await the next wave of red ink. After the third cycle not only did we have a document that we could both sign up to, but a growing sense of two-way trust and clarity. In the 35 years since then I have watched numerous senior leadership teams in the public and private sectors go round in frustrated circles waiting for clarity from their board. 'Why don't they tell us or let us decide?' is often the anguished plea!

What is needed is a healthy iterative and dialogical process that involves the board or other commissioners in senior management doing their best to provide clarity on what success would look like across a variety of dimensions, including at least:

- financial performance – capital, revenue, cost and profit;
- output – in terms of products, services, etc;
- reputation – customer satisfaction, brand reputation, etc;
- innovation – new products and services and thought leadership;
- people – attraction, retention, development, morale and productivity;
- transforming the business and its place in the sector.

This should provide enough clarity for the chief executive to select the team that he or she is confident can lead the organization and engage with all the critical stakeholders on this journey.

The leadership team then needs to work back from this draft commission and create their own mission (purpose, strategy, core values, vision), that they all feel confident and committed to achieving. Katzenbach and Smith

(1993b: 52) stress how the process of working together to create the team mission is essential:

> a team's purpose is a joint creation that exists only because of the team's collaborative effort. As such, it inspires both pride and responsibility. The better teams often treat their purpose like an offspring in need of constant nurturing and care. Naturally they spend relatively more time in the beginning shaping their purpose; but even after the team is operative, the members periodically revisit the purpose to clarify its implications for action. They continue such 'purposing' activity indefinitely.

The leadership team then need to engage the board, by showing how their mission is responding to the board's commission, in a way that puts flesh on the given bones and takes it from aspiration to a road map for the journey.

At this point they may also have to work hard with the board to close the aspiration-realism gap, realizing not everything can be achieved and agreeing priorities within the objectives and what are necessary resources to be successful; jointly handling strategic tensions and the potential risks and opportunities along the way. Often this dialogue can be helped by asking questions such as: 'What are the top five ways our plans could be derailed or fail?' or, 'What might we discover in a year's time that we already know?'

Then comes the action cycle of trying to put the jointly agreed mission into practice and quickly learning what works, what doesn't work and what you had not anticipated in the initial strategic thinking. This takes us into the double-loop between domains 2 and 3, but also necessitates a next-stage dialogue back with the commissioning group, where there is joint review, reflection and upgrading of the commission and mission.

Connecting disciplines 2 and 3: the policy into practice dialogue

While aligning the commission and mission, the leadership team needs to align their aspirations and daily practice, what they have planned to do and how they are doing it, constantly closing the rift between rhetoric and reality. I once coached a leadership team to help them develop their mission, including their core values. They ended the workshop with a debate on whether they should have the core values framed on office walls, on people's laptops or printed on coffee mats. I interrupted this premature discussion, by saying, 'Wait: these are not the organization's core values, these are your draft aspirational values. You don't yet know if you can live them.' After further discussion they decided to have them stay in draft on the CEO's office wall and that at the end of each team meeting I would help them review the meeting to discover how far the decisions they made reflected these core values, and how they had lived them or not and how they had co-created together. A month later the core values were redrafted, having been informed by experience.

The double-loop between policy and action is also at the heart of the continuous strategizing process that is central to the work of the leadership team.

Connecting disciplines 3 and 4: co-creating with the stakeholders

A university executive leadership team had done excellent work, developing their commission jointly with their council and senate, clarifying their mission together and turning it into new ways the twelve team members were co-creating leadership both in team meetings and outside. They were shocked and disappointed when their staff survey showed that many senior academics and executives right across the university spectrum had neither understood the strategy or bought into it, let alone being aligned to it and implementing it. They busily set about exploring how they could communicate and sell the strategy more. 'Right now, more communication will just make matters worse,' I challenged. 'If the staff do not own the problem or challenge, they are not going to own the solution. How can you communicate less and engage them more?'

The need for teams to be increasingly operating in dynamic dialogue within their social environmental context, rather than acting in isolation, was stressed in Chapter 1. It was also emphasized that this relationship must not be just one of responding to changes in their stakeholder community, but of partnering their stakeholders to change their social environmental context.

A high-performing leadership team can only go so far in co-creating together as a team before they need to co-create across their boundary with their stakeholders. As shown in the story above, many under-performing leadership teams fall into the trap of doing great creative work together: investigating the issues, exploring options and deciding ways forward; and then the team members are sent out individually to sell the solution to their respective stakeholder communities. Resistance inevitably arises. High-performing teams create multiple double-loops of engagement across these domains:

1 In the first cycle they listen to the needs and aspirations of their stakeholders, and inquire into the needs and aspirations of their stakeholder's stakeholders (their staff's staff; their customer's customers; their investor's investors, etc).

2 These are shared back with the team and how to align the needs of these various groups with the needs and aspirations of the team is explored. For the team to be successful, their stakeholders need to be successful.

3 The team members then engage the stakeholders with a joint exploration of how a win-win-win relationship can be created that will benefit the team, the stakeholder and the stakeholder's stakeholder, as well as the joint endeavour in which they all operate.

4 This is then brought back to the team, who connect the various emerging stakeholder engagements to further inform their next stage of co-creating the way forward and how they need to operate as a team.

It is important that in operating this double-loop there is careful attention paid to the dynamics that operate at the boundary or interface between the team and each of its stakeholders. In Chapter 5 I show ways that team coaches can attend to these dynamics.

Connecting disciplines 4 and 1: the stakeholder – commissioner's dialogue

A leadership team in the strategic health sector faced an interesting dilemma. They annually reviewed the performance of each of the provider organizations they had contracted to deliver services to the people living in their geographic area. Some contractors they praised and renewed, some they made demands on improvement and some contracts they put out to new tenders. They now realized that each year they needed to upgrade the criteria against which they were judging the providers as patient needs, demographics, health innovations and good professional practices were all constantly changing. The challenge was that the people who were regularly close to these environmental changes were the suppliers who would have to be judged by the improved criteria. With their providers they co-developed an annual cycle of regular 'green meetings' when they were working together to inform and upgrade the strategic framework, and 'purple meetings' when the purchasers had to be firmly in their governance role applying the criteria to examine the providers who had helped create the criteria.

The domains do not operate as a cascade change process, which stops with the stakeholder's stakeholders, but the connections need to be made between the wide environmental context and those responsible for the commissioning. Good boards have their non-executives meet directly with customers, investors and partners, to inquire and learn what needs to change or be improved. Other leadership teams create large system events where representatives of all parts of the system can come together to learn from each other and see the bigger systemic picture and co-strategize together. This form of activity includes the links between disciplines 4–1, but moves beyond them to discipline 5 to which we now turn.

The discipline of core learning connecting to all the other disciplines

This discipline is a higher level function to reflect on the other four disciplines. The high-performing leadership team take time out from operating in any of the other four domains, to take stock, reflect on the patterns within and between disciplines and learn more about both their own team functioning within and across the boundaries of their own team and their social environmental context. This process is most often done at an 'away-day' off site to provide the clear space in which the team can stand back, helicopter up, and look anew.

At such an event the team can focus on deeper questions about the culture of the team and the wider system. Questions such as: 'What patterns of behaviour, emotional engagements, assumptions, beliefs and mindsets are helpful and which are getting in the way of us, as a team, to more successfully serve our stakeholders and thus achieve success?' Core learning events, like the ones in the financial company mentioned earlier in the chapter, need to avoid being submerged in internal debate and be infused with the voices from the other domains, focusing outside-in, hearing how the team are being experienced by their stakeholders, what is happening in the operational life outside of meetings, how they are being viewed by their commissioners, etc.

Core learning disciplines are not just for special occasions and away-days, but need to be an essential aspect of all team meetings. Here are a number of creative ways we have discovered teams use to build core learning into their work:

- One leadership team always had three spare seats at the team table: one for the customer voice, one for the staff and one for the investor. At any time any team member could vacate their own position and go and speak as one of the critical stakeholders. At other times the CEO would invite team members to occupy one of the chairs.
- Another leadership team would start their meeting by the CEO asking to hear from the other domains:
  - Let us hear what our customers, suppliers and staff have been saying this month (4)
  - Let us hear the reports on what each of us has achieved since we last met (3)
  - Let us hear what the board is both delighted and concerned about (1)
  - Let us reconnect with our mission and the targets we set ourselves: how are we doing against our own expectations? (2)
- A large global account team in a professional services company would end its meeting by the client service partner, who led the team, asking: 'What new organizational insight and learning have we

generated about this client that could be of value to them? And what new business foresight have we discovered that could be useful for other clients in this sector?' This had to be learning that was freshly created and not known to any individual before the team had come together (4).

- In a number of leadership teams we have introduced the 'Half-time team talk' – when the team stop half-way through their meeting and each share: 'one thing I have found helpful in the first half of this meeting is ... One thing I would like different in the second half is ...'. There is no discussion as this can easily become like a post-mortem debate, but the team listening to how their co-creative dynamic is happening live in the meeting shifts both awareness and behaviour in the second half of the meeting (3).

Conclusion

Many of us spend a high proportion of our business life working in teams and much of that time in team meetings. I look back on:

- The hours spent in one team bemoaning the fact that we were too internally focused and having internal debates about why this was and what we should do about it!
- The team where everything became personalized and important discussions about the purpose and objectives of the team became ego battles.
- The team that spent all their energy trying to outwit their board and prove that the board's commission was misguided and their own mission was far more relevant.
- The team that constantly blamed their customers, partners and staff.
- The team that had very efficient meetings with high levels of agreement, but there was no commitment or follow-through once people had left the room.

I can see how each of these teams were submerged in one domain of the five disciplines map, or had slipped down the crack between the domains; how we could have done with the five disciplines map as a lifeline to help us emerge from being drowned in the dynamic and see the bigger picture.

I have also had the joy of spending time in and with teams where:

- We knew exactly what was required from us.
- We had a passion about our collective purpose, which we knew we could only achieve if we were all working at our best individually and together.

- We looked forward to meeting and there was a keen interest in each other's successes, setbacks and learning.
- There was a real sense of partnership, not just between the team members but with the board and stakeholders.
- Work was an adventure and a classroom, every setback an opportunity for new learning and every challenge a spur to creativity.

These experiences did not just occur by happenstance, or because we had colleagues we liked, but because the five disciplines were in place and also, importantly, they were in balance.

PART TWO
Team Coaching

What is team coaching?

04

A surprising finding from our research is that teams do not improve markedly even if all their members receive individual coaching to develop their personal capabilities. Individual coaching can indeed help executives become better leaders in their own right, but the team does not necessarily improve. Team development is not an additive function of individuals becoming more effective team players, but rather an entirely different capability. **(WAGEMAN ET AL, 2008: 161)**

Introduction

We have seen an exponential growth in the last 20 years of individual coaching, in the percentage of organizations using coaching, the number of practising coaches, the growth in training, accreditation, professional bodies, research and publications. Team coaching is currently about 20 years behind, with many of the same difficulties that existed in the early days of individual coaching still being prevalent. These include:

- confusion for clients over what people are offering when they provide team coaching;
- a plethora of terms and no standard definitions;
- little in the way of research, literature, models or approaches;
- a lack of established training programmes or accreditation.

In the same way that individual coaching developed from a number of different fields and professions, the same is true for team coaching. The difference is that in the world of team coaching much of what has been done to date has been called 'team development' and done within the field of organizational development. Only recently has team coaching emerged from a new synthesis of three key strands:

1 traditional consultancy approaches to team development;

2 the newer world of coaching; and

3 the learning from the fields of working with high-performing sports and professional teams.

In this chapter I will explore these three antecedent streams and then look at the various current definitions and forms of practice, and how the early pioneers have started to define team coaching. I will then propose that the field needs to build on these foundations, while expanding the scope and focus of team coaching to focus on the collective team in their systemic context.

History of team coaching

Organizational development had its early sources in the work of Lewin and the National Training Laboratories in the United States, and the work of the Tavistock in the UK. Much of the early work was carried out by sending senior executives on programmes where they would be in 'T' or training groups (NTL), Bion Study groups (Tavistock), or syndicate groups (Henley Management College), where they would learn experientially about the nature of group functioning and dynamics. This work was then developed by such writers and practitioners as Schein (1969, 2003), Burke (2002), Beckhard and Harris (1977) and Argyris and Schön (1978). As part of the growth of organizational development much work was done on looking at ways of developing teams within organizations. This led to approaches and methods for team building, team away-days and other team development activities: Douglas McGregor (1960), Rensis Likert (1967) and Bill Dyer (1977) in the United States, and John Adair (1986) and Meredith Belbin (2004) in the United Kingdom.

Bill Dyer (1977: 23) wrote about this move from 'T' groups to team development:

> As practitioners developed more experience in applying T-group methods to work units, the T-group mode shifted to take into account the differences of the new setting. It became clear that the need was not just to let people get feedback, but to help the work unit develop into a more effective, collaborative, problem-solving unit with work to get out and goals to achieve. Slowly the methodology shifted from the unstructured T-group to a more focused, defined process of training a group of interdependent people in collaborative and problem-solving procedures.

I believe we are now in the midst of a similar transition from team development that traditionally focused mainly on the internal performance and process of the team (Disciplines 2 and 3), to systemic team coaching that focuses on all five disciplines, throughout all the life stages of the team.

In the interim period between when team development was being developed and now, there have been a number of significant developments in the wider field of organizational development that have also fed into the development of team coaching. One of the most important is organizational learning (Senge, 1990, Hawkins, 1986, 1991, 1994, Pedler, Boydell and Burgoyne, 1991). We have seen a revolutionary change in ways organizations think about and practise management and leadership development. Fifty years ago the majority of leadership and management training were:

- classroom-based, away from work;
- attended by individuals;
- taught by experts;
- based on theories and case studies of past successes and failures;
- cognitively oriented.

Now it is recognized that leaders and managers learn their most important lessons on the job, facing real challenges, working with others both in teams and across boundaries, through trial and error; that effective leadership and management development needs to be:

- about cognition and affect;
- experiential and embodied;
- addressing real challenges that matter;
- collectively learning with colleagues, so the relationship develops as well as the individuals;
- through cycles of action learning (action, reflection, new thinking, planning and rehearsing and new action).

However, experience does not always provide effective learning. Most of us can go on repeating the same ineffective behaviours and somehow hope we will get a different result! To turn experience into learning requires skills in being a reflective practitioner and ways of harvesting learning, and it is rare for people to be able to do this by themselves.

One major professional services firm has a global policy that development should comprise:

- 70 per cent learning on the job;
- 10 per cent learning from workshops, conferences and courses;
- 20 per cent coaching that provides the essential glue that joins the theoretical learning and the practical learning together.

Coaching is a more recent phenomenon than team development, with its early developments in the 1970s emerging from the fields of management learning, psychology and sports coaching, but growing rapidly in the last years of the 20th century and early years of the 21st. Coaching has, to date, mainly focused on individual development in one-to-one relationships, and only recently has there been a growing interest in how to coach whole teams. However, many of the coaches of senior leaders have found that a good deal of the coaching agenda is focused on how to lead, develop and coach their team, and many individual coaches have been invited by such leaders to come and facilitate team coaching sessions.

Sports team coaching has brought about a focus on how a team can play at more than the sum of its parts, building on each person playing at their best but in a way that enhances the whole, and how a team can constantly maintain and at times restore its morale and continually raise its collective performance. It has provided approaches that visualize success, build on positives, use 'inner-game' approaches to liberate innate ability, how to rehearse collective moves, and reflect and give feedback on performances. One of the big influences on individual coaching were Timothy Gallwey's 'inner game' books (Gallwey, 1974, 1976, 1981, 1985; Gallwey and Kriegel, 1977) and they were major influences on exponents of executive coaching such as John Whitmore (2002) and Myles Downey (2003). My colleague Jonathan Zneimer, who is a Partner at Lane4, an organization that coaches both business and sports teams, writes:

> the last 30 years has seen the development of niche consultancies of sport psychologists and elite athletes who have transitioned into business consultancy. The Sporting Bodymind, set up by two psychosynthesis trained psychologists John Syer and Chris Connolly, in 1979 were perhaps the first in Europe to be employed by professional sports teams such as Tottenham Hotspur whilst consulting to blue chip organizations such as Ford Motor cars. More recently there are examples of world class athlete-led organizations such as Lane4 founded in 1995, whose MD Adrian Moorhouse, himself an Olympic gold medallist, in partnership with sport psychologist Graham Jones set about creating 'learning and lessons from high-performing environments'. Familiar names such as Coca-Cola, Nestlé and Orange have benefited from these lessons and the inspirational/aspirational model of individual and collective performance presented through the sport performance metaphor.

Weinberg and McDermott (2002) set about investigating what key aspects linked high performance in organizational and in sports teams. Interviewing ten sportspeople and ten business leaders on leadership, group cohesion and communication they discovered a level of alignment. The leaders from both organizational and sports settings agreed that an interactional style of leadership is best, but they leaned toward a more democratic style if possible. Team cohesion was commonly achieved by creating a shared vision according to both sets of leaders. Managers can learn from these aspects by revisiting the organization's vision in a democratic way – let the team refine the vision.

There is evidence that sports people, especially in team sports, are empowered to make decisions in an instant – who to pass to, what move to make. Managers can foster creativity by pushing decisions as 'far down the line' as possible, so front line people can respond quickly within the game plan. The classic example of this might be cited as 'total football' – associated with the brilliance of the Dutch national team of the 1970s and more particularly Ajax football club – invented by Rinus Michels, who managed both teams, it may well be the most appropriate aspirational team metaphor for the complete organization. Here the team players' roles are interchangeable and fluid. The creator of the goal is as valued as the goal scorer and for that matter the expectation set by the 'total' concept is that each and every player should be able to perform each role to more or less the same quality and effect. The idea of 'total business' is intriguing!

The dynamics of organizational and business teams parallel those of the sports team by demonstrating that the right people need to be in the right jobs at the right time. Imagine the unreasonable proposition of a goalkeeper attempting to play centre forward let alone be expected to become an out and out scorer of goals or a prop forward in rugby to convert to being a speeding winger. Similarly, one wouldn't expect a CFO to be able to fully 'play' the role of the marketing director. Indeed, the parallel might be enhanced further when considering interacting sports teams versus co-acting ones. A rugby, football or basketball team is considered interactive as the players' roles are diverse but require a high level of interdependence to optimize their collective performance. Equally, the nature of a cricket, baseball or indeed a golf team requires the team members to be co-active. Here the individuals often perform the same or mostly the same set of skills and it is the sum of the individual member's performance that determines the team's success. It beggars the questions to teams at work and leaders of those teams, 'what sort of team are you?', 'what sort of team do you want to become?' and 'what sort of team will best serve ourselves, our stakeholders and our customers?'

(Zneimer, 2010, personal communication)

Much of the growing interest in team coaching has come from a realization of the limits of what can be achieved through individual coaching and leadership development, which can help create strong individual leaders but unaligned, poorly functioning leadership teams. In our work across many different sectors (Hawkins and Smith, 2006), we discovered a frustration with the lack of collective leadership emerging from top teams and a growing desire for effective development of the leadership team.

These trends have led to a marked increase in the number of organizations arranging for team coaching for their senior leadership teams. These have taken a number of very diverse forms:

- a mixture of individual coaching of each team member with some sessions for the collective team;
- a series of away-day events for the leadership team;

- the team coach acting as a process consultant for some or all of the team's regular meetings;
- a mixture of the above.

Limiting assumptions concerning team coaching

The confusion has also been rooted in a number of ingrained limiting assumptions about teams and team coaching. In Hawkins and Smith (2006) we argued that one of the reasons we felt that team coaching had not received its due attention or really developed as strongly as individual coaching, up to the present, was that there are unhelpful assumptions held about the way to work with teams. Table 4.1 represents a provocation to colleagues as to the limiting mindsets we had encountered, both in team members and in many team coaches, which we considered needed an effective response for the field to develop and mature.

These limiting assumptions have flourished in the relative vacuum caused by the lack of good theoretical development of executive team coaching and, prior to 2010, no recognized training distinct from that for individual coaches, OD practitioners or sports coaches. To date those practising as team coaches have tended to be people who have had training in one or more fields and have found their own way to combine the approaches. This has led to confusion in what both buyers and suppliers mean by team coaching and a wide disparity in what is practised.

Defining team coaching

It is essential that as team coaching grows we clarify the terminology being used and assist buyers in being clear what they need and what is available. In Chapter 9 I will address the buyers and users of team coaches and discuss when to use an external coach and when to do the coaching from within the team, as well as how to find, select and work with team coaches. In this section I will clarify the differences between a number of different offerings, all of which can be seen as having their role to play as part of team coaching. These are:

1. group coaching of team members;
2. team development;
3. team building;
4. team facilitation;
5. process consultancy;

TABLE 4.1

Limiting Mindsets	Response
Team coaching only needs to happen when the team first forms	The best teams engage in lifelong learning and development
Team coaching only needs to happen when things are getting difficult	If the first time you address relationship issues is in the divorce court you have left it too late!
The performance of the team is the sum total of the team members' performance	A team can perform at more than the sum of its parts or less than the sum of its parts. It is important to focus on the team added-value
Team coaching is about helping the team members relate better to each other	Team coaching is also about how the team relates to all its stakeholders and is aligned to the wider organization's mission
Team coaching is about the team having better meetings	Team performance happens when the team, or sub-parts of it, engage with their collective task and the team's stakeholders. The team meeting by itself is the training ground, not the match
Team coaching only happens off-site in away-days	Team coaching can be assisted by off-site away-days but the core development happens in the heat of working together and with their stakeholders
Team coaching is about helping the team members trust each other	Absolute trust between human beings is an unrealizable goal, particularly in work teams. A more useful goal is the team members trusting each other enough to disclose their mistrust
Team coaching is successful if it helps create a team with no conflict	Too much or too little conflict is unhelpful in a team. Great teams can creatively work through the conflicting needs in their wider system
One can only coach teams who work together at the same tasks	A team is defined by having a shared enterprise that cannot be done by the members working out of connection with each other
Team coaching is an end in itself	Team coaching is only valuable when it is linked to improving the team's business performance and their contribution to the performance of the wider organization or system they serve

6 team coaching;
7 leadership team coaching;
8 transformational leadership team coaching;
9 systemic team coaching.

1. Group coaching of team members and action learning sets

There has been a great deal of confusion, both in the literature and in practice between team coaching and group coaching. Group coaching is the coaching of individuals within a group context, where the group members take turns to be the focal client, while the other group members become part of the coaching resource to that individual. Action learning sets are similar to group coaching with members of a set, often between four and seven in number, taking it in turn to bring current challenges they are facing, to be coached on by the other members of the set and, where present, the set facilitator. In group coaching often there is more of an emphasis on the individual; and in action learning sets, more of a focus on the challenge being presented, but this is not always the case and in both instances the focus is on supporting individuals in being the best they can be in meeting their work challenges.

Group coaching can also be carried out in the context of a team, where the individuals being coached are all members of the same team. Kets de Vries (2006, ch. 11) provides an excellent case example of using group coaching with an intact leadership team. This is further discussed in Chapter 12 of this book. Although group coaching in a team context can be a useful prelude or component of team coaching, it is fundamentally different from team coaching, for in team coaching the primary client is the whole team, rather than the individual team members.

2. Team development

Team development is any process carried out by a team, with or without assistance from outside, to develop its capability and capacity to work well together on its joint task. There have been many studies and models on how teams can mature over their time of working together. Most of the theories and our own experience would suggest that teams most often progress through a number of discernable phases. These should not be seen as predetermined or inevitable. Most often groups start by dealing with their own boundaries, membership and the group rules and expectations. Schutz (1973) calls this 'inclusion'; Tuckman (1965) 'the stages of forming and norming'. This is often addressed in the contracting stage in team development, where issues of confidentiality, commitment to the team development process, how the process will be undertaken and what will be focused on and what will be excluded need to be decided and clarified.

Soon after this period of clarifying the basic structure of formal processes of the team, the team will go through a stage of adjusting to each other and the new collective way of working, forming implicit norms and unwritten rules. This is the 'norming' stage and can often be followed by a period of testing out power and authority within the team. This can take the form of rivalry: 'Who does the best work?', 'Who most cares about the outcomes?', 'Who has the most challenges?', 'Who makes the most penetrating insightful comments?' It may also take the form of testing out the authority of the leader by challenging their approach. This is called the stage of 'fight/flight' by Bion (1961), 'authority' by Schutz and 'storming' by Tuckman.

It is only when these stages have been successfully handled that the team can settle to its most productive work, with a climate of respect for each individual and without either dependency or rivalry in its relationship to the team leader. However, the earlier phases of forming, norming and storming will reappear as new people join or new phases in the life of the team inevitably come along.

Team development can take many forms, from outward bound exercises, fun activity together to promote bonding, team analysis of its own behaviour, reviews of working processes or away-days. However, research has shown little evidence of team bonding and team activity events having an impact on team performance (Katzenbach and Smith, 1993b; Wageman *et al*, 2008).

3. Team building

Team building, which is any process used to help a team in the early stages of team development, can thus be seen as a sub-category of team development, focusing on what Tuckman would term the 'forming' and 'norming' stages. Most activities that go under this label focus on team bonding and the team understanding and relating better to each other. Some team-building sessions may use outdoor team challenges, social activities or other experiential engagement exercises. In Chapter 6, I will argue, supported by the research of Wageman *et al* (2008), Hackman and Wageman (2005) and Gersick (1988) that this stage of early team engagement is best achieved by focusing on the mission, goals and expectation of the performance of the team.

4. Team facilitation

Team facilitation is when a specific person (or persons) is asked to facilitate the team by managing the process for them so they are freed up to focus on the task. There is a wide range of areas that a facilitator may be asked to come and facilitate for a team. These include:

- to resolve a particular conflict or difficulty;
- to carry out a team review of its ways of operating and relating;
- to enable a strategy or planning process;
- to run an off-site away-day.

Clearly there are many other possible requests for team facilitation, but they all usually are inviting the team facilitator to focus on enabling the specific process and not to get involved with content or team performance.

5. Team process

Team process consultancy is a form of team facilitation where the team consultant sits alongside the team carrying out its meetings or planning sessions and provides reflection and review on 'how' the team is going about its task.

This way of providing team coaching was developed first by Ed Schein in his classic book on process consultancy (1969, 1988) and further developed by Peter Block (1981, 2000) in his equally excellent book on 'flawless consulting'. Both books should be essential reading for all team coaches, and both emphasize how to help teams reflect on how they are functioning and relating, while the teams are often caught up with the 'what' of the task and the current agenda. Schein (1988: 34) defines process consultation as: 'a set of activities on the part of the consultant that help the client to perceive, understand, and act upon the process events that occur in the client's environment'.

He distinguishes process consultation from other forms of consultancy and helping relationships, such as 'the purchase of information or expertise model' or the 'doctor–patient relationship' in very similar ways to later writers. The process consultant walks alongside the client, in a spirit of partnership, facilitation and co-inquiry. Schein (1987: 32–3) argues that process consultation is most effective when:

1 The client is hurting somehow but does not know the source of the pain or what to do about it.

2 The client does not know what kind of help may be available and which consultant can provide the kind of help that might be needed.

3 The nature of the problem is such that the client not only needs help in figuring out what is wrong but would benefit from participation in the process of making the diagnosis.

4 The client has 'constructive intent', is motivated by goals and values that the consultant can accept and has some capacity to enter into a helping relationship.

5 The client is ultimately the only one who knows what form of intervention will work in the situation.

6 The client is capable of learning how to diagnose and solve his own organizational problems.

Today in team coaching we would use less problem, diagnosis, solution language and balance a problem focus with an appreciative focus of building on what already is working well. However, many of the approaches that help the process consultant work alongside the client and gradually help the client grow their own capacity to coach themselves are still very apposite.

This process consulting may well involve a variety of feedback and inquiry processes before, during and at the end of meetings, as well as some interventions to enable the team to reflect on its processes as it proceeds.

6. Team coaching

This term has been used increasingly by coaches, moving into the area of teamwork and consultants wanting to link to the growth of the coaching industry. It has also been used very loosely to indicate anything from coaching the team leader on leading their team; coaching a number of individuals from within the same team; team building; team facilitation; team process consultancy; or one-off events or workshops.

In recent years some key writers have tried to bring clarity to the field and a number of definitions of team coaching have been put forward. In 2005 Hackman and Wageman proposed that team coaching was: 'direct interaction with a team intended to help members make coordinated and task appropriate use of their collective resources in accomplishing the team's work' (p 269). This clearly indicated that it involved work with the whole team, not just team members and emphasized the focus on task and best use of resources.

Hackman and Wageman (2005) also defined the functions of team coaching in a way that combined the performance and the process. They wrote that team coaching involved: 'Interventions that inhibit process losses and foster process gains in each of three performance processes: the effort people put in (motivation), the performance strategies (consultation) and the level of knowledge and skill (education)'. This is similar to the functions of supervision as described by Hawkins and Smith (2006), where we talk of supervision having qualitative (performance improving), developmental (educational), and resourcing (motivation and self-sustaining) functions.

David Clutterbuck (2007: 77) defined team coaching as: 'Helping the team improve performance, and the processes by which performance is achieved, through reflection and dialogue.' He very helpfully shows how team coaching needs to combine a performance and process focus, and elsewhere in his book Clutterbuck usefully elaborates on the continual learning aspects of the team (2007: 123–98). I would contend that it does not go far enough in two respects: first, it emphasizes the reflection stage of the learning cycle, whereas I would argue that team coaching needs to help a team move round the whole learning cycle of reflection, new thinking, planning and action and back to reflection. The team coach not only needs to be able to help the team reflect on its recent past, but enable the team to create new ways of thinking including shifting the frames of reference they are using to make sense of their collective experience. The team coach then needs to help the team strategize and plan new ways of engaging with their collective challenges and rehearsing new ways of being, so they can return to the task with new individual and collective embodied commitments.

Secondly, Clutterbuck's definition does not include the team engaging with their wider systemic context and how they relate with their multiple stakeholders. Like many approaches to team coaching it tends to focus from the inside-out, the team relating well together so they can perform their tasks better, whereas I would argue the team coach also needs to help the team focus from outside-in, and this will be a theme I will return to throughout this book.

In our book *Coaching, Mentoring and Organizational Consultancy: Supervision and development* (Hawkins and Smith, 2006), we defined team coaching as: 'enabling a team to function at more than the sum of its parts, by clarifying its mission and improving its external and internal relationships. It is different therefore from coaching team leaders on how to lead their teams, or coaching individuals in a group setting.' While this also combines the purpose and task of the team with how it functions and stresses the importance of looking at both internal relating and external relating, I do not think that this goes far enough. We also proposed a continuum of coaching that went from skills – performance – development – transformational. Since then we have developed further the notions of transformational coaching (Hawkins and Smith, 2010). Similarly I would propose a continuum of team coaching; see Figure 4.1. With team coaching I would suggest this continuum: team facilitation where the team coach only has a responsibility for process and not for performance improvement; team performance coaching where the team coach focuses on both team process and team performance; leadership team coaching; and transformational leadership team coaching.

FIGURE 4.1 Continuum of team coaching

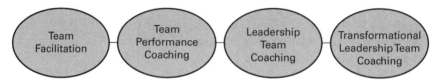

7. Leadership team coaching

Leadership team coaching is team coaching for any team, not just the most senior, where the focus is on how the team collectively gives leadership to those who report to them and also how the team influences their key stakeholder groups.

Although in Chapter 2 we mainly focused on the most senior leadership team of the organization, leadership needs to reside at all levels. A team becomes a leadership team when it focuses not just on its immediate task but also on how it can engage with its multiple stakeholder groups to co-create performance improvement for both its own outputs and outcomes, and also those of its stakeholders.

8. Transformational leadership team coaching

Transformational leadership team coaching is where any team taking leadership at whatever level, not only focuses on how they want to run their business, but also how they will transform their business. Increasingly leadership teams, at any level in the organization, are having to focus on both running their business effectively (performance) and on transforming the nature of their business. One CEO described this as having to navigate the ship through stormy seas while rebuilding the ship at the same time. Thus the coach needs to have bi-focal attention, and be able to coach the team on their current performance and on how they are leading the transformation. In Chapter 6 there are examples of this bi-focal coaching.

9. Systemic team coaching

In this book I will show how the more traditional approaches to team coaching do not go far enough and have led to much team coaching over-focusing on the internal aspects of the team and under-focusing on the external performance, when they are not meeting together but out engaging with all the critical stakeholders, through whom they make the difference. This includes not only the employees of the organization, but the customers or clients, the partner organizations or suppliers, the investors or tax payers, the regulators and the wider community and environment in which the organization operates. It is these collective and systemic aspects of the team and its context that can either enhance or undermine team performance. Furthermore, the team need to focus beyond their immediate stakeholders, to their stakeholder's stakeholders; these are their staff's staff, customer's customers, their supplier's suppliers, their investor's investors, etc, for great leaders create and enable leadership in others, and great leadership teams enable leadership in all their stakeholder systems.

Gradually I have refined a much broader approach to team coaching through a process that has included:

- research into current best practice among team coaches in several different countries;
- action inquiry into gradually refining team working approaches in the light of what worked and did not work with clients and their feedback;
- many very useful dialogues with colleagues at Bath Consultancy Group and the workshops I have led in team coaching.

This approach I have termed 'Systemic team coaching' as it is systemic in two senses. First, the focus is primarily on the team as a collective, their purpose, performance and process, and only secondarily on the personal and interpersonal development within the team. Second, the focus is on the team in their systemic context, working with them as they engage and relate to all their stakeholders. I have defined the process as follows:

> Systemic team coaching is a process by which a team coach works with a whole team, both when they are together and when they are apart, in order to help them improve both their collective performance and how they work together, and also how they develop their collective leadership to more effectively engage with all their key stakeholder groups to jointly transform the wider business.

If we now look at each aspect of this definition we can see how it combines a number of separate elements:

- *with a whole team* – team coaching is different from coaching a series of team members or coaching the team leader on how they lead the team.
- *both when they are together and when they are apart* – some teams believe and act as if they are only a team when they are together, but the team functions between meetings, when its members are carrying out activities on behalf of the team. I sometimes use the analogy that the team meeting is like a football team practising on the training ground; the match is when the team members are out representing the team back in their own parts of the business.
- *in order to help them improve both their collective performance and how they work together* – as Clutterbuck (2007), Hackman and Wageman (2005) and Hawkins and Smith (2006) all point out, team coaching is there not only to help create process improvement but also to impact on the collective performance of the team.
- *develop their collective leadership* – often I will work with senior executives who have a mindset that they are only a member of the top team when they are attending the top team meeting. High-performing leadership teams, as was shown in the previous chapter, use their time together as a team to develop their collective capacity to spend the rest of the week leading all aspects of the business in a congruent and joined up way that provides operational integration

and transformational change aligned to the vision, mission, strategy and core values of the organization.

- *to more effectively engage with all their key stakeholder groups* – collective leadership is not just about running and transforming the business internally, but also about how the leadership team engages the various stakeholders in a congruent, aligned and transformational way. These stakeholders include customers, suppliers, partner organizations, employees, investors, regulators, boards and the communities in which the organization operates.

- *to jointly transform the wider business* – as discussed in Chapter 1, to just respond to the changing context or lead what the team are overtly responsible for is no longer sufficient. The team need to take responsibility beyond their locus of control to how they will deploy their influence to develop the wider business and larger systemic context in which they operate. This is done by focusing on how they will enable the leadership of others (staff, customers, suppliers, investors, etc).

The extended team coaching continuum

Thus we can see there is a whole range of team coaching activities all of which can be useful for teams depending on their current needs. The further one travels along the continuum the more inclusive becomes the offering for the later types of coaching incorporating aspects of the former; for example team coaching may well involve team building and aspects of facilitation; systemic team coaching encompasses leadership team and transformational leadership team coaching. Thus they are analogous with Russian dolls, where the larger dolls have all the smaller dolls within them.

However, it is essential to have clarity about the nature and form of each of these different offerings so that there can be clarity of expectations and contracting between the team and their coach. Also, as later chapters will illustrate, the team cannot always see clearly what they most need, or know of forms of team coaching that they have not previously experienced and clarity can help here (see Chapter 5).

The who of team coaching

Individual coaching has increasingly been delivered in large companies by a mixture of:

- line managers coaching their own staff with or without any formal coaching training;

FIGURE 4.2

- internal coaches who have undertaken some more extensive coaching training and who often receive supervision, who give a few hours every week to coaching individuals from other departments and functions; and
- external coaches brought in to provide specific coaching for senior executives or high-potential staff.

The same pattern is also developing more slowly in team coaching. Increasingly chief executives and other senior leaders are recognizing that coaching their leadership team is a critical aspect of their role (Wageman, 2001; Wageman *et al*, 2008) and often will use their individual coach to supervise their own coaching of their team. Building and coaching a team is also becoming a more regular part of most senior leadership development programmes and a key topic in a senior leader's action learning set.

A few organizations have created a skilled group of mostly HR or internal learning and development consultants who have been trained in team coaching and who can work with teams right across the organization as required (Hawkins, 2011). These organizations often contract with an external coach to coach their most senior team, while other organizations may use a range of external providers to provide many types of team coaching. My hope is that this book will help teams, team leaders, team coaches and those purchasing team coaching for their organizations to have more clarity in what they need and buy and what they are offering and doing.

Conclusion

In this chapter we have looked at:

- the history of the antecedent streams that have contributed to team coaching;
- the current different forms of team development activities including team coaching and ways of defining these;
- the varieties of team coaching;
- systemic team coaching and how to define it.

In the next chapter we will look at the basic stages of a team coaching process and the relationship between the team and their coach, before returning to the nature of systemic team coaching and how to coach the five disciplines in Chapter 6.

The team coaching process

05

" Senior leadership teams, like other teams, need expert help in learning how to become better at working together over time. Coaching such teams is often more challenging than coaching front-line teams. High spirited, independent minded thoroughbreds are often convinced of the rightness of their ways and are not responsive to correction – even by the lead horse.
(WAGEMAN ET AL, 2008: 159)

We are coaches precisely because we recognize that change is best supported through a relationship over time. **(THORNTON, 2010: 123)**

Introduction

In their research across 120 leadership teams, Wageman *et al* (2008) found that: 'very few teams were able to decode their successes and failures and learn from them without intervention from a leader or another team coach' (p 161) and the high-performing leadership teams had significantly more coaching from their leader and peers than mediocre or poor teams. Yet as the quote above indicates, the process of coaching a team either as the leader of it or external to it, is one fraught with challenges and dangers.

In this chapter I will show how the team coach has to first be clear about his or her role and the stages of relationship between themselves and the team that is being coached. The relationship stages are addressed by exploring the CID-CLEAR model of the team coaching process. These stages apply whether the team coaches are external to the organization or internal trained team coaches, or indeed the leader or member of the team who is taking on the coaching role. For ease of narrative the model is first described assuming a team coach who is external to the team, and then how it is different for coaches internal to the team. In the following chapter I will extend this approach by exploring the different activities of the team coach in working with the five disciplines of team activity that were presented in Chapter 3 and will show how the systemic team coach extends the team's learning and engagement.

The role of the team coach

The objective of the team coach is to enable the team to improve its performance, functioning, well-being, engagement and development (see Chapter 4). The team coach does this by working alongside the team both in team meetings and off-site workshops, and in the team's engagement with its key stakeholders. The team coach may use, with the team, a wide range of:

- diagnostic instruments;
- observations and feedback;
- process interventions;
- facilitative interventions to enable the team to explore certain areas and move to new ways of operating and engaging;
- incisive questions;
- challenges about performance;
- educational inputs;
- role modelling behaviour;
- review mechanisms.

But importantly his or her role is not to:

- take over leadership of the team;
- instruct the team on how it does its business;
- become part of the team;
- take sides in internal conflict;
- go native.

The CID-CLEAR relationship process

The CLEAR model was first developed as a supervision model in 1978 and then individual coaching model in the 1980s and applied to team coaching much later (Hawkins and Smith, 2006). It outlines the five CLEAR stages of progression in any coaching relationship:

Contracting

Listening

Exploring

Action

Review

Over the years as my colleagues and I have developed team coaching we realized that there is a necessary prologue phase in team coaching that involves:

- initial exploratory discussions often with the team gatekeeper and team leader and possibly the team sponsors;
- some form of inquiry process of the team's current functioning, aspirations and coaching needs;
- some form of diagnosis co-created with the team about their current state, development objectives and possible coaching journey.

This led to developing the CID-CLEAR model.

Contracting 1

Inquiry

Diagnosis

Contracting 2

Listening

Exploring

Action

Review

As in individual coaching, this flow is never just linear, since we cycle back into contracting before and after the listening phases and again throughout the repeated cycles of exploration and action. Often the review stage is also the time when re-contracting may happen.

Contracting 1: Initial exploratory discussions

Team coaches are often called in by a team leader, team sponsor or team gatekeeper or other individuals who have a specific brief to support the team's development. The work begins right from these initial discussions, but it is important not to confuse these early talks with team members with a full contracting process with the whole team. Useful questions at this stage include:

- Why do you want help with team development now? Tell me some of the history that has led up to it.
- Why me/us? Who else are you talking to?
- Whose idea was it? Is everyone in agreement about it?
- Have you had help with team development before? What worked and what could have been better?
- How do you understand team coaching?
- What cannot be talked about in this team?
- How would you know that this development work had been successful, for the team, the team members and the team's stakeholders?

Inquiry

The inquiry phase might take many forms but is essentially about collecting relevant data and impressions about the team, their performance, functioning and dynamics; the team members and their relationships and the relationship between the collective team and their commissioners and stakeholders. The team coach may do one or more of the following:

- have individual semi-structured meetings with each member of the team;
- send out a questionnaire that asks each person for his or her perceptions on the team and what is needed;
- send out a team 360-degree feedback instrument to all the key stakeholders with whom the team interacts;
- have additional conversations with some of the most critical stakeholders; often, when working with a senior leadership team, I will also interview the chair of the board and collect feedback from the tier of management that reports to this senior team.

The semi-structured interviews need to be carefully balanced as they have several functions:

- to build a relationship and working alliance with each team member, so they feel they have been heard, you have understood their reality and they establish enough trust in you as team coach;

- to gather quality data that is comparable, which requires asking the same specific questions in all interviews;
- to ask questions that elicit right-brain knowing as well as more analytic left-brain answers;
- to be open to surprising emergent issues and data that you had not expected;
- for the interviewee to have a better understanding of why you have been invited in and how you might work.

At the beginning of each interview, it is important to state the purpose and boundaries of the interview and agree how it will be of value to both parties. I usually make it clear that I will not be feeding back any data attributable to any individuals, but will be sharing with the whole team collective themes, patterns and issues that emerge from more than one source. As in all coaching relationships the CLEAR stages apply to these initial interviews. Having contracted, one needs to listen actively, explore what emerges, agree what action both the individual and the coach can take following the interview and review the process at the end. This gives a sense that although this is a prelude to the coaching, it is also the beginning of the actual coaching.

Whenever possible individual meetings with all team members provide a solid relational foundation on which the team coaching relationship can be built, and is a worthwhile up-front investment. It may be important to ensure that as new members join the team after the team coaching has begun, that such interviews are also carried out with them.

The inquiry questionnaires might include:

- The 'what sort of team are you?' questionnaire (see Chapter 4).
- The Bath Consultancy Group High Performing Team Questionnaire (see Chapter 12 and **www.bathconsultancygroup.com**) where each team member is asked to rate on a five-point scale their view of 18 aspects of team functioning, both how it currently performs and how it needs to change in order to succeed.
- The five disciplines self-scoring questionnaire (see Chapter 6).
- Team 360-degree feedback including descriptor analysis (see Chapter 12).
- Belbin team role analysis (see Chapter 12).
- Team MBTI personality type questionnaires (see Chapter 12).

At this stage it would be wrong to overload the team members, many of whom the coach may not have met, with too many inquiry instruments. It is better to be very selective based on what has emerged from the initial contracting conversations about the team's needs. Other diagnostic tools can be used with the team later in the process as the need arises from the team itself.

What you are trying to achieve at this stage is enough data to work with the team to contract on a joint diagnosis that can lead to the co-design of the team coaching journey. Table 5.1 provides some guidance on when you might use which questionnaire.

At the same time as collecting this data on team functioning, it is essential to collect data on the team's performance. For many teams this will already exist and can be made available to the team coach. It might include:

- the team's balanced scorecard and how they are performing against each target;
- the team's priority outcome objectives and the current state of progress;
- customer, supplier, partner and/or investor feedback;
- staff attitude surveys that show how this team are seen by their staff, the value the team add to them and how they would like the team to be different;
- previous team 360-degree feedback.

Diagnosis and design

The data from all three sources (performance data, questionnaires and interviews) needs to be sorted and analysed. This is not to arrive at definitive conclusions about the team, but to develop emerging hypotheses, including the focus for the team coaching.

To carry out this analysis for teams that are on the journey from being a reasonably effective team to being high performing, we usually use the five disciplines of high-performing teams model for mapping where the team is functioning well and where it is currently challenged. This can also help in deciding the order in which the team coaching may need to travel through the five different disciplines. However, if one has been invited in to coach a team that is dysfunctional or in crisis, then we might use a different frame. This would indicate that the team needed to address Discipline 3, how it co-creates and works together, before it can engage with any of the other disciplines.

Patrick Lencioni (2002) has created a delightful fable of an imaginary leadership team that gets turned around by their new female CEO, using a simple model of 'The five dysfunctions of the team'. In Figure 5.1 I set out the model which Lencioni argues needs to be attended to from the bottom of the pyramid upwards. He includes next to each level, on the outside of the pyramid, the common indicators and causes of each dysfunction. He has developed a number of questionnaires (Lencioni, 2005) that can be used to help a team uncover and then address these dysfunctions.

Petrushka Clarkson (1995) has a useful notion that such teams often come for help because they are in danger, conflict, confusion or deficit. Each of these can elicit a 'knee-jerk reaction' from the consultant or a more useful considered response; see Figure 5.2.

TABLE 5.1

Questionnaire	When to use
What sort of team are you	If the team are struggling to decide whether to commit to being a team or stay as a work group
The Bath Consultancy Group High Performing Team	When the team are a real team wanting to explore and be coached on becoming high performing
The five disciplines self-scoring questionnaire	Generally useful for all teams where it is unclear where they need the coaching to focus
Team 360-degree feedback including descriptor analysis	When the team lack quality data on how they are seen by their commissioners and stakeholders
Belbin team role analysis	When it is clear that the team are not functioning well or under-utilizing their internal resources
Team MBTI personality type	When the team members are finding it difficult to engage, communicate and work together and there are high levels of internal misunderstanding

FIGURE 5.1 The five dysfunctions of a team

SOURCE: Lencioni (2002)

FIGURE 5.2 Team presenting issues

Diagnosis	Consultant's knee-jerk reaction	Consultant's considered response
Danger 坎	Teach Falsely reassure Rescue Contract unrealistically	Listen Acknowledge feelings Explore sources Explore nature Elicit emotional reality
Confusion 明夷	Get sucked into confusion Oversimplify Accept one frame of reference Fight Take sides	Restrain action Clarify issues Clarify roles Clarify authority Provide models and maps Explore options Assess impact/consequences
Conflict 訟	Pathologise it Fear it Minimise it Ignore it Take sides	Learn its history Welcome and understand it Model conflict handling Value the differences Validate all parties Provide arena and referee
Deficit 困	Do it for them Work with solved problems Solve symptoms Give your favourite package Assume there should be a training solution	Establish what they have Find what worked before Find out what did not work Start where they are Establish needs and wants Provide relevant input

SOURCE: Clarkson (1995)

Having done the initial diagnosis the team coach may also begin to sketch some possible maps of the coaching journey, based on the initial diagnosis. This should only be a draft sketch, as the journey needs to be co-designed with the team.

Contracting 2: Contracting the outcomes and ways of working with the whole team

Having carried out the initial contracting, inquiry and diagnosis, now comes the time to meet with the whole team and fully contract the objectives, process and programme for the team coaching.

It is useful to start such meetings with the team coach sharing the objectives for this initial meeting, such as:

- To arrive at a joint view of the current state of the team.

- To agree where we collectively would like the team to be at the end of the coaching process.
- To decide what needs to be addressed and focused on in the coaching work.
- How we need to work together to achieve the most value.
- What the coaching journey map may look like.

Having carried out some form of inquiry and initial diagnostic analysis, it is important to find a way of playing this back to the whole team, in a way that engages them not in either swallowing whole or rejecting the feedback, but as co-diagnosers of its meaning. So instead of feeding the results back in the form of a beautifully crafted report that is so polished that you can't grasp hold of it, it is better to do so in a way that is full of hooks and intriguing entry points. The purpose is not just to 'tell it as it is' (necessary though that is), but also to create a real energy of engagement and co-inquiry.

One simple way of doing this is to engage the team in digesting, sorting and prioritizing each piece of summarized data. If as a team coach you have produced a list of what the team see as the major enablers and blockers to their performing well, you might ask the team to:

1 split into threes;
2 each trio add one additional item to each list;
3 arrange the list in priority order;
4 share their lists with the other trios;
5 the whole team agree a collective prioritized list.

A similar process can be done using the high-performing team questionnaire:

1 the team look at the averaged scores and the spread of scores;
2 each member is given five sticky stars and asked to use them as representing the limited time and resource the team has to spend focusing on any item;
3 they stick one or more stars on the items they think the team should most focus on to raise their collective game and achieve their aspirations;
4 the top scored items are listed;
5 the team divide into new threes focusing on different priority areas;
6 the trios agree what actions they can take for quick wins in this area and what help they will need from the team coach to address and sustain progress in this area.

Having established a shared view of the current state of the team and what is the required difference the team wants to create, the coach then needs to engage the team in agreeing what they want to achieve from the team coaching journey and specifically what success would look like. This can be done by asking the team to work together to complete the following statements:

- This team coaching will be a success for us as individuals if ...
- The team coaching will be a success for us as a team if ...
- The coaching work will be a success for our organization if ...
- This coaching work will be a success for our clients/customers/stakeholders if ...

The coach then asks the team what they need both from each other and from the coach to achieve that success. This takes us into the important second area of contracting, which involves agreements about the relationship between the team and the coach and the process of working together. This needs to include:

a practicalities;

b boundaries;

c ethics;

d working alliance;

e the contract with the wider organization.

a. Practicalities

In forming the contract it is necessary to be clear about the practical arrangements such as the times, frequency, place, what might be allowed to interrupt or postpone the session, and the clarification of any payment that is involved.

b. Boundaries

A team coaching contract should include clear boundaries concerning confidentiality. Confidentiality is an old chestnut which is of concern to many coaches and teams they are working with. Some team coaches fall into the trap of saying or implying to the team members that everything that is shared in their meetings is confidential, only to find that some unexpected situation arises where they find it is necessary to share material from the coaching beyond the boundaries of the session.

One of the particular challenges in team coaching is where it intersects with individual coaching of team members. Generally I have found that it is too complicated to be coaching the team and also coaching some of the team members. The exception to this is coaching the team and the team leader, as long as this is transparent to all team members, and there is a clear boundary that in the meetings with the team leader as coach you do not pass judgement on team members or share information given to you individually.

Thus, in contracting the appropriate confidentiality boundary for any form of coaching it is inappropriate either to say everything is confidential that is shared here, or to say nothing here is confidential. The coach should be clear what sort of information either would need to be taken over the boundary of the relationship; in what circumstances; how it would be done; and to whom he or she would take the information. Clearly every possible situation cannot be anticipated, but such a general exploration can diminish the possibility of what may be seen as betrayal.

It is also useful to be clear about one's own supervision as a team coach, and how this works. As part of this I give an undertaking that I will treat everything they share with me in a professional manner at supervision and not gossip about their situation.

c. Ethics

Likewise it is important to clarify the professional and ethical codes of conduct that both parties may be party to. This is addressed in Chapter 10 when we look at ethics as one of the team coach's key capacities.

d. Working alliance

Forming the working alliance starts by sharing mutual expectations. It is important to discuss the style of coaching the team most want, and on which of the possible disciplines they wish the coaching to concentrate. The team coach needs to state clearly his or her preferred modes of team coaching, and any expectations he or she has of the team. It can be useful to ask the team what sort of coaching or other forms of support or development they have had in the past, what did and did not work successfully and how they would like this relationship to be different and more effective.

A good working alliance is not built on a list of agreements or rules, but on growing trust, respect and goodwill between both parties. The contract provides a holding frame in which the relationship can develop, and any lapses in fulfilling the contract need to be seen as opportunities for reflection, learning and relationship building, not judgement and defence. To make this more likely to happen it is often useful at the beginning to ask the team to think about what could go wrong in the relationship and how it will be addressed.

As well as sharing hopes, fears and expectations, it is useful to ground the discussions in an exploration of how the team coaching journey might unfold. This is where the team coach might share his or her initial sketch or sketches of a possible team coaching journey map. It is a smart move to show how this might be adapted and built on from what has emerged in this contracting, co-designing meeting and then invite discussion of what else might need to be included in the map. This process is helped by having the journey sketched on a large piece of paper, so that both the team coach and team members can add to it, possibly by adding Post-its which can be moved around.

Having explored with the team what will be helpful and unhelpful in the working relationship it is useful to discuss what might happen when the team coach facilitates events, attends regular team meetings or enables engagement with different key stakeholders:

- how and when the coach will intervene;
- what contact there will be between meetings;
- whether the team coach will have meetings with the team leader or the HR director and if so what will and will not be shared and discussed.

e. The contract with the wider organization

Last but definitely not least is the contract with the wider organization. One of the biggest quality developments in individual executive coaching has been the use of 'three-way contracting', where the coach meets with the coachee and a representative of the wider organizational system to ensure that the coaching is serving the organization's learning and development as well as that of the individual. This has been less developed in team coaching, but is arguably even more critical and important. This can be done by the team coach sharing a summary of what has emerged from 360-degree feedback on the team, and/or from interviews with key organizational stakeholders and asking the team how they will ensure they meet the legitimate expectations of these stakeholders in the coaching process.

Alternatively the team members can go out and interview the key stakeholders, and then share the stakeholders' views of how the team are currently performing and their expectations of how the team need to change and develop. In certain assignments we have brought in key stakeholders to a second contracting meeting as part of attending to the commissioning and connecting disciplines (see next chapter).

Clear contracting is not only important for the success of the team coaching, but it also models the way team members can contract among themselves.

Listening

Once a clear contract for the team development and coaching has been established, the work moves on into the listening stage of the CLEAR model, where the issues that have emerged in the contracting stage can be observed and listened to. This involves the coach in listening to the team in its work at a number of different levels. It is so easy for the coach to get lost in trying to understand the content data of the team's work that they lack the necessary listening space to listen to the other levels. Using the four levels of engagement model (Hawkins and Smith, 2006) shown here in Figure 5.3, we encourage and train team coaches to listen to:

- the data content of what is reported and discussed and the relationship of this to the agreed mission of the team (see clarifying discipline in the next chapter);

- the patterns of behaviour of the team;
- the emotional expressions and relating (through the metaphors and non-verbal communication);
- the assumptions, mindsets and motivations of the team and the team members that underlie what is said and how it is said.

This listening process needs to be active, with the team coach playing back key things he or she has heard from both the verbal and non-verbal communication, in ways that both support and amplify positive enabling interactions and help the team become aware of stuck and interruptive patterns.

The team coach in this stage might also use the privilege of being new and an outsider to ask intentionally naïve questions, such as:

- What is the purpose of your meetings?
- What do you expect from one another?
- How would you know if this meeting had created genuine value for you and your stakeholders?
- What specifically would be happening differently if you were functioning as the team you aspire to be?

Explore and experiment

In this stage the issues that have been opened up through both the inquiry and the listening stages and agreed on in the contracting can be explored and the team can experiment with new ways of operating. In the next chapter we give examples of exploratory interventions for each of the five disciplines of the team development model.

If the diagnosis and contracting stages show that there is a lack of clarity in the fundamental mission of the team, we would probably suggest a workshop with the team to clarify it, and then a joint meeting with those responsible for commissioning the team's purpose, to clarify mutual expectations and ensure they have 'co-missioned'. This is the 'commissioning interface' (commissioning discipline). If the team had a clear commission from the wider organization, but still lacked clarity of objectives, goals and action plan, the explore stage would focus on turning the mission into a team strategic plan with collectively owned team objectives (clarifying discipline).

Other teams may well need to focus on their internal relationships and team dynamics (co-creation discipline), some on the relationships with their key stakeholders (connecting discipline) while others need time to stand back and take stock, reflect and learn across all four disciplines from the perspective of the fifth discipline (core learning).

FIGURE 5.3 Four levels of engagement

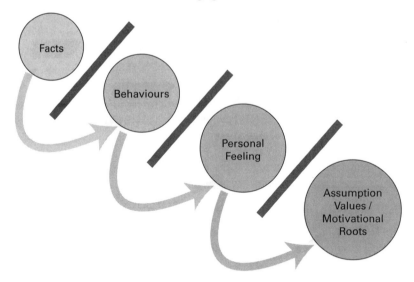

Action

Having explored and experimented with new ways of operating, the team coach then has to help the team move from awareness into action. How are they going to act differently and perform better?

Team coaching workshops can produce a lot of insight and energy, but unless these are focused on specific and prioritized new actions and behaviours, they will soon dissipate. So the challenge for the coach is to deal with the material generated in a way that moves the group to committed actions quickly and surely. One way of doing this is to use the three-way sort exercise.

Three-way sort

The team coach sets up three flipcharts, each one with a different title:

1 What we need to hold onto and build on …

2 What we need to stop doing …

3 What we need to start doing …

The team is divided into three smaller groups and each group is asked to start on a different large sheet of paper or whiteboard. The first phase of this process is for sub-teams to brainstorm responses to the question in front of them. They put down their ideas, leaving some space between each one. After five minutes each team moves to the next board to their right.

The second phase of the process is to build on the ideas left by the previous team and make them more specific. At the second board, the rule is that nobody can cross anything out, but everybody is encouraged to make more specific what is already there and add more items. If, for example, the previous group has put 'communication' on their flipchart, the second group would be asked to add their responses to the question 'communication between whom and about what'?

The third phase of the process involves the group moving onto the last board. Once again, the team members can add items that have not so far been included, but they need also to make more specific the items that are already there.

Finally, each group moves back to their original board and, having read what is there, prioritize the issues. Alternatively, every team member can be given five stars and asked to allocate them anywhere on any of the three boards next to the priority issues that need action by the team. They can allocate the five stars against issues in any way they want. This visual voting method quickly shows up how the team see their priorities and directions for moving forward.

Once the collective priorities have been agreed for the team, the hard work begins of deciding the specific actions for making change happen. We often use the six 'P' model of simple planning (Hawkins and Smith, 2006):

Purpose – What success from resolving this issue would consist of and the measurements we would use to evaluate the success.

Principles – How the change needs to be carried out in a way that is living the team's core values and the medium is the message.

Parameters – the boundaries of the change activity: what it will not address, as well as time and people limits.

Programme – the timetable of activities necessary.

People – who will be the people who will take ownership of the issue for the team and make the change happen.

Process – How these people will go about it and how they will involve the rest of the team.

Increasingly we have found that just committing to new actions at the team event is not enough, for the road to hell is paved with good intentions. So we have developed in all our transformational coaching work (Hawkins and Smith, 2010) the notion of the 'fast forward rehearsal'. The team coach takes key items where the team is committed to change and has developed and committed to a SMART (specific, measurable, actionable, realistic and timely) plan of action, and asks the team: 'How can you start living this change while you are still on this team event?'

While working with the senior executive team of a major government department the intervention the team most appreciated was trying out new behaviours on real issues. On one occasion, when they had committed to five ways they would work differently, I asked them to take a major area of current challenge for the team, and immediately start to work in these new ways. I gave them a health warning that the goal was not to do it perfectly, but have some fast and useful failures. Indeed, I added that if they did not have at least six failures in living up to their aspirations in the next 40 minutes, we probably would not be learning fast enough! As they moved from away-day behaviour, back into a demanding task meeting, as team coach I took on the role of watching the five areas of new practice. In the 40 minutes we had about four 'time-outs', where I stopped the task, had team members share what they were noticing, experiencing and feeling. I then asked them what was working in terms of effectively living the new behaviours and what could be better. In some time-outs the reflection was enough to move to a higher level of rehearsal; in others the team and I jointly devised an additional experiment for the next stage of the meeting.

Review

Having contracted, listened, diagnosed, explored, planned and enacted new action, the team need to build in a review process. As in all learning and change cycles, the team should be prepared for the fact that they will discover more about their team culture and the systemic dynamics when they try to change things. They need to prepare for disappointment when they discover that the actions they planned at a team workshop will not work out the way they expected once they are back in the ever-changing world of their work system.

Some teams build this process of tracking the progress – or lack thereof – into their regular meetings in a number of different ways:

- ensuring the mission statement is pinned up in the meeting room, and checking how the meeting decisions and meeting process align with the mission they agreed;
- having quick updates against the team scorecard when they have a meeting;
- taking a key priority action area for review at each team session;
- reviewing the meeting in the light of their planned team improvements, and each person sharing what they think has been good about the meeting and what they think could be even better next time;
- having the team coach attend their regular internal meetings or key events, and provide live coaching.

The CLEAR way of structuring an individual event

The five stages can also be used in microcosm to guide an individual meeting or workshop or indeed used by a team leader in structuring their meetings:

Contracting – What do we need to achieve today? What would success from today look like? How do we need to work together to achieve that?

Listening –Let's get all the different perspectives, hopes and fears out on the table, and make sure they are all heard before we explore ways forward.

Explore – Let's brainstorm all the elements that might be needed to move forward. What can we experiment with today?

Action – So what are we committed to doing? Who will do what, by when? What support is necessary? How can we start living that in our meeting today?

Review – So what worked well in this session? What could we do even better next time we work like this?

Some leadership teams and boards have used this model to restructure their regular meetings:

1 They start with a *check-in* and *contract* for the outcomes.

2 They *listen* to the updates and new challenges.

3 They have one or two issues for *exploration,* where the focus is to ensure generative team dialogue that produces genuinely new thinking on a critical area of performance.

4 They then have the items that need to be decided on and focus on the *action* to be taken. They also ensure they move beyond tacit agreement to demonstrable embodied and energetic commitment to making it happen.

5 The team ends with a check-out or *review*. This can involve sharing appreciations of what has been helpful in the meeting, or individual commitments of what they will be taking away and doing differently.

The team leader as team coach

Most team coaching in leadership teams is carried out not by external coaches but the team leaders themselves. We have found that the five disciplines model and the CID-CLEAR process relationship model are equally valuable for team leaders acting as the coach to their team.

When new team leaders are appointed it is important that they use their first weeks carrying out their own initial contracting inquiry and diagnosis (CID) using many of the approaches outlined in this chapter. Having done this they need to gather the team together for an off-site workshop or extended meeting, to share their initial findings and engage the team in diagnosing their own team functioning and performance, utilizing approaches similar to those outlined above. This workshop needs to then move towards forming a jointly owned plan for how the team are going to develop over the next few months and who will take what responsibility for which aspects of the plan. In the next chapter we will explicitly look at how to coach each of the five disciplines; the team leader can also use these approaches to coach his or her own team.

Conclusion

At the heart of effective team coaching is the generative relationship between the team and their coach, in which all members of the relationship should be constantly learning. Indeed I have long argued that one of the key ways of evaluating a good team coaching assignment is that all parties have learnt and changed the way they work, including the team coach. A good assignment therefore means I too have learnt, my models and methods have been changed and added to and I have used new interventions and approaches that arose from this specific relationship.

Another key way of evaluating a successful coaching assignment is that the coaching roles have been taken up by members of the team in a gradual and sustainable way, which means the team can continue to be a high performing and continually learning team, without the support of the external (or internal from another part of the organization) coach. Where the coaching is begun by the team leader, this process also applies as other team members take on different aspects of team coaching and it becomes a responsibility across all members of the team.

For the external team coach, such as myself, often the most rewarding and final review stage in the coaching relationship is going back to a team I have coached six to 12 months after I have completed the coaching assignment and helping the team review what added value has continued to be created from our work together, and how they have taken the coaching work forward and beyond anything we previously achieved together.

FIGURE 6.1 The four quadrants of systemic team coaching

	When working together	When working apart
Transformational Change	2	4
Operational Effectiveness	1	3

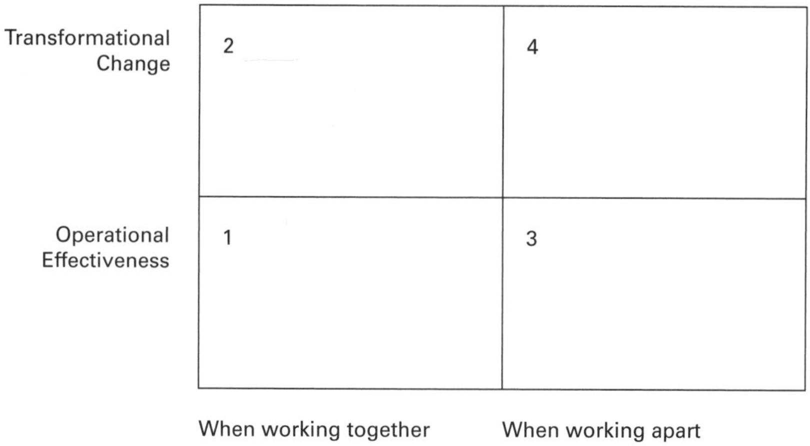

FIGURE 6.2 Scoring the four quadrants of systemic team coaching

Please score the team functioning between 1 (low) – 10 (high) in each quadrant

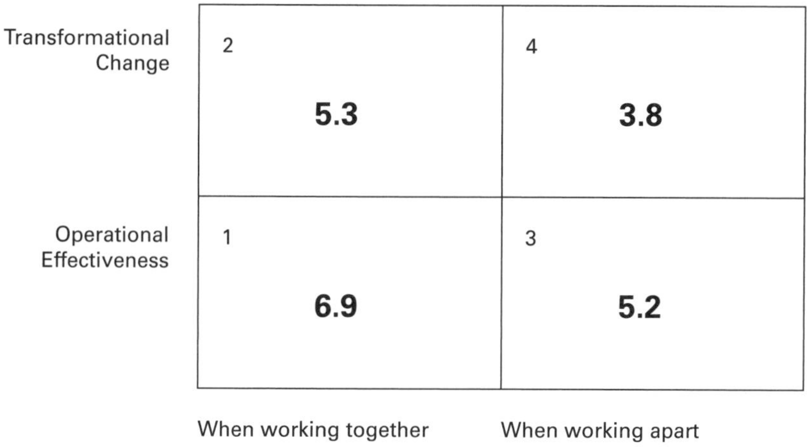

	When working together	When working apart
Transformational Change	2 **5.3**	4 **3.8**
Operational Effectiveness	1 **6.9**	3 **5.2**

The five disciplines of systemic team coaching

In Chapter 3 I introduced this model as the five key disciplines that high-performing leadership teams need to practice (see Figure 3.1 on page 36). This chapter will show how the systemic team coach can support and develop the team in each of these disciplines, with illustrations from a range of leadership team coaching relationships including the government department executive team mentioned above.

Discipline 1: Commissioning and re-commissioning

When I carried out research on leadership challenges in the civil service, a number of those interviewed commented on how 'the real leadership challenge lies at the interface between the politicians and the senior civil servants'.

In coaching a leadership team in a government department it is essential to attend to the political–civil service relationship. As part of my coaching of the leadership team I arranged to meet the Secretary of State and junior ministers to ascertain:

- What they appreciated about the leadership team and how the leadership team were transforming the department.
- What they wanted to come out of the transformation process.
- What they wanted different about how the transformation was being carried out.
- How they thought the leadership team could be more effective.
- How they thought the relationship between them and the leadership team could be improved.

This produced some very useful feedback. As coach I had to decide how to feed this back to the team, knowing from experience that just to deliver the feedback cold would create both resistance and defensiveness. I decided that I first had to awaken their active interest and curiosity. I asked them to imagine what the ministers had said, and also to list the questions they would like to have answered through listening to the feedback. As the team coach I was then able to use their answers to tailor the feedback to avoid repeating what they already knew and to address the issues they wanted to understand. This created a sense of dialogue across the boundary and avoided the one-way telling so common in the civil service. This in turn provided a basis for the team to explore how they wanted to change their relationship with their commissioners.

Another way of coaching the co-missioning discipline is to work with the board and the leadership team in a joint meeting. When I consulted to the formation of Capespan, from the merger of Outspan and Unifruco (Cape Fruit) in South Africa, we held joint team workshops for the board and senior executive teams to create their new mission. This ensured a great diversity of perspectives from executives and non-executives from both legacy companies, and included board members who were fruit growers and therefore suppliers, executives who ran the core business in South Africa, and those who ran the international marketing entities. This wider attendance ensured fuller ownership of the outcomes. However, the challenge of such an event is that we had over 30 people in the room and a great deal of politics!

Discipline 2: Clarifying

This discipline helps the team clarify its mission, strategy, collective objectives, goals and roles. Depending on what the team already have in place, the team coach can assist the team in developing or re-clarifying:

- their team mission;
- their transformation strategy;
- their transformation plan and change design;
- how the team need to meet differently for their transformation meetings from how they meet for their operational meetings;
- key roles and accountabilities for various aspects of the transformation process.

The mission of an organization, department or team is the overarching framework in which strategizing takes place. Our model of the organization mission, shown in Figure 6.3, is based on work by a number of key writers in the field (Binney *et al*, 2005; Senge *et al*, 2005).

- PURPOSE is *why* we are in business as a team, our 'raison d'être' – the difference we wish to make in the world.
- STRATEGY is *what* we focus on, our core markets, competencies and geographies, also our unique value propositions and how we differentiate our team's offerings both from the rest of the organization and the external competition.
- CORE VALUES underpin *how* we do business, the principles and behaviours that distinguish how we relate within the team to the wider business as well as to our customers, suppliers, investors and other stakeholders.
- VISION is *what we could become* as a team, if we were successful at fulfilling our purpose, focused on our strategy and behaving in line with our core values.

Peter Senge et al (1994) defined a vision as:

a picture of a future you seek to create, described in the present tense, as if it were happening now. A statement of 'our vision' shows where we want to go, and what it will be like when we get there. ... The more richly detailed and visual the image is, the more compelling it will be. Because of its tangible and immediate quality, a vision gives shape and

FIGURE 6.3 Elements of the mission

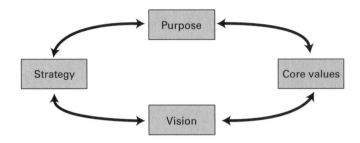

direction to the organization's future. And it helps people set goals to take the organization closer.

It is important that the team members co-create and clarify their mission together. One way of coaching this process is to ask team members to complete the following statements by themselves in a minimum of three and maximum of five bullet points. This encourages everybody to balance brevity with specificity:

1 The *primary purpose* of our organization is to ...

2 *Strategy* – To fulfil our purpose, our team needs to focus on the unique capabilities that distinguish what our team can do from the contribution of other parts of the organization. They are ...

3 The *core values* of our team, which should guide how we work and behave together and what we role-model in our engagement with others, are ...

4 *Vision* – If our team were miraculously successful in achieving our purpose, carrying out our strategy and living our core values, what we would see, hear and feel in two years time would be ...

The important thing about the responses that the team members generate is that they maximize the diversity of views, each view builds on the others and ends with a jointly created document. To maximize the 'wisdom of crowds' and minimize the danger of 'groupthink' (see Chapter 1, p 15), it is essential to start with individual thinking time and then to avoid one person reading out his or her complete answer but rather to practise a 'collective co-creative build'. This is a process where one team member offers his or her top bullet-point and then others immediately offer their statements that build on the starter statement. When this is complete, another person offers a different starting bullet-point and the team repeat the process.

Some boards prefer the executive team to produce their mission statement and then allow the non-executives to critically challenge and amplify what has been produced. In other settings the executive team and the board work separately on their mission statement, as well as their expectations and feedback to the other group. From these parallel explorations, a dialogue between the two groups can be facilitated which produces a third mission statement that is more than the sum of the two parts. This can also produce a good deal of learning for both groups.

Whichever method is chosen it is important that there is a true sense of 'co-missioning' – that a mission is arrived at through some form of collective dialogue across the boundary of the team and their wider system sponsors. Too often teams work resentfully with the commission they have been given and never take full ownership for their mission, or they develop their own mission which is not aligned to the expectations of their sponsors and those to whom they are answerable.

Having arrived at a clear and truly agreed commission and mission the executive team at Capespan needed to turn this into a clear strategy, objectives and action plan. The key questions that assisted this process were:

- How are you going to fulfil your purpose in the different areas of your strategic focus, staying true to your core values and in a way that will move you towards your vision?
- What are the milestones and scorecard by which you can chart progress towards your goals?
- What are the key strategic activities that you need:
  - to own as a whole team;
  - to allocate to small sub-groups of the team or project teams;
  - to allocate to individual team members?
- How can the team focus on business as usual and also focus on the core activities of transforming the organization and its various divisions and departments?

Discipline 3: Co-creation

In this discipline the focus is on how the team co-create and carry out their work together. It includes the operational performance and efficiency of the leadership team. As such it begins in Discipline 2, with the team clarifying their mission and agreeing ways of working and targets. Coaching stages in this discipline include the following.

First, ascertain the balanced scorecard for the team and what their specific measurable objectives are for the coming year. If there is no scorecard, then work can be done with the team to create one. As Lencioni (2005) shows in his model of the five major dysfunctions of teams, at the top of the pyramid is inattention to results, followed by lack of accountability for delivering the collective targets (see Figure 5.1 on page 71). It is very hard to be a high-performing team if the team do not have a small number of key collective targets that they are collectively and interdependently committed to achieving.

This scorecard can form the basis for an exploration with the team about how they need to work as a team to achieve and, if possible, surpass these targets. Also at this stage the team coach can help the team identify the aspects of the team culture that a) enable and b) block the team performing well against their own performance objectives.

From this a development plan can be produced with the team, which includes the development the team can do by themselves, and the areas where they will receive support from the team coach.

Areas of support to team meetings

These can include:

- *Helping the team streamline their meeting agendas,* separating out issues that are for information, for discussion and for decision, and ensuring that information exchange is done effectively outside meetings.
- *Attending their executive meetings as a process coach* and intervening when the dynamic is interrupting effective functioning (see Chapter 3).
- *Providing mid-meeting 'time-outs' and post-meeting reflection* where both team members and the coach can comment on what has gone well and what could be managed more effectively next time.

Away-day to explore team functioning

Depending on the maturity of the team and the team dynamic this could focus on a number of different dimensions:

- *The team culture.* Every team has aspects of their culture that enable them to perform well against their performance objectives and elements that block or hinder their performance.
- *Interpersonal relationships and understanding difference.* Using individual psychometrics the team could have fed back to them the different MBTI profiles, Belbin team roles and cultural differences. The team can then experientially explore how these affect the different team members' preferences and ways of engaging, and how this impacts on the team functioning.
- *Team performance functioning.* The 'High-performing team questionnaire' (see Chapter 3) can be filled in by all team members and the averaged scores and score spread fed back to the team. From this the team can decide which areas they most need to explore and

improve and what both individuals and the collective team need to commit to doing differently to improve the team performance.

- *Exploring the deeper team dynamic.* The team coach might use a number of approaches to help the team explore the more hidden and deeper team dynamics. These could include a floating team sculpt (see page 000), small groups drawing cartoons of the team a year ago, today and how they would like the team to be in a year's time, and an exploration of the culture of the team and their unwritten rules, norms and assumptions.

- *Deciding the way forward.* Having reviewed the outputs from all or some of the above, the team can decide what they need to continue, stop and start doing differently (see 'Three-way sort' exercise in Chapter 5 on p78).

At Bath Consultancy Group we have carried out our own research into what stops teams in working as more than the sum of their parts. We found the main barriers were:

- *Lack of clarity of collective focus* – if a team has not clarified their collective focus, this will cause conflict in every aspect of their functioning.

- *'Either–or' solution debates* – we have not yet discovered a team that does not have some form of repeated 'either–or' debates like:
  - Should we grow organically or by acquisition?
  - Should we centralize or decentralize?
  - Should we confront this stakeholder or maintain our good relationship?
  - Should we restructure (or not)?
  - I developed the 'Hawkins law of either–or', which says that if you are having the same either–or debate for the third time then you are asking the wrong question (Hawkins, 2005).

- *Accountability only occurs top-down – not across the team.* In some teams, members only speak when it is their area of expertise or function that is being discussed and otherwise 'keep their head down'. Team meetings become serial reports to the 'boss' and the team becomes a hub-and-spokes work group, with no real collective teamwork.

- *Doing to each other what others do to us* – elsewhere (Hawkins and Smith, 2006) we have termed this a 'parallel process', the unconscious re-enactment of what we have experienced being done to us by others. One large consultancy firm we worked with played havoc with its internal meetings by always changing the timings at the last minute and then turning up late for each other. It took us some time before we realized that this was an unconscious re-enactment of how they were treated by their clients.

- *Aiming for agreement rather than commitment* – we have witnessed many teams who have apparently made a decision which they were all going to carry out, only to find a month later that nothing had happened. We discovered that it was possible to predict when this was going to happen by taking notice of the non-verbal communication in the team meeting. The team were voting with their hands saying yes, but their bodies and tones of voice were clearly saying otherwise. As with transformational coaching (Hawkins and Smith, 2010), if the shift in commitment does not happen in the room, it is not going to happen outside it.

- *Agenda-driven rather than outcome-driven meetings* – often it can feel as if the goal of some team meetings is to complete the agenda rather than to create value.

- *Believing effective team meetings = effective team* – team meetings should enable effective teamwork during the rest of the time and not be an end in themselves. Teams are effective when they work in a joined up way, even when they are working solo or in pairs or small groups.

- *Ignoring the 'smell of the dead elk'* – many teams have issues that affect everybody, but there is a tacit agreement that nobody should mention them. It is like a dead animal under the table that everybody can smell, but nobody wants to deal with.

After we had completed our research I came across the book by Patrick Lencioni on the five dysfunctions of a team (Lencioni, 2002) and discovered a great deal of overlap. Lencioni's model (see Figure 5.1 on page 71) sees a hierarchy of five dysfunctions each building on the ones beneath it. One of the key roles of a team coach is to interrupt these interruptions, but first they have to start by engaging the team in some form of mutual diagnosis of the critical areas that the team need to focus on to become more effective.

Teams that work together regularly and intensively need to take regular time away from the pressures of the front-line work to stand back and look at how they are individually and collectively functioning, and how they relate to the wider system in which they operate. This may take the form of an away-day, or a team-development workshop, or sessions with an outside team coach, or it may be part of a larger organizational change and development programme.

Whichever way a team or group decides to manage their own dynamics, it is important to remember that the time to start focusing on what is happening in the process is when things are going well and not to wait until the group or team are in crisis. When the levels of conflict, hurt and fear rise, it becomes much more difficult to see what is happening and to take the risk of making changes. However, for some teams it is only when they hit a crisis that they create the motivation to face what is happening, since sometimes 'crises create the heat in which new learning can be forged' (Hawkins, 1986).

When working with one executive team in a large financial company we asked the team members to complete the following questions separately and then share their answers:

- The unwritten rules of this group are …
- What I find it hard to admit about my work in this team is …
- What I think we avoid talking about here is …
- What I hold back on saying about other people here is …
- The hidden agendas that this group carries are …
- We are at our best when …
- What interrupts us from being at our best is …

This was followed by each person receiving feedback from all the other team members on what they appreciated and what they found difficult about his or her contribution to the team. Then each person had the opportunity to say what he or she most appreciated and found most difficult about the team as a whole. This can also provide a basis for planning what the team need to stop, start and continue.

Discipline 4: Connecting

The focus of this discipline is on how the leadership team as a whole, as well as individually and in pairs, engages the wider stakeholder system.

We have pioneered a team 360-degree feedback process. This is not feedback on team members, but on how the team is collectively viewed by all its critical stakeholders, including its own team members (see Chapter 12). Where possible we would also coach the team in engaging directly with inquiry conversations with their key stakeholders. Doing this for all the different stakeholders provides the team with a rich field of data to explore what they need to do differently. In Chapter 3 there is a short case example of actively engaging venture capital teams in 360-degree feedback collection and ways of dramatically sharing this with the team.

As we explored in Chapter 1, it is impossible for chief executives to carry out all the stakeholder engagement necessary for a thriving organization, particularly in times of change and transformation. The leadership team members all have a role to play in transformational engagement and for effective transformation it is important that all team members are skilled and impactful in this area and can represent the team in an aligned and congruent manner.

A team coach can help a team in this discipline in a variety of ways:

- Exploring the differences between:
  - information giving,
  - communication, and
  - engagement

and then producing an engagement strategy as a key aspect of their transformation strategy.

- Having each team member assess his or her own current authority, presence, impact and leadership engagement capacity (Hawkins and Smith, 2006) and receive feedback from other members of the team and review any 360-degree or other feedback from staff and stakeholders.

- Working with the team to prepare, design and rehearse engagement events, for which they can then receive feedback from other members of the team and the coach.

- Coaching the team members live when they are engaging with their staff and stakeholders. This can include a variety of coaching approaches:
  - briefing and debriefing the leaders before and after the engagement;
  - 'pitch-side' or 'half-time' feedback and coaching;
  - help with facilitation of the event.

Besides coaching the team on their collective engagement with stakeholders, the team coach also needs to focus on how the team manages to integrate their collective leadership team role with the operational leadership of their own individual division or function. I have already mentioned in Chapter 1 the challenge of multiple team and tribal membership, and being a 100 per cent member of both the collective leadership team and the divisional or functional team one leads. It is easy to fall back to being a representational go-between or a 'torn middle' (Oshry, 1995). In this role the divisional or functional leader represents the needs, aspirations and successes of his or her own team to the senior team, while defending his or her team from criticism and protecting their budget and resource allocation. Then the unfortunate go-between returns to lead his or her own team, having to deliver the report back from the senior team and to implement any decisions the senior team have made. One faculty dean who sat on a university's executive board described his role to me as the constant deliverer of bad news, from the faculty leadership team to the university executive board and vice versa. Under pressure, it is easy to disown your membership of the senior leadership team, and to talk about 'them' as though one was not part of 'them', or to describe how you had done your best, but the decision had gone against you!

Even more destructive to organizational integration and alignment is the leader who is part of agreeing to a collective way forward in the leadership team, but ignores this when it becomes too difficult in their own division or function. The effect of this is that conflict moves out of the senior leadership team, where it ought to be addressed and resolved, and gets enacted at the next tier down, when the second tier leaders of the divisional and functional groups find they are working to different and conflicting agendas. This can descend into silo mentality, 'turf wars', and the organization competing more internally than externally (see also Lencioni, 2006; Oshry, 1995).

These are all forms of organizational splitting, very common in most organizations and separate and non-integrated team coaching for the different teams can make things worse, as the challenges can lie between the teams, not within them. A team coach can address these issues by:

- Working with the senior team to ensure that when agreements are made, the team spends time exploring and committing to how they will implement these decisions in their own areas.

- Ensuring that the senior team make a temporary decision, which they commit to pilot in each of their functions and divisions and to report back on these pilots and amend the decisions accordingly.

- By providing individual coaching to the members of the leadership team on how they connect the two aspects of their role: their membership of the top team with the leadership of their own division or function.

Discipline 5: The core learning

The fifth discipline of systemic team coaching lies at the heart of where all the other four disciplines intersect, and is the discipline where the team is not just dealing with their current operational and transformational agenda, together and apart, but able to grow their individual and collective capacity through learning together.

David Clutterbuck (2007: 125) defines the learning team as: 'a group of people with a common purpose who take active responsibility for developing each other and themselves'. This is a very useful definition but, I would slightly extend it: 'a group of people with a common purpose who take active responsibility for developing each other, themselves, their team and the wider organization in which they operate, through both action learning and unlearning'.

This is because good team learning goes beyond the learning of the individuals within the team to the team itself learning, as well as attending to the learning in the wider system. Edmondson *et al* (2001) carried out research on the effective learning of new procedures by surgical teams in hospitals, which demonstrated that 'the most successful teams had leaders who actively managed their team's learning efforts'. This is applicable to all leadership teams, who need not simply to execute existing processes, but quickly adapt to new circumstances and implement new ways of operating.

Teams are an ideal unit for action learning, as first espoused by Reg Revans in the years after World War II and used in management development ever since. Mike Pedler, one of the leading writers and practitioners, defines action learning as:

> Action learning couples the development of people in work organizations with action on their difficult problems ... (it) makes the task the vehicle for learning and has three main components – people, who accept the responsibility for action on a particular task or issue; problems, or the tasks which are acted on; and the set of six or so colleagues who meet regularly to support and challenge each other to take action and to learn. (Pedler, 1997)

A team that commit to be a learning team is investing in developing their individual and collective underlying capacity through spending time on each phase of the classic action learning cycle, shown in Figure 6.4.

We also need to bear in mind that different individuals and teams will have different learning styles which affect where they prefer to start their learning. Some people prefer to start with practical action and then reflect on what works and what does not. Others like to have the theory and explanation before planning to apply the model in action. Honey and Mumford (1992) have developed a number of methodologies for people to ascertain their learning styles. They show ways for individuals to explore how to utilize their dominant preference and also how to expand their repertoire of learning possibilities. This can be adapted by team coaches to look at the dominant learning style of the team.

We have used Honey and Mumford's (1992) work to develop our own model of learning short circuits to help teams to become more aware of their limiting learning patterns; see Figure 6.5. These need to be recognized before new learning can take place.

There are five main limiting learning styles that we have identified:

1 *The fire-fighting or compulsive pragmatist team.* This is the 'plan-do-plan-do' trap where the motto is: 'If what we plan does not work, let us plan to do something different.' The learning stays at the level of trial and error. This sort of team will tend to have a short-term tactical and problem-solving bias.

2 *The post-mortemizing team.* This is the 'do-reflect-do-reflect' trap where the motto is: 'Reflect on what went wrong and correct it.' The learning here is restricted to error correction. Here the team will over-focus on the recent past and what went wrong.

3 *The navel gazing theorists.* This is the 'reflect-theorize-reflect-theorize' trap where the motto is: 'Philosophize on how things could be better, but never risk putting the theories to the test.'

FIGURE 6.4 Action learning cycle

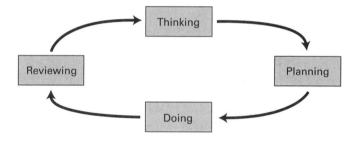

FIGURE 6.5 Learning cycle short circuits

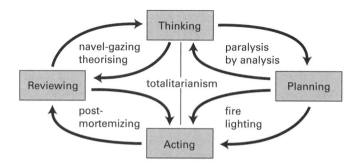

4 *The paralysis by analysis team.* This is the 'analyse-plan-analyse some more' trap where the motto is: 'Think before we jump, plan how to do it and think a bit more.' Learning is limited by the fear of getting it wrong or taking a risk. The team with this learning bias will spend a lot of time in Discipline 2, trying to analyse what is wrong, getting consultancy help on how it could be done differently, listening to change proposals but fearful about trialling approaches, or engaging with others until they are confident they have got the perfect answer.

5 *The totalitarian team.* This is the 'theorize-do' trap where the motto is: 'Work it out in theory and then tell them what we have decided.' This short trap also leads to very little leadership engagement with the wider system, only an imposition of what the team have decided, which is a great way of creating resistance and failure to win hearts and minds to the transformational or operational way forward.

Teams not only need to learn, but also unlearn, which Hedberg (1981) defined as: 'the process through which learners discard knowledge.' He goes on to say: 'Very little is known about how organizational unlearning differs from that of individuals.' But his work explores how unlearning can be blocked, particularly by the danger of too much success: 'Organizations which have been poisoned by their own success are often unable to unlearn obsolete knowledge in spite of strong disconfirmations.'

March and Olsen (1976) also warn that: 'There are times when organizations should treat their memories as enemies.' I would add to these quotes my own definition that: 'Unlearning is the process by which organizations unlock the evolving of their culture' (Hawkins, 1999).

Helping a team to become aware of the strengths and limitations of their learning style is only step one. The team coach needs to then help the team develop some new team practices which will help the team break old habits and inculcate new more successful learning habits. However, as any of us who have tried to give up a smoking, eating or drinking habit knows only too well, old habits are stronger than new good intentions. Good intentions need to be turned into committed new practice disciplines, which need some catalytic mechanism (Collins, 1999) to keep them alive.

An example of such a catalytic mechanism was arrived at in a large professional services firm where the partners recognized that a strong cultural pattern was for them to share views about other partners as gossip between each other, but rarely give direct feedback. They recognized that this had a very negative influence on leadership learning. As one senior partner put it: 'I have spent 25 years in a feedback-free zone – yet clearly other partners have heard lots of feedback about me!' The partners were wise enough to realize that all of them signing up to an agreement to not gossip about each other and to give direct feedback would not deliver a sustained shift. So, after some coaching on the nature of catalytic mechanisms the 30 senior partners involved in the workshop committed to each other that the next time another partner told them about a third absent partner (Partner X), they would all reply: 'So what did Partner X say when you told them?' When the gossiping partner then embarrassedly replied that he had not spoken to Partner X, they would respond with: 'How can I help you have that conversation?' Often the most powerful way to shift a culture is to first change the behaviour of the 'bystanders' and this is also true within a team.

The role of the team coach is to help the leadership team in becoming a self-sustaining learning team that will continue to learn and develop from its own rich experience well after the external team coach has finished working with them.

Coaching the interconnections between the disciplines

So far this chapter has concentrated on how to coach within the five distinct disciplines, but it is important to recognize that a great deal of team coaching is focused on connecting the flows between the disciplines. Above I have shown how the commissioning and clarifying disciplines need to work together, so that co-missioning leads to full ownership of the mission by both the board and the leadership team. It is also important that there is a constant cycling between Disciplines 2 and 3, so that clarity in what the team focuses on is aligned to how they are working on it together – task and process must go hand in hand. Similarly teams often need to be coached on ensuring there is congruence between how they are engaging within the team (3), with how they are collectively engaging the team's multifarious stakeholders (4). There must also be alignment between how the leadership team is engaging its stakeholders (4) and how the board and stakeholders are engaging (1) and informing the future.

The links between all the first four disciplines and the fifth one of core learning need to be iterative, where the level one learning within the disciplines can be reflected on and level-two (Bateson, 1972) or double-loop learning (Argyris and Schön, 1978) can be developed. Bateson distinguished between what he termed *zero learning* – the acquisition of data or information that does not create a difference or change – and Learning I in which skill learning is acquired through trial and error selection of a possibility within a set of options, and Learning II where second-order or double-loop learning happens from shifting the frame or set in which one is making level one choices.

These distinctions have become central to understanding not only different orders of individual learning, but also the distinctions between operational learning and strategic learning in the life of the organization. Garratt (1987) and Hawkins (1991, 1994) built on these to develop organizational learning models that showed how strategizing has both an operational action learning cycle and a policy creating cycle, and that quality strategizing entails going at least twice around both cycles. (For a fuller explanation of double-loop learning in organizations see Hawkins, 1991; and for its application to strategic decision making, see Hawkins, 1995.)

Conclusion

In this chapter I have shown the five key disciplines and the flow between these disciplines that the systemic team coach needs to be able to coach the team in. So far this has been within the context of working with the senior leadership team in an organization, sometimes called the 'executive team' or the 'operational board'.

In the next chapter I will look at how this work needs to be varied for different types of teams (virtual, project, account, etc) and then in Chapter 8 how this applies when working with the formal or supervisory board in commercial companies or the non-executive board in the public and third sector, or the cabinet board in local government.

PART THREE
Coaching Different Types of Teams

Many types of teams

07

Coaching the virtual, dispersed, international, project and account team

Introduction

So far in this book we have focused on systemically coaching leadership teams to raise their collective leadership performance. This chapter will explore how systemic team coaching also can be useful to other types of team and in the next chapter we will explore a very specific team – the board.

Types of teams

There are many different ways of classifying teams, such as by their:

- *duration* – temporary, project, stable, etc;
- *function* – finance, legal, HR, marketing, sales, production, compliance, etc;
- *customer group focus* – the X account team, the Y account team;
- *geographic spread* – dispersed, regional, national, international, virtual;
- *position in the hierarchy* – board, leadership, functional or divisional leadership, front-line, etc;

- *mode of operating* – executive (decision making), consultative, advisory, alignment, reporting, etc;
- *leadership style* – manager-led, self managing, self-designing, self-governing, etc.

David Clutterbuck (2007: 148–84; 2010: 275) provides an intriguing list based on his research in team learning, which mixes a number of these dimensions:

- *Stable teams* – where members and tasks are constant over a long period.
- *Cabin crew teams* – where the task remains the same but membership is constantly changing. Examples include film crews and some aspects of police work.
- *Standing project teams* – relatively stable new teams, drawn from a variety of other teams working usually on short-term projects.
- *Evolutionary teams* – longer-term projects where the tasks and the membership change over time, with new people taking over as the project moves into new phases.
- *Developmental alliances* – teams set up specifically for learning (for example action learning sets).
- *Virtual teams* – teams with fuzzy boundaries or geographically dispersed.

In this chapter we will look at just some of these types of teams and specific ways they can be systemically team coached. I have chosen to focus on the following types of teams: management, project, virtual, international and account, as these are all types of teams who use team coaching and have specific team coaching needs that require a special approach.

Management teams

So far in this book we have concentrated on coaching senior leadership teams, on the grounds that these have to face the biggest challenge and engage with the greatest complexity. However, team coaching can also provide great value for all levels of management teams, be they managing a function, division, production unit or support department. The five disciplines model of team coaching (see Chapters 3 and 5) applies as much to management teams as leadership teams, for all management teams have a commission to fulfil, a performance to clarify, some interdependent activity to co-create, critical stakeholders they need to connect with and the need to continuously improve through core learning.

At a simple level we can illustrate the differences between the management and leadership ends of the continuum, while recognizing most teams have a mixture of both activities:

Management is concerned with the achievement of plans through such processes as planning, delegating, project managing, reviewing, etc. The focus is on control and problem solving. *Leadership* is about aligning people to a common direction – obtaining their commitment to the realization of the vision. The focus is on motivating and inspiring.

It can be argued that all management teams have a leadership function, as they need to inspire the people they manage as well as their customers, suppliers and other stakeholders, but the leadership aspect of transforming the wider system is less prominent for management teams lower in the hierarchy, and they have additional challenges that arise from being in the middle of the organization. However, not all management groups can be classified as teams, for some are merely groupings of direct reports to a senior manager, and function as a 'hub-and-spoke' work group, which does not have a collective mission or joint interdependent activity. In this section we are focusing not on these but on management teams with collective objectives that require joint working.

I have written elsewhere (see Chapter 6) about the danger of teams in the middle of organizations becoming trapped as a 'torn middle', acting as a go-between in the conflict between those they manage and the leadership team to which they report, and at worst becoming an expensive postal service, delivering problems up the line and delivering unwanted solutions back down it. Over the 35 years I have been consulting to teams and organizations, middle managers have been greatly reduced in numbers and given greater accountability and responsibility for delivering real value, but the dangers of such dynamics still apply.

The team coach can specifically help those teams in the middle of the organization by helping them focus less on their hierarchical role and more on their horizontal role, by defining their internal and external customers and the specific value these customers need from them. All such team coaching needs to start 'outside-in', with the team finding out what their customers appreciate, find difficult and want different in both what they receive and how they receive it from this team. Only then can the team usefully explore how they can raise their collective performance in delivering the right products and services, at the right quality, at the right time and in the right way to delight their customers.

The team coach can coach the team in ways to connect with other parts of the organization to provide a more effective and aligned delivery. Many organizations suffer from a lack of middle management teams aligning their work, which causes unnecessary duplication and frustration. Many front-line staff have complained to us about how they are asked for the same information, by central support departments such as finance, human resources, internal audit, information technology, etc leading to time wastage and frustration that could have been avoided with more team work across internal boundaries.

Project teams

Project teams are a team brought together, often drawn from different teams, for a specific, defined and time-limited task.

Deborah Ancona and her colleagues at MIT have carried out very useful studies of high-performing project teams (Ancona *et al*, 2002). Their work showed that these teams shared the following characteristics:

- high levels of external focus and activity;
- extensive ties in the organization and wider context;
- expandable tiers in their internal organization;
- flexible membership – both in the team and between the tiers;
- coordination within and between tiers.

They developed a three-phase model in the life of a project team: exploration, exploitation and exportation (Ancona *et al*, 2002). I have extended this model into six Es, adding engaging at the beginning, emergence – re-engaging in the middle and ending at the end, as in my experience these are distinct phases which are essential for the project team to fully succeed. The six Es are shown in Figure 7.1.

In the first phase – 'engaging' – the team need to be selected, commissioned and then come together to 'form and norm' (Tuckman, 1965). This includes setting their goals and objectives, agreeing how they will best work together and how they will engage the external world.

In the second phase – 'exploration' – the team are combining their group-forming activities with intense activity of members going outside their own area and scouting for ideas, resources and information that might suit their purpose. Many ambassadorial relationships with key stakeholders need to be formed to ensure effective sponsorship and support.

The 'exploitation phase' contains the creative activity work of the project team, where high levels of delegated tasks, flexible membership and coordination contribute significantly to success. Hackman and Wageman (2005) cogently argue that there is another important coaching window at the temporal mid-point in the life span of the team. They argue that the team is much more ready to engage in strategy-focused coaching once they have been engaged in the joint work of the team, have the pressure of the end in sight, and have seen what is working and not working in the team's task and process performance. This leads to the 'emergence-re-engaging' stage. Depending on the progress made by the team, this may come before or after the team has got into 'exploitation'.

Then there is the 'exportation phase' where the work of the team has to be turned into action and the ambassadorial role is about selling their ideas, achieving agreement to moving forward and stimulating commitment from others to joint action.

FIGURE 7.1 Coaching project teams

Model of Key Phases

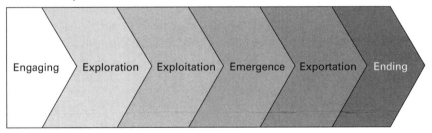

Engaging Exploration Exploitation Emergence Exportation Ending

The coach varying the coaching interventions for the different phases, developing skills and capabilities in the team and its members

A project team working on organizational change, or a design or innovation team working on bringing out a new product or service, can benefit greatly from having a team coach working alongside them. Such a coach needs to bring different experience, skills and types of intervention for each stage of the project. Hackman and Wageman (2005) built on the research of Gersick (1988) on the timing of coaching interventions and how these needed to be different for each stage of the team lifecycle. They concluded that:

> coaching interventions are more effective when they address issues a team is ready for at the time they are made ... In contrast, even competently administered interventions are unlikely to be helpful if they are provided at a time in the lifecycle when the team is not ready for them. Indeed ill-timed interventions may actually do more harm than good. (p 275)

Engaging

At this stage, the project team coach needs to help the team 'form and norm' effectively and build into a high-performing team. This includes helping them clarify the external sponsorship and commission they have been given and clarify their own goals, aspirations and outcomes (Disciplines 1 and 2, as in Chapter 6). Useful questions for this stage include:

- Who are our external sponsors?
- What mission have they given to us?
- How will they rate us as being successful?
- What is our primary purpose?
- What are the specific goals by which we will measure our success?
- What are the key things we need to get right to achieve that goal?

- What might prevent us from achieving that goal and how might we address any obstacles or pitfalls?
- What will we be proud of when we are successful?

The team then needs to look at the process aspects of how they will operate and co-create together (Discipline 3). Useful questions for this include:

- What will we need from each other to achieve that success?
- How will we need to operate as a team?
- What are the most likely ways we could run into difficulties as a team? How might we organize to avoid those pitfalls?
- How should we make decisions? Who needs to be involved in deciding, who needs to be consulted and who needs to be informed?

Exploration

This stage requires the team coach to be able to help the team:

- stimulate creativity, brainstorm and think outside the box;
- scenario plan; and
- investigate and carry out action research cycles.

If the project team are working on improving aspects of the wider organization then there are many methodologies that the team coach may bring to help the team carry out their work, such as Total Quality Management, Business Process Engineering, Six Sigma and Lean Manufacturing. There is not space here to include details of all of these, each of which has books dedicated to them.

If the project team is working on developing a new product, process or service, then once again there is a series of methodologies that the team coach can utilize for 'joint application design' or 'rapid application design'. At their heart is encouragement to think systemically and how to create a lean and effective end-to-end process. This includes the project and how to accelerate it by transcending the linear process of starting with analysis of current reality, designing and prototyping the new offering, market testing, redesigning, building, marketing and implementing. The coach may help the project team explore how they can design their own work to be less of a strung-out relay race and more a network of interconnected parallel activities. At the heart of 'lean thinking' (Womack and Jones, 2003) are the two guiding principles that provided the pillars for Toyota becoming the world's most successful car manufacturer: 'continuous improvement' and 'respect for people'. Each of these can be broken down further into defining principles.

Continuous improvement

1 Challenge – having a long-term vision of the challenges one needs to face to realize one's ambition and the culture of challenging everything.

2 *Kaizen* – good enough never is! Continuous striving for innovation and improvement.

3 *Genchi Genbutsu* – going to the source to see the facts for oneself and make the right decisions, create consensus and get results at speed.

Respect for people

1 Respect – taking every stakeholder's problems seriously and building mutual trust. Taking responsibility for other people reaching their objectives.

2 Teamwork – to develop and engage people through their contribution to team performance and through team problem solving.

'Lean thinking' has also been applied successfully to the service and public sectors. The National Health Service Institute in the UK writes:

Lean is an improvement approach to improve flow and eliminate waste that was developed by Toyota. Lean is basically about getting the right things to the right place, at the right time, in the right quantities, while minimizing waste and being flexible and open to change (NHSI 2005).

Exploitation

This stage requires the project team coach to help the team:

- Rapidly prototype and creatively experiment with possible ways forward.
- Achieve ways of seeking useful and speedy feedback from those who will be involved in deciding on, implementing and utilizing the project outputs and thus are the project team's customers.
- Redesign in the light of the feedback and what has worked and what has failed in the rapid prototypes and experiments.

Emergence: re-engaging at the midpoint review

Useful questions at this point include:

- How successful are we at fulfilling our mission?
- Where are we on the journey towards our success criteria?
- How do we need to reform our strategy in the light of our experience?
- How much are we living up to the values, norms and protocols we set ourselves? Which are proving useful and how do we need to change or add to them?
- Where have we been at our best as a team? What has enabled that? How could we be in that zone more often?
- Where have we been at our worst as a team? What patterns have contributed to that? How could we interrupt those dysfunctional patterns?

Exportation

Here the project team can be coached in connecting with all the critical stakeholders to get their 'buy-in' to the project outputs. This may involve rehearsing presentations and demonstrations of the outputs in a way that starts from the stakeholders' needs and not from the project team's solution and involves the stakeholder in experiencing the benefits. The coach may also attend the presentations and demonstrations, providing pre-, post- and mid-event coaching to improve engagement.

Ending

This is the stage when project teams are most able to stand back and harvest the learning from their work together, in order to grow their individual and collective capacities for working effectively. David Clutterbuck (2007: 166) provides some excellent questions that the team coach can use at this final stage of the project team:

- What has changed in our individual and collective knowledge, our self-awareness, our perception of reality?
- What have we learned about team formation?
- How have we used this learning?
- What is the process of capturing and sharing this learning?
- How can we make sure it is available to others?
- How can we build on this learning?
- How can we continue to learn from each other once the project team is disbanded?

Virtual teams

Increasingly team coaches are working with teams that are geographically dispersed and only rarely (and sometimes never) meet face-to-face. This requires new ways of operating for the team and the team coach and different and additional skills and methods.

Lipnack and Stamps (1996) give a useful definition of virtual teams:

A virtual team, like every team, is a group of people who interact through interdependent tasks guided by a common purpose.

Unlike conventional teams, a virtual team works across space, time, cultures and organizational boundaries with links strengthened by webs of communication technologies.

For a virtual team to work really well they need some face-to-face time to build their ability to develop relationships and a sense of collective purpose. Manfred Kets de Vries (2006) describes the challenge well:

In the cyber society of today – in the virtual teams that are becoming ever more common in the global marketplace – the building of trust is even more important and even more of an uphill battle. To make virtual teams effective, an enormous investment in relationship-building needs to be done up front. It's impossible to e-mail a smile or a handshake ... Personal relationships and face-to-face communication, not electronic communication, build trust. And yet only when a significant degree of trust exists between various parties can one expect effective interaction between individuals and groups located in different parts of the world. Without the glue of trust, teams don't work well and virtual teams don't work at all. (p 299)

Yet with the increasing globalization of all forms of organization, and the cost of travel in terms of money, time and world resources, we will need to evolve ways of building trust with less face-to-face time than we have previously been used to. As team coaches we need to develop new skills and methods to coach on video and audio meetings of the team, ensuring that relationships are built and misunderstanding checked out. We also need to remember that there is less informal space before and after meetings to process communication than there is in face-to-face meetings.

My colleague Chris Smith, when he was head of Leadership Development for Cable and Wireless, proposed five conditions for success with virtual teams:

1 Consciously build the team.
2 Develop an enabling leadership style.
3 Provide appropriate technology for communications.
4 Map the matrix and manage the network.
5 Develop, recognize and reward virtual team work.

He suggested that the signs that a virtual team were in trouble were:

- members cannot easily describe the team purpose;
- communications are formal, stuffy or tense;
- great deal of participation – little accomplishment;
- talk but not much communication;
- disagreements are aired in side conversations;
- decisions are made by the leader with little interest/involvement from the rest of the team;
- members are not open with each other;
- confusion about roles leads to duplication or gaps in activity;
- team has been in operation for three months and has never reviewed its functioning.

This is a very useful checklist for any virtual team or team coach.

It is important that the team coach is working live with the team when they are working virtually, joining teleconferences or web-based discussion groups. A coaching web-based workroom and different forms of e-coaching can also be useful in such settings.

International teams

Often but not always virtual teams are international teams, and international teams will often, but not always, function mostly as virtual teams.

Canney Davison and Ward (1999: 11) define an international team as: 'a group of people who come from different nationalities and work interdependently towards a common goal'. The multi-country context can bring with it many additional complexities and challenges. Canney Davison and Ward (1999: 12) list:

- working on a complex task;
- having an impact in more than one country;
- serving a very wide set of customers;
- solving problems in many areas simultaneously;
- expecting to have a significant impact;
- different cultures and backgrounds.

They point out that the cost of establishing and maintaining internationals teams means that the expectations on them are necessarily high, which adds to the already considerable challenges. Canney Davison and Ward (1999: 16) go on to provide a useful table of the advantages and disadvantages of such international teams; see Table 7.1.

TABLE 7.1

Advantages of International Teams	Disadvantages of International Teams
Enables global strategies to be created that are sensitive to local requirements	Individuals can feel torn between loyalty to the team and to their local manager
Enables the organization to benefit from a diversity of perspectives that more closely match the preferences of its client base	It can be difficult to reach a consensus on a way forward
Increases organizational learning about global market	Language and communication difficulties mean that it can take longer to reach an optimum level of effectiveness
More efficient use of resources – avoids duplication of effort	Remote working can feel very isolated and demotivating and harm family life. It is also easy to get distracted on local issues
High level of intrinsic rewards, learning a lot from different people, different parts of the company, and learning different methodologies in tackling problems	Potential for increased conflict due to different opinions
Extends international development opportunities beyond traditional expatriate manager	Certain cultural habits such as talking about oneself, pointing, types of food can be offensive to people from other cultures
Being 'special' can increase morale	These teams need high initial investment in people, training and technology to avoid very expensive mistakes
Team leaders and members usually increase their skills with communication technology	Difficult to create equitable reward and evaluation
Enables broader targets to be set that will have an impact in many different countries simultaneously	

Gregerson *et al* (1998) carried out a survey of Fortune 500 companies in the United States and discovered that 85 per cent do not think they have an adequate number of global leaders and 67 per cent think their existing leaders need additional skills and knowledge in working globally. Various studies have identified the qualities needed by an effective global leader; these are summarized by Hawkins and Smith (2006) and shown in Table 7.2.

The team coach must be able to help the team leader and team members in such international teams develop more of these capabilities for working globally. This means they themselves must develop these skills. Senior executives in international organizations need to develop these skills and be able to work transculturally.

Zulfi Hussein writes about this challenge in relation to mentoring: 'In order to mentor a person from a different culture the mentor needs to be able to determine how their own culture and the culture of the mentee will impact their communication' (Zulfi Hussein, in Megginson and Clutterbuck, 2005: 98). He goes on to emphasize the importance of what he calls 'cultural literacy', which he defines as understanding the values, beliefs and symbols of the dominant culture, one's own culture, the mentee's culture and the culture of the organization in which the mentee works.

This is an even greater challenge when as an international team coach you need to relate well to the many different cultures that may be present in the team. This can be accentuated if as the team coach you come from the culture of the country where the organization is based and can be seen as identified with the dominant group. In Hawkins and Smith (2006) we wrote about the need to work through dialogue that was reflective on our own cultural norms and patterns, many of which we might not be aware of.

It is important to take steps to understand other cultures, and we have found that our usual stance of openness to inquiry serves us well. This is partly because we generally believe that an open attitude to learning means that we ourselves keep alive and creative rather than become formulaic in the work, but also because, if we are to really honour rather than deny cultural diversity, we need to find ways of dialoguing across difference. So dialogue is at the heart of what we do. If we see our task as merely to understand the other's perspective then no real meeting has happened. We are ourselves absent. In a supervisory relationship this means not only a willingness to encourage and explore difference in the relationship, but also an attitude of open inquiry towards ourselves and our relationship with our clients.

Tyler *et al* (1991), as quoted in Holloway and Carroll (1999), distinguish between three stances in responding to culture:

- *The universalist* denies the importance of culture and puts difference down to individual characteristics. In counselling, a universalist will tend to understand all difference in terms of individual pathology.

- *The particularist* takes the polar opposite view, putting all difference down to culture.

- *The transcendentalist* takes a view that resembles our position quite closely.

TABLE 7.2 Effective global leaders and global consultants

Identity	Conceptual ability	Interpersonal relations
● Positive self-concept	● Global socio-economic perspective	● Interprets behaviour carefully
● Authenticity	● Contextual thinking (Helicopter/space shuttle)	● Matches styles on context
● Adaptive to others		● Makes self understood
● Sees self/own culture in context		● Respects people equally
● Guided by principles		● Open to influence
● Open to differences		

Coleman (in Holloway and Carroll, 1999) discusses this perspective as follows:

> Both the client and the counsellor have vast cultural experiences that deeply influence their worldviews and behaviour ... it is the individual who has to make sense of and interpret those experiences. The transcendent or multicultural perspective suggests there are normative assumptions that can be made about individuals based on cultural factors such as race, gender and class, but that it is just as important to understand how these normative assumptions become reality through the idiosyncratic choices made by individual members of a group.

Eleftheriadou (1994) makes a helpful distinction between cross-cultural work and work that is transcultural. In *cross-cultural* work we tend to 'use our own reference system to understand another person rather than going beyond our own world views'. *Transcultural work* denotes the need to work beyond our cultural differences and be capable of operating within the frames of reference 'natural' to other individuals and groupings.

The ability to work in this way is important: entering in to the terrain of the other is a key part of honouring the diversity that they bring with them, so being able to adapt to it is a significant skill to learn. At a deeper level, however, there is a more generative dimension in which both parties move beyond honouring the difference that each brings – and mutually create an additional shared language and set of frameworks for their inquiry. An open attitude to inquiry enhances the ability to work transculturally from a transcendentalist perspective. This inquiry optimally takes place within a dialogue in which both parties participate in the learning.

In coaching a number of international teams we developed a culture awareness exercise which can be carried out in diverse pairings:

Person A states: 'What I would like you to know about my cultural background …'.

Person B replies: 'What I heard was …'.

Person A clarifies any misunderstandings.

Person B then responds by stating: 'How I would act differently to respond to what you have told me is …'.

Person A then lets person B know which of these responses they would find helpful.

Client or customer account teams

I was invited to help a global account team of one of the world's largest professional services firms. Various senior partners, drawn from different lines of service (audit, tax, corporate finance and consultancy) and different geographies had flown in especially for this half-day account meeting. For the first hour most of them were alternating their attention between listening to the updates from colleagues on what they were doing with this joint client and working on their Blackberries. There was little sense of joint endeavour or joint value creation. After an hour I called a time-out and asked: 'What new learning or knowledge have we created that none of us knew before we arrived at this very expensive meeting?' There were blank stares, and one or two started to mention information they had discovered from a colleague. I repeated the challenge, realizing that many of them had no notion of how a team could generate new thinking and knowledge that was not already inside an individual. After some explorations of how this might happen, they changed their whole meeting format and evaluated every future meeting on what percentage of the meeting time had been spent in information exchange and how much in generating new knowledge through thinking together. They went on to explore how in each meeting they could generate both new business foresight as well as company insight that would be of value to the company, and how to deliver it in a way that built the depth and breadth of their collective relationship with the client company.

Another growing area of practice for team coaches is coaching account teams. An account team is a multidisciplinary and/or a multi-regional team brought together from across a company to focus on the relationship with one key customer or client organization. My colleagues and I have worked with a wide variety of account teams. In the professional services these have included organizational consultants, lawyers, accountants, auditors, tax advisers, financial advisers and sometimes a mixture of different professionals coming from different advisory firms. We have also worked with account teams in retail products, manufacturing and financial services.

In this work our focus is to help the client account team provide a service to their shared client that is more than the sum of its part, and where the team are more integrated than the client organization. Inevitably the account team can begin to take on some of the dynamics of their client organization and so much of this team coaching is similar to team supervision, where one needs to focus both on the account team and the needs and dynamics of their client. (For a case study of working with an account team's dynamics and how it paralleled the client dynamics, see Hawkins and Smith, 2006: 195–6.)

Developing the account team

The team coach may also develop an ongoing relationship with the account team where they coach not just the team functioning (Disciplines 2 and 3) but also the developing relationship with the client system (Disciplines 1 and 4). From our experience of combining the role of account team coach and systemic shadow consultant with a number of global account teams in major professional services firms, I developed with the help of colleagues and key clients a model of 'Account transformation'. This model has not only been used with a wide variety of accountancy, consultancy, legal and financial companies working with global clients, but also with product companies that wanted to develop long-term partnerships with their key customers.

The account transformation model in Figure 7.2 identifies four potential types of relationship roles with clients:

1 *Solution supplier* is the area where current needs, known to the client, are delivered by the account team as the supplier. Here the work is often won through competitive tender and tightly specified by the purchasing department.

2 *Strategic adviser* is the section where future needs, known to the client, are anticipated and where the team adds value to the client's forward strategy through adding their own expert knowledge about the sector trends.

3 *Integrated trust* is the area where current patterns, processes, culture and needs, hidden from the client's view (blind spots) are revealed compassionately and appreciatively by the account team – so that the client experiences the team as adding value in areas they could not originally have foreseen.

4 *Performance partner* is the section where there is joint investment and shared risk between client and consultant team, focused on addressing future needs that cannot be predicted with certainty.

FIGURE 7.2 Account team transformation model

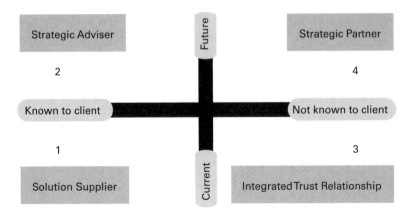

Each relationship role requires a different language and mode of engagement from the consultants:

1 As a *solution provider,* the language is most often couched in terms of the client bringing problems and the consultants bringing solution. The language is one of technical expertise.

2 As *strategic adviser* the language is more focused on challenges and opportunities, and is future-oriented.

3 As *trusted adviser* the language shifts to focusing more on patterns, processes and culture. Instead of concentrating on the immediate problem, attention shifts to the systemic patterns and dynamics of which this problem is just one symptom.

4 As *performance partner* all the above languages may be in play, and the language of joint endeavour and creating win-win relationships is essential.

Each relationship role also requires the account team to bring different values and expertise. As *solution provider* the account team brings their technical expertise or their product – for example, to restructure, cut costs, manage an acquisition, provide legal representation or provide photocopiers. As *strategic adviser* they bring 'business foresight' – their understanding of the business and the business context, not only as it currently exists, but as it is developing into the future.

As *trusted adviser* one is bringing 'organizational insight', gleaned from having worked with the organization at different levels and in different ways. Elsewhere I have defined organizational culture as what you stop noticing when you have worked somewhere for over three months, and have illustrated this by quoting the Chinese proverb: 'The last one to know about the sea is the fish.' The trusted adviser can bring insights about the culture as it manifests when you try to change anything in the organization.

So instead of just helping it carry out a successful acquisition or major change project, the account team can increase the organization's acquisition or change capability for future such activities, through understanding better what blocks and what succeeds in their particular culture.

As *performance partner* the value the account team bring includes a joint commitment to a shared endeavour with their client/customer/partner organization. This role needs to encompass the value brought from all the previous three roles, but also the skills and capacity in partnering and ways to create win-win relationships.

Often account teams lack the discipline and the skills to generate the collective knowledge, to deliver the added value of business foresight and organizational insight, which would differentiate them from other product or service providers. Often we have found that account team meetings are an exchange of information and a check on the progress on each assignment. The team coach's role is to provide both processes and facilitation to explore the trends in the wider sector and also the cultural patterns and processes of the company with which they are working. The account team coach then helps them travel the journey from being one of many suppliers the client uses – through the stages of becoming a strategic and trusted adviser – to being a long-term performance partner that is key to the client company moving forward. The team coach can do this through:

- Coaching the team in discovering the client/customer's explicit and implicit 'commission' and their underlying needs (Discipline 1). The core question the team coach helps the account team answer is: 'What can you uniquely do that will enable your client/customer to succeed in their market-place?'
- Helping the team 'clarify' their mission and strategy with their client/ customer and work out the steps to get there (Discipline 2).
- Attending account team meetings to help them move from an emphasis on exchanging updates and information to generating new collective thinking that produces customer insight and business foresight that can add value to the customer organization (Discipline 3).

In today's marketplace, having a quality product or service at the right price and delivered in a timely and effective way is an essential prerequisite to compete for business. To stand out, an account team needs to not only focus on their customer but their customer's customer. The account team needs to get alongside their customer and help them succeed with their customers through the product or service they provide and with the value of their organizational insight and business foresight.

Conclusion

In this chapter we have explored how team coaching can be adapted for management, project, virtual, international and account teams. These are just a few of the great variety of different types of teams. As the field of team coaching grows there will be much further development in adapting team coaching to a greater range of team situations.

In the next chapter we will explore one more particular type of team, that of the board of the organization.

Coaching the board

08

> *The directors determine whether or not a company survives and thrives. The extent to which the board liberates or constrains the energies and talents of the people of a company is determined by the competence of the directors and* how effectively they work together as a team. **(PETER MORGAN EX-DIRECTOR GENERAL OF THE INSTITUTE OF DIRECTORS, QUOTED IN COULSON-THOMAS, 1993: 222)**

Introduction

In Chapters 5 and 6 we looked at coaching the executive or leadership team of an organization, and in this chapter we will turn our attention to coaching the board. As the quote at the beginning of this chapter states, the board of the company is pivotal to the success or failure of a company, and teamwork in the board is crucial to effective board performance. Coulson-Thomas in his 1990s survey of 218 directors in the UK, 75 per cent of whom were chair or CEO of their companies, found that teamwork was the number one challenge they listed, and yet very few boards had engaged in any formal team development activities or team coaching. Since then the challenge and demands on boards have increased exponentially, with many national and international reviews of governance and board functioning and changing legal responsibilities.

Those who coach boards may use many of the same skills as they do for coaching leadership teams and a number of the same methods and skills are relevant. However, the context and the role of the board necessitate a distinct approach to board coaching, which I will outline in this chapter having first explored the changing challenges for boards and what makes for a high-performing board. Most of the chapter focuses on the private sector board, but much of the approach is both relevant to, and has been used with public and voluntary sector boards, and I will address these directly at the end of the chapter.

The growing challenges for boards

Over the last 30 years corporate governance has become a key business issue and an area of development and change. There have been events and trends that have spurred inquiry and changes in standards of practice. For example:

- Incompetence and corruption have been highlighted in the media, with some legal cases setting new precedents in countries based more on case law. Contrary to the beliefs of some governments on the right of the political spectrum that market forces would automatically function for the greatest social good it has become clear that more regulation was necessary.

- This has been further intensified by the financial and banking crisis of 2008–09, with unprecedented collapses in major banking institutions (Swords, 2010).

- Concentration and coordination of shareholder power through institutional investors and fund managers have resulted in a demand for higher quality reporting and greater transparency of the board's decisions and workings.

- Globalization of companies and national economies has resulted in a growing pressure for international standards.

- Greater speed of change and complexity has required boards to be more able to learn and help their companies learn and adapt, and to create new models of leadership.

- There has been an increase in awareness and active interest of all stakeholders in company activity partly facilitated by the internet and communications technology.

Coaching the board

Boards are increasingly expected to carry out and publish a review or audit of their own role, performance and functioning. Some boards have used this as an opportunity to have external help from a board coach, to carry out a board review/audit and this may well move on to the board coach working with the board on some of the identified areas of improvement. Increasingly the public sector is also requiring its boards to be regularly reviewed.

Another common way that team coaching enters the boardroom is when a team coach has been working with the executive team and has involved the board as part of the process, and the board have recognized that as part of the organization moving forward they also need to look at their role and performance.

When coaching boards, the stages in the coaching relationship as outlined in the CID-CLEAR model (see Chapter 5) would still apply, with the coach having to undertake:

- initial contracting – often with the board chair and board gatekeeper;
- some inquiry process using interviews with the various board members and a board review instrument;
- some form of diagnostic process to make sense of the emerging issues and a way of engaging the board with his or her findings and developing an action plan for how he or she will develop the board in the light of these findings.

With some boards the process of coaching may end here, but other boards may engage the coach to help with the improvement process.

The five disciplines of team coaching (see Chapters 3 and 6) all apply to board coaching, but the journey through the five disciplines is often very different, due to the different context and responsibilities of the board. Often the board audit or review means that the coaching starts in Discipline 5 'Core learning' and then moves to Discipline 2, 'Clarifying' the role and functions of the board.

As part of this process it is important that the coach helps the board also move into Discipline 1 'Commissioning'. Boards receive their commission from their shareholders (or members) as well as from the legal, fiduciary and governance standards in the jurisdictions in which they operate. This necessitates attending to the relationship between how the board see their role, function and mission, and the legal, fiduciary and governance standards required in the various country jurisdictions that are relevant to their operation and for their sector and type of organization. In most countries there are specific regulations for publicly listed companies, other non-listed limited companies with shareholders, partnerships, public sector organizations and charities.

In the inquiry phase it is also important to find out the expectations of the board from its shareholders, or in the case of charities its members, or in the case of a partnership its partners. Some boards have regular mechanisms for collecting this feedback; others may ask the coach to initiate such a process. At a minimum it is important to inquire into formal and informal feedback (and complaints) that have been received, as well as issues that have emerged over recent annual general meetings of members or shareholders.

Only when the board coach has helped the board clarify its role and commission is it sensible to move on to help the board clarify how it has added value to the enterprise through its various functions and how it could increase the value of its role (Discipline 2). Later in this chapter we will look at the key functions of a board, which can provide a framework for considering the value a board creates in each of these major functions.

From this foundation the board can then consider Discipline 3 and look at how it 'co-creates' as a team and the dynamics of how it works together. Finally, the board coach can help the board attend to how it connects (Discipline 4): how it communicates with, learns from and engages with all its critical stakeholders. For boards these stakeholders include:

- investors, shareholders, members, partners, the general public (depending on the type of board);
- regulators – auditors, tax offices, government departments, sector and profession regulators, etc;
- customers, clients or service users;
- staff and employees (especially the executive team);
- suppliers and partners;
- the communities in which the business operates.

One of the most critical relationships for any board is between itself and the executive team that report to it. We shall consider this relationship in the section on coaching the board in how it connects.

Clarifying the role of the board: Disciplines 1 and 2

As part of the initial inquiry the coach should ascertain how each member sees the role and functions of the board and then link these to both the legal and fiduciary requirements that operate in the countries where they do business and the best practice governance standards currently operating for their type of organization.

The UK Cadbury Report was one of the first to clarify Corporate Governance:

> Corporate governance is the system by which companies are directed and controlled. Boards of directors are responsible for the governance of their companies. The responsibilities of the board include setting the company's strategic aims, providing the leadership to put them into effect, supervising the management of the business and reporting to the shareholders on their stewardship.

> (Cadbury Committee 1992)

The underlying value of the business represents more than shareholder interests (though shareholder value may be emphasized sometimes to the exclusion of others). The value of all types of assets, resources and capital are included: physical, financial, social and human. The social capital covers both the company's relationships and its reputation in the eyes of customers, investors, suppliers, business partners and current or potential employees.

The human capital includes the knowledge, learning capability and loyalty of employees. Compliance with social and legal responsibilities increasingly includes ensuring that business activity does not inflict unacceptable costs or losses on the local community or natural environment, and monitoring risks at all levels.

Within this purpose statement there are a number of dilemmas represented by different needs, stakeholders and timeframes. Four major dilemmas facing directors were identified in the UK Institute of Directors paper on the standards of the board (1995):

1 be entrepreneurial and take risks to drive the business forward – while exercising prudent control;

2 be knowledgeable about the actions and workings of the company – while standing back from the day-to-day and retaining an objective long-term view;

3 be sensitive to pressures of short-term local issues – while being informed of broader trends in society, in the competition and internationally;

4 focusing on commercial realities – while acting responsibly towards employees, society and the natural environment.

To be effective in handling these and other dilemmas the board needs to conceptualize its role as:

● at the boundary between internal organization and some of its key stakeholders – rather than at the top;

● directing – rather than managing or fulfilling a professional function, so board members see directing as a proper job and give time to it;

● working for the good of the whole company or enterprise – rather than just representing a function or single stakeholder or party interest;

● learning and leading learning within the process of formulating, implementing and reviewing strategy – rather than staying with current assumptions and reacting too late to changes around them.

This last part of a board's role has been particularly elaborated and emphasized by Bob Garratt's books on the learning and development of boards, *Fish Rots from the Head* (1996) and *Thin on Top* (2003). As well as being sensitive to relevant trends and changes in their external environment, the board members learn from the customer through educating and valuing their employees as a source of information on customers, and stimulate inquiry by asking questions and creating dialogue with others inside and outside the organization. The board creates the emotional and social climate for learning from mistakes as much as successes, and for tolerating uncertainty. The board should never underestimate its role in setting the tone for how the organization operates and the coach needs to constantly challenge the board 'to be the change they want to see'.

The functions of the board

When asked by the *Financial Times* what he saw as the main functions of the board, Niall Fitzgerald, who had been CEO and Chairman of Unilever and had become Chairman of Reuters, said:

1 Decide which skills are needed on the board.
2 Agree the strategy and keep it under review.
3 Focus on profitable growth with acceptable risk.
4 Safeguard the brand and corporate reputation.
5 Give directors access to detailed information.
6 Expose the board to younger talent in the company.
7 Discussion should be open, candid and trusting. (Boardroom Agenda by Niall Fitzgerald, *Financial Times*, 27 September 2005)

In helping a board review its performance the team coach needs to be able to help the team look at its various and at times conflicting functions. A board needs to maintain a balance between attending to the external and internal environment. It must also create a balance between attending to the long-term policy and strategy issues on the one hand and to the short-term monitoring of current performance and accountabilities to shareholders or regulators on the other. These different functions need to be held in dynamic tension. Bob Tricker (1980) first set these out in a model. Bob Garratt's (1995) version, presented here in Figure 8.1, made some changes to it (placing learning at the centre). The model can be used for framing the various areas of board focus.

The arrows represent the four major functional areas within a cycle, with each function having a rhythm or cycle of its own. In one board I coached we used this model to develop a better rhythm of reviews linked to the different board functions:

- policy review: annually;
- strategy review: six-monthly;
- operations review: monthly;
- governance and board review: annually, three months before policy review.

The board needs to set aside the time for thinking strategically and for the stewardship of the enterprise. Often boards can become legally-oriented or administrative, with structures and agendas that become ends in themselves and block the board dialoguing in a way that is generative, and thinking and learning together.

FIGURE 8.1 Functions of the board

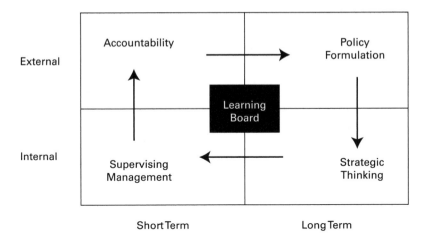

Effective board leaders relate the short-term to the long-term and the particular to the general in their day-to-day actions and communications: they show or state explicitly the links between specific decisions, plans and evaluations and the overall direction and vision. Just as with the five disciplines of leadership teams, the flow and connections between these functions is as important as the activity within them.

The functions in the four areas of policy, strategy, supervising operations and external accountability (as outlined by Bob Garratt and Bob Tricker) cover:

1 Policy formulation
  - monitoring the external environment;
  - stating purpose;
  - creating vision and values;
  - shaping the development of corporate culture and climate.

2 Strategic thinking
  - positioning in changing markets or social context;
  - setting corporate direction;
  - formulating strategy;
  - reviewing, deciding and allocating key resources;
  - deciding implementation process.

3 Supervising management
  - overseeing management performance;
  - reviewing key business results;
  - monitoring budgetary control and corrective action.

4 Accountabilities
- reporting to shareholders or owners;
- ensuring compliance with regulators;
- responding to other stakeholders;
- ensuring reviews of the board and board directors.

In each of these areas the board will need to develop methods of organizing discussions and board information flow, ways of developing policy, vision, strategy and culture with the organization, and procedures for scanning, monitoring, audit and control – as well as ways of working together and reviewing its own collective and individual director performance (see below).

1. Policy formulation

Boards need to have a:

- framework for thinking about the environment (political, physical, economic, social, technological, trade, legislative and ecological) and ways of sensing and scanning changes relevant to the enterprise;
- process of reviewing purpose in the context of the changing environment and of renewing the vision in relation to purpose, core competencies and values;
- review process to look at leadership practice based on an understanding of how leadership cultures are formed, maintained and changed.

2. Strategic thinking

Boards will need methods and models for organizing thinking, information and dialogue following a sequence from industry and market analysis to the assessment of the firm or business and development of an overall strategy, then functional strategies (marketing, production, finance, human resources, etc), resource allocation and business planning.

3. Supervising management

Boards will need to design key performance indicators, and the information systems to support them, for all levels of management. This would cover the business drivers and reflect different assets, systems or functions and management of strategic projects. The front page would be a 'dashboard' for the board. These indicators can include business ratios, finance, risk management, customer perceptions, human resources and key assets such as physical, social, human and supply chain.

4. External accountability

Methods of reporting back to shareholders and other stakeholders will be needed: committees and procedures for financial audit and regulatory compliance, and for audit of the selection, performance and remuneration of board members. Customer or employee surveys are often part of the supervision of management. Some companies now have a subcommittee for an environmental protection audit.

One way a board coach can help a board review these functions is to present the model and ask the members to explore what they have done well and what they could improve in each of the main functions. This information can be collected through individual interviews with board members or a questionnaire, and used to initiate a dialogue leading to a plan of action. Alternatively, this can be carried out live with the board by having the main areas up on different flipcharts and asking board members to post comments on different coloured Post-its, representing positives and improvement areas, on each board. The board members can then split into sub-groups, each tasked with sorting the comments on one of the boards and drawing up the key themes and recommendations for improvement. This later method ensures greater participation and ownership of the issues and encourages the dialogue to be more between different board members than a debate between the coach and dominant board members.

Structure of the board

How a board fulfils the different functions mentioned above depends on what form of board structure has been adopted. Sometimes the performance of the board is limited by its structure. There is no right structure that will meet all needs or be appropriate for all contexts, and whichever structure is chosen creates different boundaries and potential fault lines. It is important for board chairs, non-executives and board coaches to understand the basic range of board structures, in order to facilitate an informed discussion on whether a board has the suitable structure to carry out its purpose.

There are four main different forms of board structure, and these are in some ways evolving and converging across the world. There are differences according to country culture/history/traditions and the size and ownership (public or private) of the company. Public sector governance structures are taking on some of the characteristics of the private sector particularly in Europe and the United States.

The four main types of board structure differ mainly in the number and independence of non-executives, the separation of executives and non-executives and the balance of powers and liabilities between them, and the legitimacy and use of constructive criticism, conflict and diversity. The first two, executive and non-executive boards, give power more to the executives or non-executives; the other two, two-tier or unitary boards, can have more balance of power, but not necessarily, as it depends on their composition and functioning. Each has its particular advantages and disadvantages, and can be found in different sizes of business or countries.

1. Executive board

Here there are no non-executives: a dominant chief executive, perhaps a chair who may or may not be excluded, and other executive directors who may see their relationship with the CEO as primary, thus increasing his or her power. Because the chief executive is dominant the board may be weaker on monitoring what is happening outside the organization, suffer from lack of diversity and debate, and clone membership, style and assumptions.

This form is found in smaller companies with owner directors, family businesses and subsidiaries of multinational companies. However, increasingly even in smaller and family owned businesses, there is growing use of non-executive and independent directors.

In this type of board, there is a danger for the team coach of being pulled into the missing role of the non-executive and being invited to give advice and become a major contributor. If this happens the coach needs to name this pattern, renegotiate the contract and boundaries and invite the board to consider whether they need a non-executive. In family firms the board coach can also be pulled into the role of family therapist or mediator, and this pattern needs to be named and the contract returned to or renegotiated.

2. Non-executive board

This usually comprises only non-executives, who may or may not be independent. They decide on policy, direction and strategy and delegate the execution to the CEO; they also retain the liability. If the CEO is not a member of the board this distances the board from what is going on in the business. If the CEO is a member and the only executive present, he or she can have great power as a gatekeeper of the flow of information. This can suppress debate and criticism and the organization may orient itself too much around the CEO to the neglect of the customer. This structure is found often in the United States and in New Zealand, and also in public service and charity organizations with boards.

With this structure the board coach can end up addressing the conflict between the board and the executive team, with access to one side of this relationship only. Alternatively he or she may be drawn aside by the CEO to become their ally in managing this interface.

3. Two-tier or 'senate' boards

This is comprised of a supervisory board and an operational board. The supervisory board addresses the strategic issues and informs the operational board of its strategic intent, and receives and reviews performance figures from the operational board. The supervisory board is composed of non-executive directors, but they may not be independent. The operational board represents the different interests in the company and can include trade union representatives.

While this can balance powers between constituencies of interest, the disadvantages are that there may not be enough independent members of the supervisory board and many of those on the board may represent interlocked interests of bankers or shareholders, or local and national political interests. If the two boards become too tied up with national, local or organizational politics then they become separated from each other and the policy, strategy and operations functions are no longer integrated. This structure is found in Germany, the Netherlands and France.

The challenge for the team coach is to create a contract where he or she can coach both boards as well as addressing the relationship between the two boards. I have done this by having separate sessions with both boards before bringing them together for a joint workshop.

4. Unitary board

This includes both executive and non-executive directors as its name suggests, and usually both a chair and CEO. All directors are equally liable for the performance of the enterprise. The executives are responsible for agreeing and executing strategies and for the supervision of management, whilst receiving scrutiny, support and criticism from the non-executives. The non-executives play a key role in policy formulation and ensuring accountability, especially externally to shareholders and other stakeholders – protecting their interests.

The advantages are that there can be more integration of different perspectives and interests. The risks are that the non-executives and executives may not be independent enough. Audit of their selection, appraisal and remuneration is therefore critical, as is their induction and training. This is found most often in the UK and commonwealth countries.

5. Advisory boards

These are used by smaller companies or companies venturing into other countries for the first time to give them access to other knowledge or networks, or to represent other nationalities.

Board committees

These are used for specific business requirements or for ensuring conformance with external accountabilities or required standards of board practice. The most common are:

- audit committee: financial compliance;
- nominations committee: board member selection and appraisal and contracts (length of tenure, etc);
- remuneration committee: board member and senior executive pay, pensions and performance bonuses.

Other less common board committees that are used in some organizations:

- environmental audit committee;
- health and safety committee;
- intellectual property committee.

Other board committees may be set up for succession planning or human resources, new product or market development, or any issue relevant to the business.

The dynamics of the board: Discipline 3

While the board members have clarified their role and functions and aligned these with legal and stakeholder expectations, the board coach will most often find that a number of board dynamics and conflicts emerge that affect the way the board works and co-create together. The coach must not fall into the trap of just seeing these as interpersonal conflicts. Even more so than with leadership teams, the board will represent different stakeholder interests and the boards need to find ways of holding these in contention and resolving any emerging conflicts. The most common board conflict is between the chair and the CEO, with the chair most often carrying the interests of the shareholders and the CEO more focused on the needs and interests of the customers, suppliers and staff. The board coach can help the board by gently asking them to mention which stakeholder group they are currently concerned about or consider themselves to be representing. This can help the discussions to become clearer, less personalized and with more collective awareness of systemic contentions. One of the key tasks of any board is to constantly find the best integration and alignment of all stakeholder interests.

In addition, board members will often have a range of personal interests that overlap with the work of the board, such as:

- involvement with customer or client or potential competitor organizations;
- differential shareholding in the company;
- being employed by the company;
- involvement with suppliers or partner organizations that the company is working with;
- involvement with professional bodies or trade associations which interact with the company;
- government or political involvement.

It is good practice for boards to keep a record of all potential conflicts of interest publicly registered by all board members. The declaration on a register of such interests is only a first step in the process, for a healthy board also needs to have a culture of such interests being noted and dealt with when they become pertinent in the board's ongoing business.

When working with the newly formed board of Capespan mentioned in Chapter 6, I facilitated the board in drawing up its policy on 'Conflicts of interest', which given that most of the non-executive members of the board were suppliers to the company, was a complex process. During a break, the then CEO took me aside and challenged me that we had dealt with the formal aspect of conflicts of interests but had not addressed the dynamic in the room. I asked him what he suggested we did next. 'That is what we pay you for,' came his blunt reply, just as we were about to reconvene! As we restarted I repeated his challenge to the whole group and then asked the 30 people present to look at the list of potential conflicts of interests they had all jointly created and agreed to before the break, and to stand up if they currently had one or more conflicts of interest as listed. At first no one moved. Then one or two slowly got to their feet. Only then did the dynamic start to manifest. Heated exchanges began, with board members saying to others things like: 'Well if x is standing you should be standing as well.' Gradually about half the board members in the room were standing. I then asked those who were not standing to pair up with someone who was standing and:

1 ask them to list all their potential conflicts of interest;

2 then to tell them what they would like them to do about these conflicts, both in board meetings and outside, to effectively manage these conflicts of interest;

3 get their agreement to a plan of action;

4 tell them how they would support them in carrying out this plan of action.

The process had now moved from a form-filling piece of bureaucracy to a co-creative active process.

Coaching the board on how it connects: Discipline 4

In 1995 The Royal Society of Arts, Manufacture and Commerce in the UK launched a major project to look at the nature of 'tomorrow's company'. This had wide representations from different businesses, professional bodies and academics. One of the most important outcomes from their work was the recognition that boards were often over-focusing on their shareholder or member interests and insufficiently focusing on the interests of their other stakeholders. One of the results that derived from this project was a new format for company annual reports, in which the board/company reported on the value it had created for each of the following stakeholders:

- investors;
- customers, clients or service users;
- suppliers and partners;
- staff and employees;
- communities in which the organization operates; to which we have added:
- the natural environment.

This entails being clear about what the company had received and delivered to each of these stakeholder groups and the added value created.

In coaching the board in how to improve its connectivity with all its stakeholders, the board coach needs to return to some of the data that have emerged in Discipline 1, or in the inquiry phase of the board coaching. The effectiveness of a board's connection with its different stakeholders is fundamentally based on the ability of the board to listen to the feedback from all these different stakeholders groups. In coaching boards we have used a range of 360-degree organizational feedback methods, so the board could see the complete range of stakeholder perceptions and requests. These have included 'Descriptor analysis' (see Chapter 12), which has the benefit of providing a simple yet subtle feedback on how the organization and its current leadership are perceived and the difference the stakeholders would like to see. This can provide the basis for tracking changing stakeholder perceptions over time. Ultimately the value of a business is rooted in the wide range of perceptions stakeholders hold about the company and therefore it is a key area a board should monitor. Yet so many boards that we have coached, while looking separately at: customer satisfaction rates, regulator reports, shareholder complaints, competitive positioning in key markets, staff surveys, etc; lack a way of seeing how collective perceptions of the company are changing and fail to be aware that there is an echo chamber between the stakeholders who constantly influence each other.

One group of board coaches I supervised had a very significant impact on the board of a major bank, by videoing the various board members being interviewed on their vision and aspirations for the bank and then interspersing these clips with clips of various customers and stakeholders saying how they currently experienced and perceived the bank. The contrast was dramatic and led the board to urgently address how to close the rift between their rhetoric and the reality at the daily stakeholder interfaces.

The board coach, having helped the board listen to many stakeholder voices, can help the board members decide how and what they would like each of the stakeholder groups to be thinking, feeling, doing and saying about them in the future and work with the executives to design an engagement process that shifts perceptions. As with coaching leadership teams on their engagement (as described in Chapter 6, Discipline 4) the board can also be coached on their important engagement processes (AGM, press briefings, meetings with regulators, road show meetings with key investors, etc). These can be in the form of rehearsals, live support at important engagements with pre-, post- and mid-term coaching, or even facilitation of important conversations.

Coaching the board on how it learns and develops: Discipline 5

As stated above, board coaching will most often start in Discipline 5 with the board coach being brought in to help carry out a review of the board performance and functioning, both for and with the board. As shown above, such a review will involve looking at all the five disciplines of team coaching as well as the different board functions. How the board members engage with this process indicates how open to feedback and learning they are and how effective they are at attending to their continuous improvement. Another area that the board coach may be asked to facilitate as part of the review is the contribution and performance of the individual board directors.

Individual board director development

Good boards will have:

- an induction process for new board directors;
- a statement of the requirements and expectations of a board director;
- a list of the competencies, capabilities and capacities expected of board directors;
- suggestions for board director training that can be undertaken. This may include individual coaching available to a new board director specifically on this role.

To exercise the many board functions effectively there are some generic director competencies in chairing boards and being a director. These include:

- *Conceptual*: the ability to use imagination and think conceptually and to value this as important: broadening and changing orientation towards time (thinking in relation to the past, present and future), using hard and soft data, exercising critical thinking and asking discriminating questions, recognizing and working with different thinking styles in other people and cultures. Seeing patterns across data, incidents, events and stories and relating these patterns to policy are part of the key ability in moving between detail and the broader picture.
- *Political*: the extension of interpersonal awareness and competence to understanding and responding to board dynamics and politics, and to

building up and exercising influence effectively, especially as an independent non-executive.

- *Personal:* the confidence and maturity to develop an independence of mind and to take personal risks in challenging those in authority and others, or asking questions that might come across as ignorance – and in being open to challenge, conflict and criticism in return. Being able to design structures to regulate and contain this.

The coach may help a board review the performance of each of its directors by carrying out a self- and peer assessment for each board member, where each board member rates his or her own performance and contribution and also provides feedback for all the other board members (see the 360-degree feedback processes in Chapter 12). This may be fed back to each individual director by the board coach, the chair of the board, another nominated director or a combination of the three. This can lead to making agreements on how their contribution can be enhanced going forward. In two of the boards I myself chair, I play an active role in delivering feedback to all the other board members and receive regular feedback myself, collected and delivered by the senior non-executive who is chair of the nominations and remuneration committee.

The board coach may also coach the board in how the feedback and development plans of the individual board members can be appropriately shared with the whole board team.

Conclusion

With committees reporting or having reported on corporate governance in many different countries and with companies and directors brought to court for cases of corruption or negligence, reforming codes of practice in corporate governance has been an issue in many countries with more developed economies and stronger governments in the last decade. Making large corporations more accountable is a natural concomitant of the growth in size and power of multinational enterprises. International law and codes of practice have lagged behind this development.

Two broad conclusions can be drawn. First, boards in publicly listed companies will need to maintain a competent standard of directing and of strategic management of their business both for their own survival in a changing and competitive environment and to meet the expectations of their shareholders. This means attending to all the main functional areas and the five disciplines of high-performing teams/boards.

Secondly, the greater independence of non-executive directors, the auditing of the selection and appraisal of directors and generally the demands for compliance with the consensus on codes of practice will help break up any comfortable collusion amongst board members and stimulate effective thinking, dialogue and decision making. This will make the non-executives a real force, but increase the risk of them having more of a policing role and potentially being in an adversarial relationship with the executive.

With more active involvement of shareholders, greater awareness of all stakeholders and their needs and extensions of legal liability, boards will find it tougher to tackle commercial realities and to consider the needs of the whole system. This is already leading to a greater need for skilled board coaching, and the number and capability of board coaches is in most countries lagging behind the need.

PART FOUR
Selecting, Developing and Supervising Team Coaches

How to find, select and work with a good team coach

09

In search of perfection

Nasrudin was helping a company look for a new chief executive. They had tried all the top recruitment and headhunting firms in the country and in desperation turned to Nasrudin.

Over dinner they started to ask him some questions about himself. Having discovered that he was not married, they asked him had he ever come close.

'Indeed yes,' he replied. 'When I was young I was very keen to marry the perfect wife. I travelled through many lands looking for her. In France I met a beautiful dancer, who was joyful and carefree, but alas had no sense of the spiritual. In Egypt I met a princess who was both beautiful and wise, but sadly we could not communicate. Then finally in India after much searching I found her. She was beautiful, wise and her charm captured the hearts of everybody she met. I felt that I had found the perfect wife.'

Nasrudin paused with a long sigh. So one of the senior managers eagerly asked:

'Then did you not marry her, Nasrudin?'

'Alas,' sighed Nasrudin, 'she was waiting for the perfect husband.'

(Hawkins, 2005)

Introduction

I n this book I have so far argued that the world needs far more high-performing leadership teams and shown how Wageman *et al* (2008) found in their research that one of the enabling conditions for highly effective leadership teams was 'competent team coaching'. In Chapters 3 to 7 I have set out to describe what competent coaching looks like whether delivered by an external or internal team coach or by the leader of the team.

Before going on to describe the training, development, supervision and methodologies for team coaches, this short chapter will consider how teams can find, select and manage their relationship with a good team coach, whether he or she is internally or externally sourced. In this process it is also important that the team explores what it can do itself to raise the coaching levels in its team by utilizing team members in coaching roles and by developing the team coaching skills of the team leader. Bath Consultancy Group has successfully developed and led a programme for improving the team coaching skills of team leaders for two large global companies. When a team does decide to bring in a team coach from outside its own resources, one of the most important keys to success is finding the right coach for your team at this stage in its development, and this is far from being an easy task.

Earlier in the book I wrote about how team coaching is now at a similar nascent stage to where individual coaching was 20 years ago. This stage is characterized by:

- a lack of clear definitions of different types of team coaching and of a theoretical framework;
- a growing number of practitioners, but without clarity on their offerings or professional training routes and lack of accreditation specifically for team coaching;
- a lack of supervision that is specially focused on the systemic nature of team coaching;
- buyers knowing they need help, but not having frameworks for working out what sort of help they need or for contracting with suppliers through a shared language;
- buyers not knowing how to assess both quality and fit between available team coaches and the specific needs of the team.

To address some of these market confusions I have developed the following seven-stage approach for teams and organizations that want to find, select and work successfully with a quality team coach.

An approach to finding, selecting and working effectively with a quality team coach

This approach has seven stages. The first three start some time before the team coaching fully begins and the last continues after the team coach has exited. The stages are:

1 Specifying and defining the need and hoped-for outcome.
2 Finding suitable candidates for the role.
3 Selecting the team coach with the best fit to the specification and the team's needs.
4 Contracting with the selected coach.
5 Developing the relationship, with regular reviews.
6 Evaluation.
7 Ending and beyond.

I will now explore each of these stages.

1. Specifying and defining what the team need

On the journey to finding the right team coaching for your team, the first step is to start with creating the specification. This has three necessary aspects:

a What is the current state of the team?
b Where does the team want to get to (starting with the end in mind)?
c What does the team believe will be helpful?

a. Defining the current state of the team

Defining the team's present level of development can be made easier by using the five disciplines model (Chapter 3) and the stages in team development models (Chapter 4). These provide a language for teams to begin to explore where the team are in their developmental journey and to frame what help they are looking for from a team coach. Often team leaders, team sponsors or organizational gatekeepers can fall into the trap of defining the team by their dysfunctional behaviour or current conflicts. This can inadvertently set the frame for the team coaching to be about resolving conflict or solving interpersonal problems.

b. Defining the success criteria for the team

If you do not know what success will look like and how it will be measured, you are far less likely to achieve it. Thus it is important, before inviting in external coaching, for the team to undertake some work to define what success would be like for them. Some of this will be based on their external commission and on the current metrics used to measure success in the organization, as well as any current 360-degree feedback mechanisms. However, it is also important that the team look at their own success criteria, not just for external performance but also for how they function and how they serve the needs of the team members. The team can use the five disciplines model to create their own success criteria in each of the five disciplines (Chapter 6).

c. Defining the specification for the team coach

Having defined the present state of the team and where they want to journey to, it is important that the team define the help they want from a team coach on this journey.

Useful questions for the team to consider include:

- *Range*: Do we want a team coach that can help us with all the five disciplines or just some of them?
- *Focus of role:* Deciding which of the following is required:
  - team facilitator, who will facilitate some specific processes;
  - process consultant, who will coach the process of our meetings;
  - team coach, who will coach the team on performance and task as well as our process;
  - systemic team coach, who will coach the internal performance and task, and also how the team engage with their commissioners and stakeholders.
- *Style:* What style of intervention do we want from our team coach: how challenging do we want him or her to be? How much do we want the coach to have an educative/developmental role? How active do we want him or her to be in meetings/team workshops and between events?
- *Experience:* What range of experience do we want from our team coach? Is it important that he or she has experience in our sector? Should the coach have experience of international or virtual teams?
- *Difference:* What difference and similarity to us do we want the coach to have?
- *Involvement of individual coaching:* Do we expect the team coach to also carry out any individual coaching of the team leader or team members? What will be the nature of this individual coaching?
- *External or internal:* Does the team coach need to come from outside the organization or do we have suitably skilled internal team coaches in other parts of the organization? Will the internal team coaches have sufficient authority and influence to help the team achieve its development?

2. Finding suitable candidates

The best way of developing a longlist of possible team coaches is to:

- ask colleagues both in your company and beyond who they have used and would recommend;
- ask HR or the Leadership and Development function to create a list of possible people for you, based on your initial specification;
- approach the major coaching organizations and ask them for their lists of accredited coaches who are experienced and trained as team coaches and have supervised them. (Most of the major coaching organizations are listed at the end of this book; however, to date none of the professional bodies specifically accredit team coaches although APECS is embarking on this process.);
- approach reputable organizational development consultancies that specialize in team development and, if required, also specialize in leadership teams, board development, organizational change and transformation, etc.

3. Selecting a coach

Having established a longlist of 10 or more, a simple questionnaire sent out with the specification for the type of help you are looking for could include the following:

a Please define the type of team coaching you offer.

b What is your model for high-performing teams and how do you help teams achieve that?

c Please describe the types of teams you have worked with and the difference you have helped to create in team performance and functioning.

d Please describe your typical team coaching process, in terms of length, process stages, types of contact with the team, and evaluation.

e What training have you received in team coaching?

f What supervision do you specifically receive on your team coaching? From whom? How frequent is it?

g Please describe a time when you have taken team coaching to supervision, and how this has transformed what you subsequently did to help the team.

h Please describe an ethical dilemma you have encountered in team coaching and how your training, supervision or ethical framework helped you resolve this.

The answers to these questions should provide enough material to ascertain the level of fit, and the answers to questions e–h should help in evaluating the quality of the team coach. These will assist in reducing the longlist to two or three possible team coaches that you would like to meet.

In the process of selecting from the shortlist it is important that the possible team coaches meet as many of the team as possible. At a minimum they should meet the team leader and at least two team members that represent different aspects or themes within the team. It is also important that they meet the organizational gatekeeper (who may well be a member of the Human Resources department) and the sponsor of the team coaching from the wider system who has an interest in the team's success. This can be the person who the team leader reports to, and in the case of an executive leadership team could be the chairman of the board of the organization.

It is helpful for this smaller group to discuss their most important requirements of a team coach with the wider team, as well as specific questions they want answered by each shortlisted candidate. This provides a basis for checking out their thoughts and feelings with the whole team as well as pursuing questions that follow up the questions and answers in the list above on fit and quality.

The selection group may also find it helpful to use the wider list of team coach capabilities and capacities that are described in Chapter 10, and together decide which of these are essential for their purposes and how they will assess these in the shortlist contenders. In individual coaching, large companies more frequently use assessment centres for selecting their approved list of external executive coaches and include in the assessment process a live coaching session with a volunteer from the organization's executives. This is clearly harder to carry out for team coaching. Occasionally a team will invite a team coach to attend one of their meetings and offer feedback as part of the selection. Another alternative is to ask the prospective team coach to facilitate an exploration of the team's needs with a small group comprising the team leader, the gatekeeper and one or two key members. This provides a live experience of the team coach in action, how he or she operates and the insight he or she can bring.

4. Contracting

Having found the right coach, it is important that the works starts with a good two-way contract. Much of what needs to be included in the contracting process is covered in Chapter 5, which is addressed to the team coach, but at a minimum the team need to ensure they have a contract that includes:

- two-way expectations, including how success will be evaluated;
- the length and frequency of the engagement;
- what activities will be involved: interviews, workshops, attending meetings, coaching alongside major engagements, individual sessions and with whom;

- any financial arrangements;
- working protocols on such issues as confidentiality, what will be shared with whom, access to stakeholders, privileged information, etc;
- how reviews of the process and relationship will be carried out (see below).

5. Developing the relationship, with regular reviews

As in life, finding and selecting the right partner is only the first step in a successful partnership (see the Nasrudin story at the beginning of the chapter!). Right from the beginning it is important that the team and their coach build in regular reviews to the team coaching process. Some of these reviews need to be with the whole team and some with the smaller group of team leader, gatekeeper, sponsor, etc. These reviews need to look back at the starting contract, measure progress, reflect on what has been most and least helpful and what has enabled or blocked progress. They can be used as a basis for re-contracting the next stage of the team coaching.

It is unrealistic to expect that the team coaching relationship will run smoothly and be without its own relational difficulties. Often some of the difficult dynamics and patterns within the team will be re-enacted within the relationship with the team coach, and so the ability to reflect consciously on this relationship is a key part of the coaching journey. Teams that decide to change the team coach at the first signs of difficulty in the relationship miss out on the learning that could arise from exploring how to work through these difficulties and transform the relationship. However, the review process should also consider how, over time, the role and contribution from the team coach can be transferred to team members and/or whether a different form of external help is needed.

6. Evaluation

Having defined the current state of the team and the success criteria for the coaching programme, it is important to have an evaluation process that measures progress along this journey. I have found evaluation is most useful if it includes qualitative and quantitative measures (see Table 9.1) for each of the five disciplines of high-performing teams (see Chapters 3 and 5).

7. Ending and beyond

Ending the team coaching relationship should be a process and not an event. It should include the opportunity to:

- stand back and reflect on the journey that has been undertaken together;

TABLE 9.1

Discipline	Quantitative Evaluation	Qualitative Evaluation
1. Commissioning	Performance assessment of the team by those they report to against agreed Key Performance Indicators (KPIs)	Alignment of perceptions between the team members and those they report to
2. Clarifying	Performance measures against the mission and strategic objectives set by the team, including financial measures (revenue, share price), market share, overhead reduction, etc	Clarity of the mission, vision, strategy and core values in those who report to the team and other key stakeholders. Descriptor analysis (repeated)
3. Co-creating	Length of meetings and amount covered. Perceived alignment by staff and stakeholders	High-performing team questionnaire (repeated)
4. Connecting	Staff satisfaction surveys, customer, partner and other stakeholder surveys	Descriptor analysis
5. Core learning	Percentage of agreed new ways of operating being implemented and at what speed	Self- and peer feedback mechanisms

- give two-way feedback on what has worked well, what has been difficult and what in retrospect could have been better;
- harvest the learning that the team has acquired and plan how this will be sustained after the team coach leaves;
- explore and plan how responsibility for the coaching and learning processes can be taken up by team members.

As a team coach, I often find it useful to have a final session with the team leader that directly addresses how he or she can take on more effective team coaching as part of his or her role.

Conclusion

In this chapter I have shown that successful team coaching begins some time before the team coach arrives, with the team undertaking a thorough process of specifying their current state and developmental aspirations. This sets the context for deciding what coaching resources are needed, both from within the team and from external sources. I have provided a series of guidelines for specifying, finding, selecting and contracting with a team coach, utilizing the five disciplines model of teams and the CID-CLEAR model of the coaching relationship presented in Chapters 3, 5 and 6. In the resources section at the back of this book there are further suggestions for help in finding the right external help.

In the next chapter we will consider what makes for a competent team coach and then how to help team coaches develop these capabilities. The penultimate chapter then looks at team coaching resources (diagnostic tools and team coaching methods) that can assist the coach. The following chapter on team coaching supervision is, I believe, at the core of continuous personal and professional development. It provides the connecting web between the learning that comes from books and courses and the competencies, capabilities and personal development that arise in the heat of the practice of team coaching and lie at the heart of being effective as a good team coach.

Developing as a team coach

10

It is not what you have experienced that makes you greater, but what you have faced, what you have transcended, what you have unlearned.

(BEN OKRI, 1997: 61)

Introduction

There is a growing demand for experienced and effective team coaches and yet to date there is a dearth of training courses for team coaches and professional accreditation processes. Many of those offering leadership team coaching have gradually moved into the area from their core offering, whether in individual coaching, organizational consultancy or as an HR or learning and development professional. As I have shown in earlier chapters, this previous training provides useful skills that can be incorporated into team coaching, but they are an insufficient basis for being an effective team coach. Some may have moved into being a team coach from having led a wide variety of teams themselves. This chapter is partly written for those who are embarking on the transition into team coaching, to help them navigate the development pathways, and partly for experienced team coaches to stand back and review their practice and reflect on what elements of their own continuous personal and professional development they should focus on for further development.

In this chapter I will first address the transition into team coaching from individual coaching, organizational coaching or sports coaching and the necessary demeanour required from a team coach, before sharing some of the most common questions that team coaches ask in the early stages of their development. I will suggest some possible answers.

The transition

From individual coaching

I have argued elsewhere that good individual executive coaching always has at least three clients: the individual executive, his or her wider organization and the relationship between the two. Much individual coaching has over-focused on the needs of the individual coachee and under-served the needs of the organizational client. There are too many coaches who lack either an interest or an understanding of wider organizational and systemic change and so end up providing a form of counselling at work rather than effective coaching. This tendency can be carried over into team coaching where the coach mainly focuses on the needs of individual team members and the personal relationships between them, and forgets that the key client is the team as an entity, how it performs and relates to the wider system in which it operates.

Like a good sports coach the leadership team coach has to care more about the team than any of the individuals within it. This requires a fundamental shift in perspective, in how one looks and listens and resonates. You may remember the 'magic eye' pictures that were popular in the 1980s. At first they looked like a random mixture of different coloured shapes. Only if you were able to defocus your eyes from the normal way of looking could you see that there was an interesting three-dimensional picture lying behind and within the form you first saw. Some people would look for a very long time, getting more frustrated, as they could not unlearn their normal way of seeing and failed to see the 'hidden image'. Most people who persevered found that gradually they learnt to look differently and they became better at speedily deciphering new pictures and seeing in this new way.

As a team coach, one needs to have the skill to defocus from the enormous amount of personal and interpersonal verbal and non-verbal data to see the collective pattern that lies behind and within the overall team picture. Then one needs to defocus again from looking at and listening to the team dynamic to focus on the team nested within its systemic context of the wider organization and its many stakeholders. In many years of training and supervising team coaches and consultants, I have found that this refocusing does not come naturally, particularly in the western white culture which is primarily oriented to the individual (Ryde, 2009).

Some of the questions I may ask as a team coach supervisor to help team coaches re-focus, can sound very foreign to many individually-oriented coaches, but they unearth illuminating responses:

- What colour are the spaces between the team members?
- If the collective team had a voice what would you hear it saying or asking for?

- What rhythm does the team have? What harmonics do you hear underneath these individual melodies?
- If the team were a country, a meal, a work of art, a vehicle, a piece of music – what would it be?
- What is happening in the spaces between the team and their stakeholders?
- What is the dance between the team and their commissioners?
- How do you show empathy to the whole team, as opposed to the sum of the members?

The ability to look and listen differently is only the first step. Individual coaches can also get stuck focusing on Discipline 3 of the five disciplines model and be trapped with the limiting assumption that if the team members get on well with each other and co-create effectively in their meetings, then they will perform better (see Chapter 4). The research on teams (Katzenbach and Smith, 1993a and b; Wageman *et al*, 2008) suggests that team performance only improves if the coaching focuses on all the disciplines and not just on team relationships and dynamics.

From being an organizational consultant

The transition from being an organizational consultant is often very different. Here the consultant, depending on their training, may focus on the performance of the team and believe that this can be improved by just concentrating on the structures, selection or work processes. Depending on their orientation they may well get stuck over-focusing on Discipline 1 or 2, and fail to address the deeper dynamics and blocks to progress that lie in Discipline 3. They may well fall into the trap of not realizing that it is not sufficient to re-engineer the organization unless you also enable the team to rewire their relationships.

The organizational consultant may also lack some of the coaching skills and fall into the trap of being more an adviser to the team than enabling them to create their own solutions and ways forward. In his work training process consultants, Schein (1969) devoted a lot of his attention to helping more expert-driven consultants to learn the skills that left the ownership of these issues with the teams they were working with, for without ownership it is unlikely that the team will develop commitment to the actions that emerge from the work.

Stepping into the role – the necessary demeanour

In Islam and Sufism there is a lovely Arabic word *adab,* which means to act in a manner fitting the role one is called upon to play. There is the proper *adab* of the host as well as the proper *adab* of the guest, of the teacher and of the pupil, etc. Part of becoming and developing as a team coach is learning and deepening the proper *adab* of the team coach. This cannot be defined in a series of bullet points, but can be suggested and is mostly learnt through watching others and through one's own direct experience, noticing when one is in the right zone and when one has fallen out of alignment, both through one's own sensing and through feedback from the clients.

As indicated above, stepping into the role requires a shift in focus and an ability to constantly move one's attention from individual to relationships, to the collective team, to the team in their organizational context, to the wider system and back again. This requires practice and in the early stages of training nearly all team coaches find it exhausting until they have begun to develop the necessary emotional and cognitive muscles to do it with ease.

Adab also requires being at ease with oneself, being authentic and transparent, while at the same time being happy to fade into the background, still with full attention at all levels. One needs to be at ease with whatever emerges, be it conflict in the team, anxiety, attacks on you as the team coach or getting stuck in the process.

In the capacities outlined below I explore the need to stay in the zone. This involves avoiding falling into deference and rising into arrogance. A quiet but strong and holding presence (Scharma, 2007; Senge *et al,* 2005), connecting with all team members and key stakeholders, but giving preference to no one individual or sub-group is of the essence. The coach must be willing to support and challenge as necessary, acting with fearless compassion (Hawkins and Smith, 2006, ch. 15). Also the *adab* requires a willingness to get it wrong, or be seen to get it wrong and be gently curious about one's own and other's 'mistakes'. One of my earliest teachers of group work, Marcia Karp, was fond of the saying 'A Mother's place is in the wrong!' and 'Motherhood is a cold cup of tea.' I now know that both these phrases also apply to team coaches. The *adab* of the team coach has to be maintained through the meal and refreshment breaks of team workshops, when team members will want to continue conversations with you.

We never fully acquire the *adab,* but perhaps over years we become more comfortable in stepping into the role and finding it more familiar. Nor do we ever arrive at the end of the developmental journey. In writing this book I have regularly reminded myself that being a team coach is not about getting it right, but about being creatively in the service of the team being the best they can be and facing the challenges that their environment is posing.

Below I explore further some of the capacities that are at the heart of the role of team coach, but first I will explain how I understand the difference between capacities, competencies and capabilities and discuss some of the key skills and behaviours that support us stepping into the role.

The core capabilities

So what are the differences between competencies, capabilities and capacities? In Hawkins and Smith (2006) we defined these differences based on earlier work done by Mike Broussine (1998):

'Capabilities', like 'competencies', can be learnt and developed, they are about know-how. However, the difference between the two is seen in the way the learning is generated. Competencies can be learned in the classroom, but capabilities can only be learned live and on the job. The danger is that one can acquire a very large tool-kit of skills, without developing the capability of knowing when to use each skill and in what way. Supervision has a vital role to play in helping the supervisee turn their competencies into capabilities, and to ensure that the capabilities are held within an ever increasing capacity to work with others with fearless compassion.

'Capacities' relate to one's being, rather than one's doing. They are human qualities that can be nurtured and refined. Capacities can also be thought of in their root meaning of the space you have within you for containing complexity. We have all met people who seem to have little internal space from which to relate to you – and others who carry a seemingly infinite internal spaciousness, which tells you that they are fully present with whatever you feel you need to share or do.

Capacities are not things to be acquired or places to arrive. Each capacity takes our whole life to develop and development is not a uni-directional process. Without attention to our practice and supervision, each of these capacities can atrophy within us, and our effectiveness decline. Development and learning is for life, not just for school. The joy is – there is always more to be learnt.

As part of writing this book I wrote to a wide range of friends and colleagues who are experienced practitioners in team coaching and asked them the question: 'If you were responsible for teaching a new cadre of team coaches in just three months and were restricted to teaching them only five things, what would they be?' Putting all their answers together gave me a list of over 50 key skills, reflecting the many different development routes and training that current team coaches have received, and would require a lifetime's training course! On further analysis certain key patterns begun to emerge. But before you read these, perhaps you could take a pause to see how you would answer the question.

Competencies and capabilities

The first set of basic competencies and capabilities that emerged from the research align well with the stages of the CID-CLEAR process model, although many who responded did not know this model:

1 Can effectively contract and review (and re-contract) with the gatekeeper, the team leader, all the team members and the team collectively, and those representing the wider organizational authority on the objectives, success criteria and process of the work to be undertaken *(contracting)*.

2 Can build fast rapport with a wide range of team members, including the nominal authority (usually the team leader) and the team member who brings the biggest challenge to the status quo *(Inquire)*.

3 Can listen and observe at depth to the issues of all team members and the collective team issues and pattern *(Inquire)*.

4 Can diagnose collective team culture and dynamics and systemic patterns and feed them back in ways that create new insight and mindset shift in the team. This is both at the initial planning stage and through the work as a process consultant *(Diagnose)*.

5 Can feed back the results of the diagnosis and use this as a basis to develop a working alliance and contract with the whole team, which includes success criteria, process of working together and mutual expectations *(Contract 2)*.

6 Can use a range of incisive questions, facilitation methods and team coaching tools that enable the team to explore their own *(Explore)*:
   - fundamental purpose and commission (Discipline 1);
   - team purpose, strategy, objectives, goals, roles (Discipline 2);
   - norms, protocols, ways of working together, including the team at their best and their worst (Discipline 3);
   - engagement with all its key stakeholders and how it enables those stakeholders to engage with their stakeholders (Discipline 4);
   - integration, reflections and learning across all the domains and engage in double-loop learning; can enable the team leader and team members to work as coaches to each other and the team (Discipline 5).

7 Can enable the team to move to new behaviours, emotions, beliefs, purpose and action, and create commitment that goes beyond agreement and good intent *(Action)*.

8 Can ensure regular reviews of the work with the team leader, the whole team and other key stakeholders that help take the work to a higher level or end appropriately *(Review)*.

Systemic capabilities

The second set of capabilities that emerged from the group of experienced practitioners was that they nearly all mentioned a range of understandings that underpin working with teams within the context of wider system dynamics. I have clustered the responses into four areas that each comprises a different systemic dimension. These are:

1 *Connecting system levels.* Have an understanding of how group and team dynamics are different from individual or interpersonal dynamics and can articulate their personal model and how you apply it.

2 *Development over time.* Have an understanding of the phases of team development and how to adjust one's own role accordingly.

3 *Power, politics and difference.* Can understand and appropriately work with the dynamics that may be covert, political or power-based.

4 *Connecting team coaching to organizational change and development.* Understand how the coaching project fits in with and supports the wider strategic, culture change, leadership development and organizational development processes of the wider organization.

Capacities

The group of responders also mentioned a range of capacities:

1 'Self-awareness – aware that you are the instrument'; 'to be the change you are encouraging in the team'.

2 'Self-ease'; 'to be at ease as things unfold and to intervene less'.

3 Neither falling into deference (see Hawkins and Smith, 2006, Appendix 1) or the arrogance of knowing better than the team, but staying in the zone of mutual inquiry, combining, challenge and support.

To these I have added some further generic capacities we included in our list for coaching supervisors, but can be seen as equally necessary for team coaches:

4 appropriate authority, presence and impact;

5 relationship engagement capacity;

6 encourages, motivates and carries appropriate optimism;

7 working across difference, transculturally sensitive to individual and team differences;

8 ethical maturity;

9 a sense of humour and humility.

Capacity 1: Self-awareness and listening to the collective team

A key capacity for a team coach is the ability to listen to the collective team and not just to separate individuals. This requires being able to tune out from the individual focus and tune into a collective one. One way to develop this capacity is to listen to each person both verbally and non-verbally as representing different aspects of the collective, not as voicing their personal position. Team coaches need to listen not just with their ears and brain but with the whole of their body. My colleague Malcolm Parlett terms this 'embodied listening', where our whole being becomes a resonance chamber for receiving the non-verbal communication, in body language, interpersonal contact and rhythms of the voices. This helps the coach to engage at the four levels of engagement outlined in Hawkins and Smith (2006) and illustrated here in Figure 10.1.

To make sense of the resonances that the team coach is receiving, there is a need to be very aware of one's own natural body and emotional rhythms, one's own feelings and tendencies to react, in order to ascertain what one might be registering from the team. This requires high degrees of self-awareness as well as sensory acuity to the team.

Capacity 2: Self-ease

In the early stages of being a team coach, most practitioners find they are driven by a need for the team's approval and to 'prove their worth'. This can lead either to a tendency to over-intervene or to a pattern of waiting until one has an impactful finely engineered insight or intervention with which to impress the team. The danger with the first tendency is that it can limit the space for the team members to take leadership or coaching roles within the team and can diminish the impact of what is said. In the latter pattern, often by the time one has carefully crafted the insight, feedback or intervention, the moment has passed and the offering lands as out-dated commentary.

The other key aspect of this capacity is the ability to tolerate ambiguity and 'not knowing' and to have responsibility without control. Lack of this capacity can cause team coaches to try to control rather than guide or facilitate the team process, or to move to premature resolution of complex issues. It can also lead to team coaches falling into deference or arrogance and losing a sense of partnership.

Capacity 3: Staying in the partnership zone

Team coaching is at its best when the coach is neither subservient to the team or its leader, nor trying to dominate or control what unfolds. In Hawkins and Smith (2006) there is an extended section on the danger of deference, written by my colleague Nick Smith.

For some of us, this could be triggered by people we see as in 'high authority', for others it may be settings of extreme formality. The deference threshold is where we hand over our ability to create transformational impact for any one of a multitude of reasons. The arrogance threshold is

FIGURE 10.1 Four levels of engagement

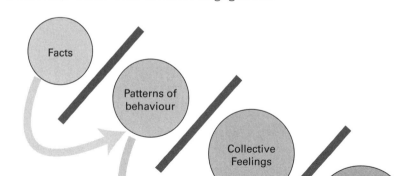

where we take unilateral power or control and start to believe we know better. Knowing what triggers our deference and arrogance is a good starting point on the journey to always being ready to engage with someone else from our own depth and strength. It is by being knocked from our centre that we lose that capacity, and by maintaining our centeredness that we can offer it to others.

Capacity 4: Taking appropriate leadership

Many in the coaching profession have argued that the coach's role is to support others' leadership and not to take leadership. However, leadership is not just a role we inhabit – it is also an attitude to life and its challenges. Leadership begins when we stop blaming others and making excuses when things go wrong. Leadership begins when we start to explore 'How can I best make a difference?'

Team coaches need to develop their leadership capacity in their own roles. This is explored in Hawkins and Smith (2006) where we wrote:

> Some people have argued with us that it is wrong for coaches to take leadership for that could mean the coach becomes inappropriately directive. We argue that there is an essential and appropriate form of leadership, which needs to be developed by the coach or organizational consultant if they are to balance support and challenge with the interests of the multiple clients they need to hold in mind. The coach or consultant has to be able to challenge executives and, at times, represent the needs of the wider system. On many occasions we have been asked:

'When do you know it is appropriate to challenge your client?' and 'What moral authority do you have to challenge your client?'

To both of these questions we answer from a systemic perspective:

'When we genuinely feel that the client is not in alignment with themselves or with the larger system of which they are part, and we sense we are representing the needs of the larger system.'

The larger system might be:

- their own long-term needs rather than the situation to which they are immediately reacting;
- the team they are part of;
- the needs of the whole organization;
- the needs of the stakeholder system;
- the needs of the sector or profession and its purpose.

The follow-up question is then:

'Why are the needs of the organization more important than their immediate needs?'

Our belief is that only by acting in alignment with the systems you are part of, are you truly serving your own long-term needs. The environmental law that a species that destroys its habitat sooner or later destroys its own chances for life can be seen as a metaphor for what happens at other systemic interfaces. Only by serving the wider system are we truly serving our own long-term needs.

As coaches, mentors, consultants or supervisors we need to be able to speak our truth, to name what we see, hear, feel and understand – and to do so with *fearless compassion*. This courage to take leadership within the relationship needs to be balanced by an appropriate humility and openness. It is important to avoid knowing better or knowing first. To speak one's truth but always with an element of uncertainty, recognizing that we never have the complete picture or a full understanding, and neither does the client. Through dialogue we can with the help of the disciplines of our craft, develop a fuller picture and understanding than both perspectives put together.

One model that has helped team coaches develop their appropriate leadership has been the model of authority, presence and impact that I first developed in the 1990s, developing partners in one of the big four professional services firms. In this model, shown in Figure 10.2, we divide personal power and influence into three main aspects.

1. Authority
This derives from what, or who, you know or what you have done in the past. Your achievements and experience may be embodied in titles,

FIGURE 10.2 Authority, presence and impact

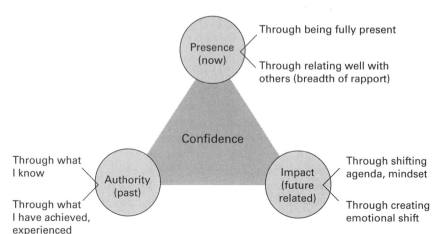

qualifications or role. It may also be embedded in your curriculum vitae, references, how you are introduced or how you refer to knowledge and experience. To carry true authority in your being is embodied in how you enter a room, how you greet another, and also in how you hold your experience open as a resource for others while not imposing it on those who do not ask. To fully take authority, I need to take my rightful space without embarrassment, to stand my ground, on my ground and be well grounded physically, intellectually and ethically.

Exercising and referencing one's authority can open doors and achieve initial attention. However, it doesn't, by itself, create lasting relationship or effect change. Over-exercising or over-referring to one's authority invariably creates a negative effect with other people wondering why you are trying so hard to promote yourself or resenting what they consider to be showing off.

2. Presence

This is the ability to be fully present with a quality of immediacy and to develop relationship and rapport quickly and with very different types of people. People who have a lot of presence command attention and respect in a wide range of situations and a large number of people find them easy to relate to.

To have high quality presence requires a meta-awareness, which embraces and comprehends what is happening on all levels for both oneself and others. This includes the levels of thoughts, feelings, actions and intuitions:

> Unless we develop in our presence we are not wholly here. We exist in our thoughts, in our desires, but not in our Being. And therefore we cannot fully relate because we are not fully here. Without presence our dialogue is primarily mental or emotional.

(Helminski, 1999)

With presence we demonstrate poise and grace and provide a spaciousness for others to connect with us. It also involves 'becoming open to what is seeking to emerge and discovering our genuine source of commitment' (Senge *et al*, 2005).

3. Impact

'Impact' is the Yang, or outgoing energy to the Yin, or attracting energy of 'presence'. It is concerned with making a shift live in the room, which will create a shift in commitment and actions to go forward. People with high levels of impact can shift the direction of a meeting, conversation or event. They have the ability to intervene in a way that shifts or reframes the way issues under discussion are being perceived and addressed. The other aspect of impact is the ability to shift the emotional climate of a meeting, relationship or conversation by the skilful introduction of a different emotional energy, such as the introduction of humour, assertive and focused challenge or by changing levels in the discourse and give expression to collectively felt but unnamed feeling.

Impact opens doors and windows to new possibilities and connects to depths not previously realized. It brings into the room candour and directness that takes the focus to the core of the matter and creates the alignment behind realizing and enacting new possibilities.

Capacity 5: Relationship engagement

At the core of all the people professions is the capacity to relate to others. Often the members of the teams we coach will be people from very different backgrounds to ourselves and experiencing the world very differently. These team members become our teachers in finding new ways to expand our capacity to relate and engage. Our partners, children and friends often become our teachers in new ways of relating, especially when we experience them as difficult! In my research on personal and professional development in the teaching profession a new model was shaped to help teachers explore their educative capacity. I have since developed this framework into a more generally applicable model of 'relationship engagement capacity', shown in Figure 10.3. (There is a related self-assessment questionnaire and process available from the author.)

Capacity 6: Encourages, motivates and carries appropriate optimism

All leaders and team coaches need to remain aware that there is always a danger as we develop our leadership and coaching capacity that we become too dominant in the relationship, and create feelings of either inadequacy or dependency in others. We always need to reflect on issues about dominance – but also consider how we can open doors for those we work with to

FIGURE 10.3 Relationship engagement capacity

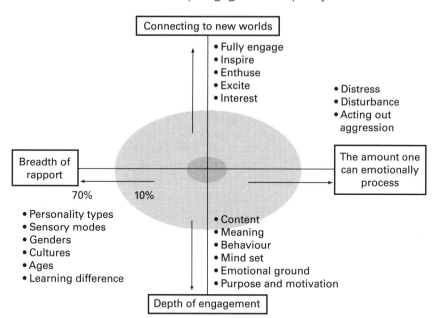

unfold their own coaching capacity. A good leader creates leaders, or to put it another way, a good leader liberates dormant leadership in others and a good team coach enables team members to develop their own coaching capacity.

A central skill of the team coach is to develop the coaching capacity in the team leader and right across the team members so the developmental coaching continues long after the team coach finishes the assignment.

Capacity 7: Working across difference – transcultural engagement

Most teams that one coaches include a range of differences that have an impact on how the team functions. These include:

- gender;
- ethnic and national backgrounds;
- age ('Baby boomers' speak a different language to 'Generation Y');
- 'old timers' and 'new comers';
- loyalty to different legacy companies that pre-dated a merger or acquisition;
- customer facing and support departments;

- different functional loyalties – finance, marketing, production, sales, HR, etc with mean different stakeholder interests (investors, customers, suppliers, employees, etc);
- position in the hierarchy.

As Judy Ryde (2009) so cogently argues, to work well with differences, we need to start by looking in the mirror. We need to become aware of our own often taken for granted culture that we take to work with us; this includes our colour, nationality, gender, age, class, and professional background. We have to be aware of how this affects what we see, hear, feel and understand, as well as the impact we will have. As team coaches we need to be comfortable in having these aspects of ourselves commented on by ourselves and the team members, as this is often a necessary precursor to exploring some of the important differences within the team.

Capacity 8: Ethical maturity

Michael Carroll (1996) articulates how acting ethically is full of complexity and ambiguity. He provides a very useful four-stage process for ethical decision making:

a *Creating ethical sensitivity* – involves becoming aware of the implications of our behaviour for others and insight into the possibility of ethical demands within interpersonal situations.

b *Formulating a moral course of action* – represents how the interplay between the facts of the situation, professional ethical rules and our ethical principles may jell into a moral course of action.

c *Implementing an ethical decision* – refers to the need to follow through and implement the ethical decisions made whilst coping with the resistances both inside and outside, such as politics, self-interest, protection of a colleague, fear of making a mistake.

d *Living with the ambiguities of an ethical decision* – indicates that coping with doubt and uncertainty is a vital capability for containing a moral dilemma.

To become capable of managing all four stages well, it is important not only to encourage all practitioners to develop their own ethical rules, ethical principles and explore with peers common ethical dilemmas, but also to practise working directly with ethical challenges.

Some of the common ethical dilemmas that team coaches bring to supervision include:

- individual team members sharing confidential views with the team coach they do not want shared with the team;
- the team leader asking the team coach to comment on the performance of individual team members;

- the team coach being asked to individually coach some of the team members, but not all, either by those individuals themselves or by the team leader;
- senior management wanting the team coach to report on the performance of the team they are working with.

Many of these dilemmas can be addressed by exploring what is disconnected within the organizational system and coaching the reconnection, rather than the coach becoming caught up in enacting the split or becoming the 'go-between'. From this, certain ethical principles for team coaching emerge. As team coach:

- I am there to serve the collective team in being more effective at meeting its purpose and performance objectives. I am not there to serve any individual or factional interests that are not in service of this wider purpose.
- I am there to comment on and facilitate the collective performance, functioning and dynamics of the team. I am not there to comment on the performance, functioning and dynamics of individuals.
- I am there to facilitate more effective and direct communication and engagement, both within the team and between the team and its stakeholders. I am not there to act as a go-between for non-communicating parties, unless some form of mediation is specifically contracted.

Capacity 9: A sense of humour and humility

While trying to develop all the competencies, capabilities and capacities mentioned above, there is a great danger of taking oneself far too seriously. In Hawkins and Smith (2006) we wrote: 'The ability to laugh at oneself is, we believe, a prerequisite for thriving in the role of team coach. We have to be able to sometimes laugh at and with our clients, at the absurdity of what we humans get up to. But first we must laugh at ourselves.'

Katzenbach and Smith (1993b) discovered that one of the elements that most distinguished 'high-performing teams' from 'effective teams' was that they had fun together and laughed at themselves. These teams took seriously the achievement of their collective purpose and exacting performance goals, but could laugh and tease each other.

Laughter has been shown to have beneficial effects on the body and health, releasing endorphins and vitalizing our systems. It also can create more space in our minds, becoming aware of how we are making connections and be a way of making contact across difference. In the *Wise Fool's Guide to Leadership* (Hawkins, 2005) I have used humour to provide an 'unlearning' curriculum for leaders, which is equally applicable to team coaches. Humour is a great teacher that can delicately embrace a paradox, or help liberate us from our fixed ways of seeing the world.

In the conclusion of Hawkins and Smith (2006) we wrote:

Humility is strengthened by being able to laugh at oneself, but it is also fundamentally about avoiding the trap of omnipotence. This requires the recognition that ultimately it is not us as coaches and consultants who help others to develop and change, we are only the stewards, who maintain the enabling space in which learning, change and transformation can happen. We clear the space for grace and learning to emerge and polish the mirror so that reflection can be more accurate.

Team coach dilemmas

Over the many years I have been supervising and training team coaches a number of key dilemmas and questions continually emerged. When I carried out the short collaborative inquiry among team coaches in various countries, I also asked them what questions they thought the book most needed to address. From both these sources I have chosen the core dilemmas and questions that team coaches (including myself) seem to find at the cutting edge of their practice. I hope your question or dilemma is represented here, even if in a different form from how you would frame it. If not then send me an e-mail and I will do my best to engage with your question, either directly or in later editions. **Peter.Hawkins@BarrowCastle.co.uk**.

1. *What are the advantages and disadvantages of coaching the team and the team members?*

Over the years I have worked with a number of leadership teams where I was both the team coach and coaching all or a significant number of the team members. As I have researched this area more thoroughly, I am much more circumspect about when and how I mix these roles. Trying to combine individual coaching with team coaching has the danger of pulling the team coach into over-focusing on the individual and interpersonal agendas, rather than prioritizing the collective team and wider system agendas. Also, I now would avoid coaching some but not all the team members, as this has the danger of being seen to be aligned with some parts of the team and their agendas, more than the others. The exception to this is that I will sometimes combine team coaching with coaching the team leader specifically on their role as team leader and team coach, for often he or she will have to take up some of my role between my engagements and after I withdraw.

2. How do I deal with the team leader being the problem?

First, be careful with how you might be drawn in by the team to see the team leader as the problem, which can lead to scapegoating the leader for disowned collective failings. Perhaps reread the story at the beginning of Chapter 1 and ask how you can help the team take responsibility for addressing the weaknesses of their boss, for there is no perfect leader. However, if you do find yourself in a situation where the team have constantly tried to address the issues with the team leader who seems impervious to hearing or learning, then there is a role for the team coach to explore what other forms of helping the team leader address these issues can be facilitated.

3. How should I balance being non-directive and being focused on the team's performance?

In the field of counselling and psychotherapy, Carl Rogers (1967) would emphasize 'the need to start where your client is', and Sheldon Kopp (1988) would say that it is vital to 'be where your client ain't'. Of course they are both right! It is important not to come across as critical and knowing better than your client team what is good for them. However, we do have a responsibility to hold up the mirror and help the team face what they are not seeing, hearing or addressing. We might do this in a number of different ways:

- by amplifying some of the marginalized voices in the team;
- helping the team clarify who they are here to serve, and what being the best they could be would look like. These questions and the explorations that need to follow them are about helping a team create a performance drive that is outer-focused, but motivated from within. Performance is not about meeting numerical targets but about becoming excellent in meeting the real needs of those you serve;
- carrying out a team 360-degree feedback to present the voice of the team's commissioners, customers and other stakeholders and help the team honestly address what they need to shift in their performance to meet the legitimate needs of their various stakeholders.

4. What if the team want to focus on one of the five disciplines, but as team coach I think the real need lies in another of the disciplines?

Telling the team what is good for them is rarely the most effective route to change, and can create more resistance. In Chapter 6 I described giving a leadership team a version of the five discipline model and asking them individually to score their team performance in each of the five disciplines on a 1–10 scale. When they saw the averaged scores, it was then possible to ask them where they thought we most needed to focus in our work together, and got an answer that was less biased by their wanting to stay in their comfort zone.

Another useful option, as with many coach dilemmas, is to share the dilemma with the client: 'I notice there is a big lobby to focus on how you as a team relate together, but my sense is that there is a more urgent need to get clarity on the team's mission first. I wonder how we might reconcile these different perspectives.'

5. What if a number of the team are not committed to the team coaching?

When some members of the team are great advocates of team coaching or your being the team coach, and others in the team are resistant, the advocates evangelizing harder often intensifies the resistance. For the work to proceed well you need to be on the side of both groups. I will often step back at this point and say I am not yet convinced that team coaching is the answer for the team, or even if it was, that I am the right person to do it. But I can sense there are some things the team want or perhaps need to discuss and if it was helpful I am happy to talk to each person and listen to the different agendas and share these back with the team, and only then address what is the right way to work on these different agendas, and whether or not they need any help from me or another team coach.

Conclusion

I do not believe that the nine capacities which I have described are in any way exhaustive. However, in the research all nine capacities were mentioned by at least one experienced team coach as important to their practice and were also mentioned as part of what they consider to be the core curriculum for team coaches. As we wrote in Hawkins and Smith (2006):

> Given that a core purpose of coaching is to develop the human capacities of our clients, it is essential that we have a clear understanding and recognition of each of these capacities both in ourselves and in others. However much we have developed any of these capacities, there is always further to go! Sooner or later life will provide us with a challenge that demonstrates the limits of one or more of our capacities, and the opportunity to develop further.

Supervising team coaching

11

At the core of continuing professional development is continual personal development, where our own development is weaved through every aspect of our practice. When this happens every coachee becomes a teacher, every piece of feedback an opportunity for new learning, producing practices that support the balanced cycle of action, reflection, new understanding and new practice. Elsewhere (Hawkins and Smith, 2006) we have shown why we believe that having supervision is a fundamental aspect of continuing personal and professional development for coaches, mentors and consultants. Supervision provides a protected and disciplined space in which the coach can reflect on particular client situations and relationships, the reactivity and patterns they evoke in them and, by transforming these live in supervision, can profoundly benefit the coachee, the client organization and their own professional practice.

(Hawkins, 2010)

Introduction

In the last chapter I wrote of the complex range of skills and personal capacities team coaches need to develop to be a master of their craft. However, this is only the foundation and the journey to mastery in the very complex field takes many, many years. The key element to supporting this ongoing development is quality supervision, from someone who is trained and experienced in both team coaching and supervision.

Effective team coaching requires someone who can maintain the difficult boundary position of working closely with the team while remaining independent of the team dynamics and culture, and who can be aware of the systemic dynamics both within the team and between the team and the wider systems that the team are nested within. To be able to sense and make sense of these complex system dynamics is almost impossible if one is working alone, but it becomes possible with good quality supervision.

What is supervision?

Previously I defined supervision as:

> The process by which a coach with the help of a supervisor, can attend to understanding better both the client system and themselves as part of the client-coach system, and by so doing transform their work and develop their craft.
>
> (Hawkins and Smith, 2006)

To this could be added:

> Supervision does this by also attending to transforming the relationship between the supervisor and coach and to the dynamics in the wider contexts in which the work is happening.

Coaching supervision has three elements:

1 Qualitative: – providing an external perspective to ensure quality of practice.
2 Developmental – mentoring the coach on their development in the profession.
3 Resourcing – Coaching the coach on their coaching practice and work life. (Hawkins and Smith, 2006)

Coaching and mentoring have been areas of enormous growth in the last 10 years (Jarvis, 2004 and Berglas, 2002). Despite this, coaching supervision was noticeable by its absence in the first 20 years of this new profession. In the early part of the 21st century very few coaches were receiving supervision (Hawkins and Schwenk, 2006), and those who did so were going to supervisors trained in psychotherapy or counselling. It was not until 2003 that the first specific training was offered for coaching supervisors and 2006 that the first research was published (Hawkins and Schwenk, 2006) and the first book specifically on coaching supervision was published (Hawkins and Smith, 2006).

In the four years since the research, we have seen a significant growth in the practice of coaching supervision, with all the major professional coaching bodies recommending it as an essential aspect of continuing professional practice and development and many more companies requiring supervision for all their internal and external coaches. There has also been growth in the amount of training for coaching supervisors; the UK has led in this field, and such training is now being seen in other countries. However, the growth in specific supervision for team coaching and training for supervisors in this area is still lagging behind, although beginning to be available in one or two places (see Resources section).

Supervision is even more essential for team coaching than it is for individual coaching, as it is nigh on impossible for an individual coach to be aware of the many levels of the team dynamic as well as the wider systemic context of the team. Additionally the team coach has often been brought in by the team leader, or a sub-section of the team, and may struggle to be accepted by the whole team and the team sponsors in the wider system as someone who can be trusted to work in the interests of the whole team. For the coach to build and maintain a working alliance with the whole team requires constant vigilance. Often I have found that one can be doing perfectly adequate team coaching, but be undone as a coach by unseen team and organizational politics outside of the sessions one is attending.

I have written elsewhere (Hawkins, 2008, 2010; Hawkins and Smith, 2006) of the potential dangers of coaches going to psychologists or psychotherapists for supervision and how this can accentuate the danger of the coaching over-focusing on the individual client and under-serving the organizational client. There is now a new challenge, which is that those who are practising team coaching are going for supervision to coach supervisors who are individually-oriented, and accentuate the danger of the coaching over-focusing on the personal and interpersonal dynamics of the team and under-serving the collective aspects of the team in its systemic context.

There is a shortage of skilled supervisors who are trained not only in coaching and coaching supervision, but also in team coaching and the supervision of team coaches. In this chapter we will explore the process of supervising team coaching. However, this chapter is also relevant to those who supervise coaches who work with individuals but where the team context is important. This may include those who are leading teams, going on to the board for the first time, leading a project team, or just being a member of one or more teams.

Different contexts for supervising team coaching

The supervision of team coaches can take place in a variety of ways:

1a as part of one-to-one ongoing supervision that might focus on individual and team coaching work;

1b one-to-one supervision specifically focusing on team coaching practice;

2a as part of a group supervision in which individual and team coaching are addressed;

2b group supervision specifically focusing on team coaching practice;

3 as part of a shadow consultancy to a team of consultants and team coaches who are all working with different teams within the same organization.

There are benefits and disadvantages to each of these approaches. Approaches 1a) and 2a) would be most common when the coach has a mixed portfolio of individual and team coaching and has an individual or group supervisor who is experienced in supervising both individual and team coaching. Approaches 1b) and 2b) would be more beneficial when a large part of the coaching practice of the supervisees is team coaching, or when the supervisor they go to for supervision of their individual coaching is not experienced in supervising team coaching.

Approach 3) shadow consultancy, is most beneficial if one is carrying out team coaching as part of a wider organizational consultancy assignment that involves a range of other colleagues. In this instance the supervisor needs to be skilled in working with the wider organizational and system dynamics, as well as working with the parallel processes and team dynamics that often will play out across the organizational consultancy team (Hawkins, 1998; and Hawkins and Smith, 2006, ch. 11; the section on Account Teams in Chapter 7 of this book). I have found that in such forms of supervision often the most difficult dynamics to attend to as the shadow consultant or team supervisor is that of the consultant team. Some of these dynamics will be parallel processes from the client organization, while some will be playing out the dynamics of the consultancy organization and others might well be specific to this particular assignment team. Often the dynamics are an entangled mixture of all three of these and each of these frames has to be held in parallel.

What is important is clear contracting in the supervision process (see Hawkins and Smith, 2006), and for the supervisor and supervisee to clarify whether team coaching will be included in their supervisory relationship, or whether it would be better taken to another supervisory setting. I would recommend that supervisors do not just drift into including team coaching supervision, and should only do such supervision if they are experienced in team coaching themselves and have had some training in team coach supervision.

Another danger that can apply to all of the five contexts for supervising team coaching is being overwhelmed by the amount of data presented. By its very nature the team coach has to carry data, not only about the team, their history, task, process and dynamics but also about the individuals in the team and their interpersonal dynamics, and also about the organizational and wider system context in which the team operate. Often a team coach will feel overwhelmed by all the data he or she is trying to hold, process and make sense of; and will then parallel this process by attempting to overwhelm the supervisor with large amounts of data, emerging in a confused and chaotic way (much as it may have emerged for the coach). It is important that the supervisor does not become flooded in parallel and can, at the very least, comment on this process as it happens. One of the consequences of this is that an inordinate amount of the supervision time will be given over to listening to the story, with too little time left for exploring what is happening at greater depth and looking at what needs to shift not only in the team, but also in the relationship between the coach and the team and in the coach themselves.

It is always important to remember that no matter how fascinating the team might be to hear about, the only part of the system you can influence in the supervision is the team coach and it is here that the supervision will have the most impact.

The six-step team coaching supervision model

To help with these dynamics and complexities, I have developed a specific team coaching supervision model which, although designed for use in supervising team coaching in a group setting (approach 2b), can be adapted for the other supervision contexts. This model provides a discipline and framework that ensures the balance of attending to the minimum requisite amount of data to be able to explore the many levels of dynamic (individual, interpersonal, team, organization, wider system, coach relationship with team and team coaching sponsors), before moving on to discover live what needs to shift in the team, the coaching relationship and in the coach. Along with my colleague John Leary Joyce of the Academy of Executive Coaching, we have twice led workshops with over 90 people, working in parallel in 13 supervision groups, each of which completed a significant piece of supervision on a specific piece of team coaching in 45 minutes, by following the model.

Step 1: Contracting

It is important that the process starts by asking the team coach/supervisee what they want and need from the supervision of this team. This can most usefully be done by starting with the end in mind and asking them: 'For this to be a successful supervision for you and the team and the client organization, what do you need to leave this session having achieved?' then to ask: 'What do you most need from me as supervisor and the other supervision group members to achieve that success?'

Whatever emerges from these two questions needs to inform the balance of the attention in the rest of the process, and the process should end by checking back and looking at the contractual goals for the session and how they have been addressed and met.

Step 2: Setting the scene

The team coach is asked to take less than one minute to say what type of team he or she is working with and some brief data on the team.

Step 3: Exploring the dynamics

The team coach is invited to draw on a large sheet of paper symbols, images and colours representing the individual team members and then the connections between them and the stakeholders who surround the team. This is a form of picture sculpting (see Chapter 12):

a *Individuals:* what is happening for the individuals in this team?

b *Interpersonal:* what is happening in the spaces between the individuals?

c *Team dynamic:* this can be elicited by asking: 'If this team were a piece of music, a meal, a geographical place, etc what would it be?'

d *Team mission and intent:* What does the team want/need/aspire to achieve that is currently beyond their reach?

e *Stakeholder engagement:* Who are the key stakeholders the team needs to engage with and what needs to shift in each of these relationships?

f *Wider systemic context:* What is the shift the team need/want/aspire to create in their wider systemic context and what needs to shift in the team to be the change they want to see?

Step 4: Clarifying the three-way contract and intent and deciding where on the coaching continuum the work needs to focus

a The team coach is invited to step into the role of the collective team and, speaking as the team, states what the team want and need from the team coaching and the team coach.

b The team coach is then asked to change back to being the team coach and voicing his or her intent/interest/investment in working with this team.

c Then the coach is asked to move to the side and step into the role of the wider organization or system in which the team exist. In this role they are invited to voice what the wider organization wants and needs from the team coaching. They can be asked their view of the return on investment the organization is looking for. They may also be asked how the senior members of the organization that the team report to want to stay engaged with the process and outcomes of the team coaching.

Step 5: Developing the shift required in team and team coach

The team coach is encouraged to answer the following questions, based on what he or she has discovered in the first three steps:

a What is the shift needed in the team to meet the aspirations of all parties?

b What is the shift required in their relationship with the team?

c What is the shift required in them as the coach, to be the change they want to see in the client?

d What is their specific commitment?

In this process it is important to facilitate the team coach moving to embodied learning (see Hawkins and Smith, 2010). This may entail the coach rehearsing the most important lines he or she needs to use when next meeting the team, or finding and enacting the right emotional state to shift the dynamic within themselves.

Step 6: Review

It is important to end the supervision by returning to the contract and checking with the supervisee what has been most helpful from the session and anything that could have been even more helpful for his or her work and learning. This is important for the supervisee, supervisor and the supervision group to have affirmed what they have done and to continually learn and increase their collective capacity to supervise team coaching.

Variations on the process

This step model has been used in all five of the supervision contexts mentioned earlier in this chapter.

When used in individual supervision I have found it helpful for both the supervisor and supervisee to be up out of their chairs in the exploration stage, supporting the supervisee in drawing the picture sculpt and moving into different positions for speaking as the team, the sponsoring organization and as themselves. This creates more energetic and embodied learning, with more chance of the supervisee entering the emotional life of the team they are working with and leaving with more embodied commitment.

When this model is used in shadow consultancy, it is important to spend more time on Step 3, e and f, to explore how the work with this team fits with the overall organizational development assignment. In addition, at the end of the process we would also spend time harvesting the learning for the benefit of understanding the wider system (see Hawkins, 2011, for a fuller description of ways of harvesting the organizational learning). I do this by addressing the following four questions:

1 How well aligned is this team to the strategy and developmental journey of the wider organization?

2 What are the cultural patterns we have noticed in this team?

3 How are these similar and different to the cultural patterns we have noticed elsewhere in the organization?

4 How should the answers to the first three questions inform our work with this team and elsewhere in the organization and the wider system?

Sculpting the team

Another variant on the model is a 'Team sculpt'. This is a method that can be used in any setting if there is the time available and an experienced supervisor who is appropriately trained. This approach was developed from the work of Moreno, the founder of psychodrama and sociodrama and a contemporary of Sigmund Freud. When Moreno met Sigmund Freud later in life, a long time after they had both left their native Vienna, he is reputed to have said: 'Mr Freud, you analyse men's dreams, I give them the courage to dream again.' The stages of the 'team sculpt' approach are:

Stage 1: Instead of drawing the team members, the supervisee uses members of the supervision group to play different team members, placing them symbolically in relation to the centre of the team and in relationship to each other. The supervisee then shows the group member how to take up a pose that represents their way of being in the group. Having placed all the key team members, the supervisee is asked to choose somebody to be placed in the right position to represent themselves as team coach. This is often very telling.

Stage 2: The supervisee then speaks as each enacted team member, and themselves as team coach. They do this by placing his or her hand on their shoulder and speaking as that team member, stating how they feel in this team.

Stage 3: Each person who has been enrolled as one of the team members is invited to make a statement beginning: 'In this position in the group I am aware of and I feel …'.

Stage 4: All the members are given the opportunity to explore how they would like to move to a different position in the group and what such a move would entail for them and what would be needed from others. For example, one person who has been sculpted on the outside of the group might say that he would ideally like to be right in the middle of the group. Having expressed this desire, he would be invited to find his own way of moving into the centre and seeing what that shift felt like for him and for the others in the middle.

Stage 5: Those sitting outside the dramatized team are asked to reframe the group by being asked: 'If this group were a family what sort of family would it be? Who would be in what role? If it was a country, play, sport, television programme, etc, what would it be? Who would be in what role and what would be the transactions?' It is also possible for the groups to try out their own frames. There are countless possibilities – meals, animals, countries, modes of transport, myths, Shakespearean plays, and so on.

Stage 6: The sculpt can then be further developed by having the supervisee place other individuals to represent key stakeholders in relation to the team and repeat stages 2 and 3 for the members of this wider system.

Stage 7: A chair can then be placed in a suitable position to view the whole sculpted system. Members of the group can be invited to take it in turns to come and stand on the chair and to close and open their eyes and sense a blink impact of witnessing the whole, and to say: 'If I were the creative coach to this system I would …'. The supervisee, having heard the responses of others, can then be asked to stand on the chair and make his or her own statements of commitment of what he or she will do differently as a result of the supervision. The person can then hear how people respond in the roles they are occupying.

Stage 8: As with all such techniques it is important to use a method to de-role those playing other people. The one most frequently used is to invite each person (possibly in pairs) to say one way they are like the person they have played and two ways they are very different.

In Chapter 12 there is a description of how to use team sculpting live in coaching a whole team.

Example of the six-step process

I sat with the three of the senior HR team for a large retail organization. We were there to help one of the three who was part of a leadership team and also had responsibility for coaching the team of one of the most successful and dynamic brands, but knew the team were stuck in how to take the business on to the next level.

As I asked her to tell me briefly about the team, I could feel the energy suck away from both the storyteller and those listening, including myself as she struggled to tell us everything that was going on. After less than five minutes I stopped her and wondered out loud whether this was what their top team meetings were like. 'Energy death by over-reporting?' Her deep sigh confirmed the parallel.

Rather than tell us about the team, I invited her to draw the team, its stakeholders and its relationships and explore through this pictorial sculpt what needed to shift. Her energy increased and excitement grew around the room as new connections emerged from the page and the patterns that needed to be addressed crystallized.

Reflections on the six-step supervision process

This six-step process builds on the CLEAR model of supervision outlined in Hawkins and Smith (2006) and described in Chapter 3 as a coaching process:

Contract

Listen

Explore

Action

Review

This model suggests that supervision should always start with contracting, then listening at depth to the situation being presented by the supervisee, then moving into different ways of exploring the presented issues before moving to new action and ending with review.

In this six-step team coaching supervision model, I have created two steps for the explore stage: one that explores the team and their systemic context; and one that explores the relational field between the team, the coach and the sponsoring organization. The first explore stage allows the coach to stand back and review the team he or she is working with through a variety of different lenses, whereas the second explore stage encourages the coach to step into the various roles in the relational triangle of the team coaching.

The model is also informed by our 'Seven-eyed supervision model' (Hawkins, 2010; Hawkins and Shohet, 2006; Hawkins and Smith, 2006). This model, shown in Figure 11.1, has been developed over the last 25 years and is now used widely in many parts of the world. The model shows how supervision can focus differentially through seven separate lenses. The purpose of the model is to provide a complete range of different areas that can be focused on in supervision and the range of styles necessary. It is based on a systems understanding of the ways things connect, inter-relate and drive behaviour. It illustrates the way in which the systemic context of the coachee can be mirrored in the coaching relationship and how the dynamics of the coaching relationship can be mirrored in the supervisory relationship. Set out below are the seven areas of potential focus that can be useful to both supervisor and supervisee in reviewing the supervision they give and receive and help them discover ways they can expand their supervision practice.

FIGURE 11.1 The seven-eyed model of supervision

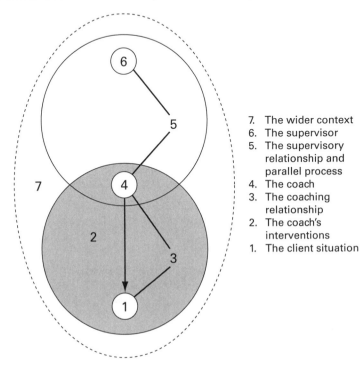

7. The wider context
6. The supervisor
5. The supervisory relationship and parallel process
4. The coach
3. The coaching relationship
2. The coach's interventions
1. The client situation

1. The coachee's system

Here the focus is on the team and the content of the issues they have brought to the coaching and the wider issues of their organization. It includes not only the issues the team want help with, but also how they present and frame these issues.

2. The coach's interventions

Here the focus is on the interventions the coach made and alternative choices that might have been used. It might also focus on a situation in which the coach is about to intervene and explore the possible options including the likely impact of each.

3. The relationship between the coach and the coachee

Here the focus is on the relationship that the coach and team create together.

4. The coach

Here the focus is on the coach themself, both what is being re-stimulated in him or her by the team's issues as well as the dynamics of the client system, and themself as an instrument for registering that which is happening beneath the surface in the team and the coaching relationship.

5. The supervisory relationship

Here the focus is on the live relationship between the supervisor and the coach. The focus needs to include what the coach has absorbed unconsciously from the team and their wider system and how it may be being played out in the relationship with the supervisor. Sometimes the coach can treat the supervisor, unconsciously, in a parallel way to how the team client has treated him or her.

6. The supervisor self-reflection

The focus here is the supervisor's 'here and now' experience with the coach and what can be learnt about the coach/team/coaching relationship from the supervisor's response to the coach and the material presented.

7. The wider context

The focus here is on the organizational, social, cultural, ethical and contractual context in which the coaching is taking place. This includes being aware of the wider group of stakeholders in the process that is being focused upon: the client organization and its stakeholders, the coach's organization and its stakeholders, and the organization or professional network of the supervisor.

Using all seven modes

In talking to supervisors and coaches who have approached others in search of help in exploring coaching situations, we have discovered that often supervisors are stuck in the groove of predominantly using one of the seven modes of working. Some focus entirely on the situation with the team and adopt a pose of pseudo objectivity (mode 1). Others see their job as coming up with better interventions than the coach managed to produce (mode 2). This can often leave the coach feeling inadequate or determined to show that these suggested interventions are as useless as those previously tried.

Other coaches have reportedly left supervision feeling that the problem with the team was entirely due to their own pathology (mode 4).

'Single-eyed vision', which focuses only on one aspect of the process, will always lead to partial and limited perspectives. This model suggests a way of engaging in an exploration that looks at the same situation from many different perspectives and can thus create a critical subjectivity, where subjective awareness from one perspective is tested against other subjective data, achieving not objectivity but appropriate complexity.

Each mode of supervision can be carried out in a skilful manner but it will prove inadequate without the skill to move from mode to mode. The most common order for moving through the modes is to start with mode 1, talking about specific coaching situations, then to move into modes 3 and 4 to explore what is happening in the coaching relationship and for the coach/supervisee. This may well explore the here and now relationship in the room between the coach and the supervisor (modes 5 and 6), and/or bringing into awareness the wider context (mode 7). Finally, having gained new insight and created a shift in the supervisory matrix, the attention may turn back to mode 2, to explore what different interventions the coach might use in the next session to create the needed shift in the coaching relationship. The coach might even try out some of these interventions in what we term a 'fast-forward rehearsal'. Our experience shows that if change starts to happen live in the supervision, it is far more likely to happen back in the coaching relationship (see Hawkins and Smith, 2010).

If we look back at the team coaching process outlined earlier in the chapter, we can see how this follows the seven-eyed model. It is important that the supervisor starts by attending to what is being presented about the team in steps 2 and 3 using the skills of mode 1. Then there is the focus on the relationship between the coach and the team and the wider organizational client in step 4, using the supervision skills of mode 3, and how this particular assignment is impacting on the coach and his or her own particular patterns (mode 4). In addition the supervisor needs to be attending throughout to how the supervision impacts and affects them as supervisor and the supervision group (mode 6) and the relationship between them, the supervision group and the supervisee (mode 5). The supervisor needs to be aware throughout of moving between the focus on the team and the focus on the wider systemic field in which the team, the coach and the supervision reside using the whole range of mode 7 supervision. Finally, in step 5 the supervisor is using mode 2 skills to focus on the shift required in the team coach and the next interventions he or she is committed to making with the team.

In the supervision of team coaching in a group context, it is particularly common for the team dynamic to be paralleled in the supervision group. This can be played out by different members of the supervision group picking up on very different aspects of the team dynamics, or taking sides between various parts or individuals within the team, or even playing out the conflict that is explicitly or implicitly happening in the team. When this occurs it is important that this is recognized and used in the service of more fully understanding the team dynamic (mode 5) or indeed the wider system conflicts (modes 5 and 7).

Conclusion

We are constantly learning from each cohort of new trainees about the fascinating craft of supervising coaches. Increasingly we are reminded that at the heart of being a good team coach or coaching supervisor is not academic knowledge, nor an armoury of tools and techniques, but a dedication to developing one's human capacity to be fully present for another and acting with what we term 'ruthless compassion'. For it is the ruthless compassion we can bring that ultimately allows the fear and anxiety that pervade so many work situations to be overcome, and for our clients to find new strength to act courageously.

In this chapter I have strongly advocated the importance of supervision for all team coaches no matter how experienced they are, for not only can no individual see the whole system he or she is working with, but we also quickly become part of that system. It is very difficult to see the sea in which you are swimming. Even when there are two team coaches working with the same team, supervision is essential, as the relationship between the two coaches can easily be affected by absorbing the dynamics of the team and the wider system, which they then can act out in parallel process.

To meet this need for supervision of team coaches we need more experienced and specialized team coach supervisors, and to attain that goal we need more training programmes and courses that provide specialized training in supervision of teams and organizational and systems dynamics. I hope this chapter will provide team coaches and their supervisors a new model of carrying out such specialized team coach supervision as well as showing how the CLEAR and seven-eyed coaching models can be adapted for supervising team coaching.

Team coaching methods, tools and techniques

12

> *If the only tool you have is a hammer, you tend to treat everything as if it is a nail.*
>
> **(OLD SAYING OFTEN QUOTED BY ABRAHAM MASLOW)**

In coaching teams, all tools require an artisan, or perhaps at times an artist. It is good to have a well-loaded tool-box, but this is not simply a process of attending as many seminars as possible on new approaches. Acquiring new tools can become a preoccupation at the expense of learning to wield the ones we already own with mastery skill, as all artisans must. In the end it is our judgement and our experience-honed instincts that lead us to pick up a particular instrument. **(CHRISTINE THORNTON, 2010: 125)**

Introduction and principles for using tools and methods

In this chapter I will outline a number of methods, tools and techniques that are useful for coaching different kinds of teams and team situations. A number of these have been referred to in previous chapters in their relevance to specific team situations. For convenience I have organized them in three main clusters:

1 *psychometric instruments* that can be used to explore the personal and interpersonal relationships with the team;

2 *team appraisal questionnaires* and instruments including a team 360-degree feedback instrument;

3 *experiential methods* for exploring the team dynamics and functioning.

However, before sharing this toolkit it is important to consider some of the principles for using tools. These are expressed very eloquently by Christine Thornton (2010: 126–27) who offers seven sage pieces of advice:

1 Keep in mind that all tools are simply a means of starting a conversation that the team need to have with each other. (I would add 'or a conversation they need to have with their commissioners or stakeholders'.)

2 Tools help mainly by giving a structure to the conversation that helps people feel safer at the beginning, to equalize the risk and the discomfort, to depersonalize any difficult feedback, and to give the team a sense of working towards a goal. (I would call this 'creating a common language' for an issue.)

3 The importance of timing and context.

4 Any model is ultimately a way of simplifying ... complex realities so we can grasp them and talk about them. So chose a tool that is simple enough to be grasped and used by the team.

5 Think about the likely effect of the tool on this team's situation.

6 Be eclectic in your sources – go beyond the coaching and management literature. Have a magpie eye for what may be useful. Remember the power of the internet search engine.

7 Build your own library of favoured tools.

1. Psychometric instruments

There are a number of useful psychometric tools available that can help teams understand the different personality types, preferences and world-views of each of the members. Here are some that have been used widely in team coaching.

Myers-Briggs Typology Inventory

This is used in organizations for selection, assessment, individual and team coaching. In the team coaching aspect MBTI can be used to help teams that are conflicted, and who see fellow team members' different ways of coping and working as hindering overall productivity. A team analysis of MBTI scores, can be framed as ways of helping the team positively use their differences.

Increasingly we find that most members of leadership teams know the simple (four-letter) version of their MBTI score. It is based on work done by the mother and daughter team of Myers and Briggs in the 1950s, which built on Jung's insights on personality types. By plotting an individual's preferences along four dimensions of personality traits, they created a four-box system of 16 personality types:

Introversion – Extroversion

Sensation – Intuition

Thinking – Feeling

Judging – Perceiving

Depending on your preference along each of these dimensions, this will locate you in one of the 16 dominant personality groupings. (It should be noted that there are more complex depths to the model that can be explored.)

Each team member's personality type can be shared in the group and the team coach can help the team realize how this will cause them to view the same issue and each other very differently and thereby generate more respect for, and find better ways of utilizing, their differences. One way of helping is to clarify how the individual's natural preferences will tend to generate individual reflex reactions. Such personal reflex reactions will normally reinforce conflict in a team rather than understanding. By showing what preferences are in abundance in the team and which are absent, the team coach can help the team explore how such bias might be affecting critical areas of team performance, such as communication, decision making or problem solving.

In some large teams we have drawn the dimensions on the floor and asked people to locate themselves in their part of the map. With those who also share their personality type we asked them to discuss and then share with the group:

- what distinguishes their small group;
- what they would like others to recognize about them;
- what others most often misunderstand about them;
- how they think the team can best utilize their distinctiveness.

The usefulness of the spatial mapping is that it makes clear what personality types the team has most dominantly and what personality types it lacks. Team members who understand the typology can be invited to enter the space representing missing personality types and describe how they would see the team from that perspective.

I once worked in a consultancy team where nearly all the team members except me were extrovert, intuitive, feeling and perceiving types; only the team manager preferred the sensing and judging dimensions. The exercise made the team realize how infuriating it must be for the team manager that the team members would sit around and endlessly discuss different ways of looking at a problem but never arrive at a concrete conclusion! Even when they did conclude something they were prone to revisit the decision at frequent intervals.

There are other personality type inventories that can also be used including Manfred Kets de Vries' (2006) 'Personality Audit' and 'Spiral Dynamics' (Beck and Cowan, 1996).

Leadership styles inventories

There are a number of instruments that look at different leadership styles. Some that we know to be useful in helping teams explore different leadership styles include:

- *Situational Leadership,* Hersey and Blanchard (1977), which explores leaders' preferences in relation to task and relationship dimensions.
- *Conflict Styles Inventory,* Thomas and Kilmann (1974), which looks at different approaches and responses to conflict.
- *Global Executive Leadership Inventory*, Manfred Kets de Vries (2006), which provides self and 360-degree feedback on 12 dimensions of leadership behaviour: visioning, empowering, energizing, designing and aligning, rewarding and feedback, team building, outside orientation, tenacity, global mind-set, emotional intelligence, resilience to stress and life balance.

Manfred Kets de Vries (2006: ch. 11) provides a very good case study of using 360-degree feedback based on the Global Executive Leadership Inventory and the Personality audit in a group coaching context within a team, where each team member had an extended time to share their inventory feedback, hear how the other team members responded to this and discuss how they could develop their contribution to their role, the team and the organization in the light of these discussions.

Kets de Vries convincingly argues the benefit of group coaching within teams with team members sharing their personality inventories and 360-degree feedback:

> When people get to know each other better, when they understand each other's leadership styles, when they have a good sense of each other's competencies, when they understand the nature of each other's work, there is a greater likelihood that they will trust each other. In the transitional space of the coaching workshop, people open up and begin to share information, talking about the issues that preoccupy them. They stop beating around the bush, they stop playing politics, and they start to support each other.

(Kets de Vries, 2006: 299).

Such group coaching of team members is often a very good prelude to team coaching, for it is difficult for team members to focus on the collective needs of the team and the wider system before they understand each other and feel their own needs have been recognized.

Belbin Team Role Analysis

In the 1970s, Dr Meredith Belbin and his research team at Henley Management College set about researching the performance of teams to ascertain what made some teams perform better than others. From their work they discovered what Belbin later called the 'Apollo syndrome'. This emerged from studying the performance of small syndicate groups on the executive training programme, when undertaking what was called the 'Executive management exercise'. They experimented with putting those with the highest scoring intelligence in what was termed the 'Apollo group' and found to their surprise that these teams functioned worse than average when competing with groups of more average ability. As the research progressed, it revealed that the difference between success and failure for a team was most linked to the team having a good balance of helpful behaviours across the mix of the team members. Belbin identified a number of separate clusters of behaviours, each of which formed distinct team contributions or 'team roles'.

Belbin defines team role as: 'a pattern of behavior characteristic of the way in which one team member interacts with another where his performance serves to facilitate the progress of the team as a whole' (Belbin, 2004: 191). His further research showed that different individuals displayed different team roles to varying degrees.

The nine team roles

1 *Plant:* these tend to be highly creative and good at solving problems in unconventional ways and provide fresh and original thinking for the team.

2 *The monitor evaluator:* provides a logical eye, makes impartial judgements where required and weighs up the team's options in a dispassionate way. They also provide a useful reality check by investigating whether there are the resources to carry out the proposals.

3 *Coordinators:* were originally called 'chairs', for they provide the focus on the team's objectives, draw out team members and delegate work appropriately.

4 *Resource investigators:* provide an external focus spotting resources in terms of ideas, people and market opportunities that may support the plan.

5 *Implementers:* take the ideas and make them happen through project plans, delegation, clear objectives and timelines.

6 *Completer finishers:* provide the dogged energy to see tasks through to completion and the attention to detail to ensure the highest standards of quality control.

7 *Team workers:* provide the emotional and practical support to the team and help the team to work well together.

8 *Shapers:* shape the way the team efforts are applied. They will often frame the challenges and objectives and impose some shape on the discussion and outcomes of the group.

9 *Specialists:* supply knowledge and skills in rare supply and prefer to contribute on that limited front.

Each role brings a necessary contribution to the team, but also has a limiting down side, which needs to be recognized and compensated for by others, to create a well-balanced team.

In using team role analysis we have found that although individuals have a tendency that draws them to playing some team roles more than others, how they will score on a Team Role Inventory is very context-specific and will vary depending on the team they are currently working within.

Where we have found the Team Role Inventory to be valuable is where a complete team fill in the Inventory with reference to that team context. The results can then be charted on a complete team basis, with team role scores totalled. This provides a very useful representation of what roles the team is over-endowed with and what roles the team has in short supply. Also we have found this visual table to be useful in showing who carries what role for the team. Through the team analysis, often quiet and little noticed team members can be seen and appreciated for making an important but previously overlooked contribution.

We also have found it useful to help teams interrupt the pattern of recruiting more team members like themselves and thus reinforcing the team's imbalance. A team of 'plants' are attracted to creative, out of the box thinkers, but recruiting more of them leads to great creative brain-storming meetings and debates, but little implementation! Likewise I have worked with a senior financial team that wanted to recruit more 'monitor-evaluators' like themselves, but were able to see that this would mean they were even better at killing off any new creative thinking.

Leadership engagement capacity

Theirs is a self- and peer assessment tool to help leaders look at their personal capacity to engage with a wide range of others, both within the team and across their stakeholder community. It is based on the relationship engagement capacity described in Chapter 10. The full questionnaire is available from the author.

2. Team appraisal questionnaires and instruments

The Five Disciplines Questionnaire

This questionnaire was developed by Peter Hawkins with help from colleagues at Bath Consultancy Group, based on research into high-performing teams, influenced by the research of both Katzenbach and Smith (1993b) and Wageman *et al* (2008) and research into team coaching. (Bath Consultancy Group holds the copyright on this questionnaire and a databank of responses. If you would like to use it, please contact the Group; details are in the Resources section.)

Team members are asked to score each of the 18 elements on a 1 (low) to 5 (high) scale, where:

5 = The team is a role model or exemplar that others could study in this area.

4 = The team does this consistently well.

3 = The team does this well sporadically but is not consistent.

2 = The team rarely does this but recognizes its importance.

1 = The team neither does this well nor focuses on it.

Team members are asked to score all elements on the chart (shown in Table 12.1) and, for two scores, to think about what most needs to change in this element, both in the team and in their own contribution. This ensures that they are not just judging the team, but taking personal responsibility for how the team can develop.

The team scores can then be collected and a visual representation of the average score and the range can be shown for each category. The team can see where there are differences of opinion about current competence and need for change. This in itself can become a very creative focus for team discussion.

In addition, for each of the five disciplines an aggregate score can be produced, both for the perception of the current performance and where the team thinks it needs to be. This is achieved by adding all the scores for questions 1 to 3 and dividing by the number of people in the team, and then by 3 and putting the result into Discipline 1; doing the same with questions 4 to 6 and putting the result in Discipline 2; and the same for questions 7 to 12, but this time dividing by the number of people in the team and then by 6 and putting the result in Discipline 3. Questions 13 to 15 are divided by the

TABLE 12.1

Discipline	Indicator	Current rating 1 low - 5 high	We need to be at? (1 – 5)	Shift needed in me and the team to achieve future rating
1. Clear commission	1. The team has a clear commission and mandate from the wider organization and those it reports to			
1. Commission collective performance	2. Achieving team goals is recognized and rewarded above achieving individual goals			
1. Commission selection	3. The team has been selected to have a good range of the necessary complementary skills			
2. Clarity of purpose	4. All team members can clearly articulate and own the overall purpose			
2. Clarity of goals	5. The team is working towards agreed goals in an effective manner			
2. Clarity of action	6. The team commits to clear actions with accountability and follow through			

TABLE 12.1 continued

Discipline	Indicator	Current rating 1 low - 5 high	We need to be at? (1 – 5)	Shift needed in me and the team to achieve future rating
3. Co-creating	7. Clear and shared ways of working			
	8. Team members are mutually accountable not just for their own areas but for collective goals			
	9. The team maintains a high level of morale and commitment			
3. Co-creating in meetings	10. Everybody is fully engaged and involved, the team makes good use of its diversity			
	11. The outcomes are better than any individual could have arrived at by themselves			
	12. Team members leave the meetings feeling more focused, supported and energized			

TABLE 12.1 continued

Discipline	Indicator	Current rating 1 low - 5 high	We need to be at? (1 – 5)	Shift needed in me and the team to achieve future rating
4. Connecting with Staff	13. The team members can engage employees at all levels as transformational leaders			
4. Connecting with Stakeholders	14. The team relates well to all its key stakeholders with team members representing the whole team			
4. Connecting with the changing environment	15. The team scans its stakeholder environment and constantly attends to changing needs and perceptions			
5. Core Learning	16. The team regularly and effectively attends to its own development			
	17. The team attends to developing each of its members			
	18. All team members give good real-time feedback and provide support and challenge to each other			

number of team members and by 3 and go into Discipline 4 and finally the same process is used for question 16 to18 and the result is put into Discipline 5. This helps the team focus on where there is the largest gap between aspiration and perception of current performance and where team coaching might be most helpful.

An example is given in Figure 12.1 of a team that considered their co-creating and core learning were much closer to what they thought was needed than the quality of their connecting with stakeholders or their external commissioning. There was a smaller but significant gap in the discipline of clarifying. After the team had discussed the aggregate scores, it was decided to start by the team having a workshop to 'clarify' its own sense of mission and then a joint session to explore this with the board non-executives and create a better 'commission'. The joint session also carried out a stakeholder analysis, which later was developed in a plan for better 'connecting'.

Once the team agree what change dimensions are critical to success, they can clarify the behaviour changes that will be needed in them individually and collectively to close the gap between aspiration and reality.

Team 360-degree feedback

This is fundamentally different from individual 360-degree feedback for team members. It is a method for obtaining feedback on how the team is collectively viewed by its key stakeholders. These may include:

- staff who report into this team;
- other parts of the organization that regularly interface with the team;
- those the team report to;
- customers (internal and external);
- partners, suppliers and other external bodies;
- investors and regulators.

Most team 360-degree instruments have to be carefully tailored for the particular team situation, but there are some generic questions that are always useful. These include:

- What do you most appreciate and value about what you receive from this team?
- What most disappoints you about what you receive from this team?
- What would you like to see different in what you receive from this team?
- What do you most appreciate and value about how this team engages with you?
- What most disappoints you about how this team engages with you?
- What would you like to see different in how this team engages with you?

FIGURE 12.1 The five disciplines of team coaching with questionnaire scores

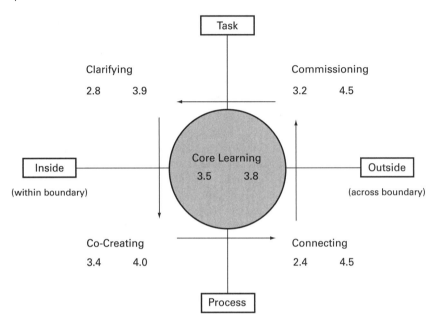

These questions can also be scaled, asking the stakeholders to score their satisfaction/dissatisfaction with what they receive and how they are engaged. It is usually most helpful to collect qualitative answers to open questions and quantitative scores and to show them on graphs or tables, particularly if the questionnaire is going to be repeated a year later as this helps track improvement/decline.

Another instrument we have designed to bridge the qualitative and quantitative feedback in a way that can be tracked over time is 'Descriptor analysis'.

Descriptor analysis

In many organizations I have asked the question: 'How do you connect the data you get from your customer feedback, your staff attitude survey, your press analysis, regulator and company analysts' reports and investor feedback?'

So far I have never had a fully satisfactory answer, but nearly all the senior executives I have asked found it an important question. One chief executive replied: 'If we could integrate all that feedback, we would have a powerful aerial view, which would transform our ability to steer our organization!' Unfortunately, in most organizations the sales department manages the customer feedback, the marketing department manages the press analysis, the Human Relations department manages the staff attitude survey, Corporate Affairs manages the investor feedback and the financial director manages the analysts' and regulatory reports.

Multiple stakeholder perceptions, when they are joined up, provide a valuable intermediate measure of change in organizational performance and value creation. We developed a methodology that can collect and integrate 360-degree feedback on the organization (and sometimes also its collective leadership) from a wide range of stakeholder positions.

The process, illustrated in Figure 12.2, begins with an analysis of:

a all the descriptors (adjectives and descriptive phrases) in the organization's literature (annual reports, mission statements, visions, core value statements, CEO speeches, etc);

b all the descriptors used in the data currently collected from different stakeholders;

c the key challenges, dilemmas and questions currently engaging the organization at a strategic level, garnered through group, team and individual interviews.

We then build a word search instrument that includes:

15 top descriptors from a);

15 top used descriptors in b);

15 descriptors from our word bank that reflect the key themes and dilemmas garnered from c).

This word search is included as part of a 360-degree feedback questionnaire sent to representatives of all the identified stakeholder groups, with the request that they underline three descriptors that they believe most accurately reflect how they see the organization today, and circle three descriptors that they would like to be able to use to describe the organization in two or three years' time. From this 'quick-to-collect' data, a quantified 'league table' can be produced of the most underlined descriptors that correspond to today's perception and of the most circled descriptors that represent the perception of what is expected in the future.

Sometimes we do a parallel word search on how the collective leadership of the organization is viewed. This can dramatically show what needs to shift in the leadership culture prior to achieving a shift in the organization so that the perception of the organization moves toward that which is desired.

The outcome can be built into an ongoing barometer that can be used to regularly review progress. This is done by building the 10 highest underlined descriptors and the 10 most circled descriptors into a shorter word search that can be integrated into all current stakeholder feedback mechanisms.

FIGURE 12.2 Descriptor analysis process

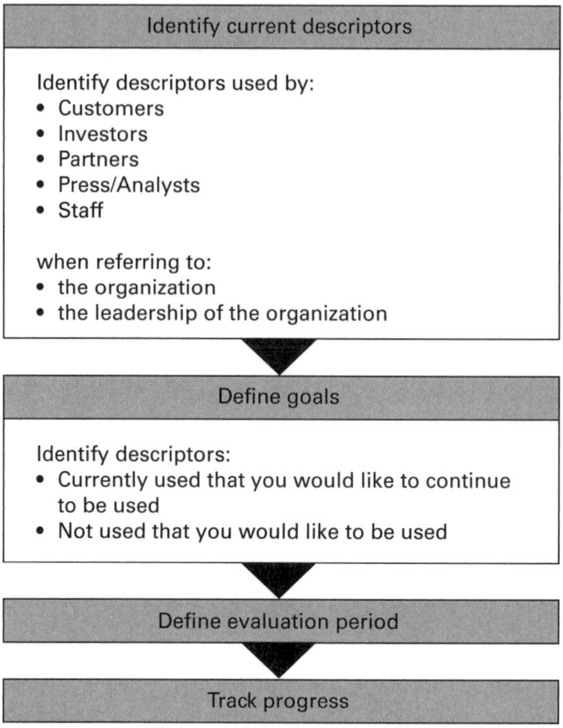

One large British financial organization we worked with some time ago wanted to move from being currently seen as 'Bureaucratic, British and Institutional' to being 'Leading, European and Innovative'. It geared its culture change and leadership development processes to the goal of creating this shift, and gradually over the next three years it was able to see how each of its stakeholder groups was reporting a shift in how they perceived both the organization and its leadership, towards the vision of how the company wanted to be seen.

3. Experiential methods for exploring team dynamics and functioning

Appreciative Inquiry

Appreciative Inquiry seeks out the very best of 'what is' to help ignite the imagination of 'what might be'. The aim is to generate new knowledge which expands 'the realm of the possible' and helps the partners of an organization envision a collectively desired future and then to carry forth that vision in ways which successfully translate intention into reality.

(Cooperrider and Srivastva, 1987)

The key feature of Appreciative Inquiry (AI) is its focus on what currently works well as a starting point for improvement and change. The assumption is that at some time, for instance in using it for team development, there have been experiences or moments when the team have worked well which they can identify and build on to vision how they want to work together well in the future. This grounds the vision of the future in the present and has a powerful effect in amplifying what works well through stories told of these experiences.

AI challenges fundamental assumptions about change processes, such as our reliance on deficit-based problem-solving approaches and can be very useful in working with teams. It uses a four-stage model, known as the four Ds – discovery, dreaming, design/dialogue and delivery.

1. Discovery

Here the team coach asks the team to describe 'a time when you feel the team performed really well'. This can work as a series of inquiry interviews prior to the group process or a pairing process in a group, which leads directly to sharing stories:

- What were the circumstances during that time?
- Describe a time when you were proud to be a member of the team group. Why were you proud?
- What do you most value about being a member of this team?

Getting people to tell their stories is a key part of the AI process, which people really enjoy once they get started, and which works well in pairs, allowing people to ask questions, encouraging them to suspend assumptions and jot down notes for each other. The process of listening is important. AI has been described as inquiry with the heart, so it requires empathy, staying with the positive frame, asking curious questions, finding out about the context, and hearing the story. The listener actively participates in the inquiry through asking questions and sharing experiences and excitement rather than being a neutral observer.

The next stage is hearing stories or excerpts from the stories in the whole team, which can take time, to uncover themes. This is a crucial stage in creating a group inquiry and retaining the power of the individual experiences.

2. Dreaming

The next step after collating themes is dreaming of 'what could be' – creating a desired and compelling image of the future of the team, based on the best of what is already happening.

Provocative propositions describe 'an ideal state of circumstances that will foster the climate that creates the possibilities to do more of what works' (Hammond and Royal, 1998). They are symbolic statements grounded in the stories told, and the process involves:

- Finding examples of the best (from stories).
- Determining what circumstances made the best possible (in detail).
- Taking the stories and envisioning what might be. This can be done by applying the question 'what if' to all the common themes and writing affirmative present tense statements incorporating the common themes.

Some examples:

- Our customers have a pleasant experience when they talk to us.
- We anticipate their needs and have the information available when they call.
- We continually learn as we work.
- We achieve together and are mutually accountable.
- We accept challenges as a team, not as individuals.
- We own the process and we challenge the process.

The proposition needs to be a stretch, a challenge and bold – again the power is in the process as these examples may seem tame to others (like any other vision statement) but will not seem so to the group who were engaged in the experience of creating them.

3. Design/Dialogue

In a team this stage applies to the need to decide what changes are being made as a result of the visioning and how the propositions can be lived out in practice.

In a team development process a team would typically reconvene to apply propositions to operational issues and use dialogue within the wider organization to consult on implementation plans. The team might split into 'issue teams' based on different propositions such as shared team leadership, communication, culture and fun.

4. Delivery

This is the stage of deciding on changes and carrying them through whether as a team or an organization. In a strategic planning process it may also involve agreeing meaningful performance indicators and transition plans.

Whilst the creation of the propositions serves as a guiding light for action in a team or organization, too often the process may stop with the creation of the vision. This may be the weak link in AI, as there can be an assumption that change in behaviour will follow.

Commitment to action works best when tested by what this would mean in everyday action and resolving what may get in the way of enacting the propositions they have created together. The change also needs to start in the behaviours and actions while on the workshop (see Chapter 5, Action Stage).

Solution-focused Team Coaching

'A team is not a problem that needs to be analysed and solved but a potential to be unfolded' (Meier, 2005: 5).

Solution-focused approaches to coaching and change build on the work of AI and provide some additional useful tools and question sets. Meier (2005) sets out a useful eight-step process for coaching teams, which is very similar to the CID-CLEAR coaching process in Chapter 5:

1 *Preparing the Ground* – the coach agrees the scope of the work and how the coach and the team will work together.

2 *Expectations and Goals* – this is similar to the second contracting phase in the CID-CLEAR model (Chapter 5), where the team individually and collectively generate statements about what success from the team coaching would look, sound and feel like, and what difference it would create.

3 *Hot Topics* – the team generate all the areas where improvement is aimed for. This can be done by team members individually putting their view of the key improvement areas on separate Post-its and placing them on a large display wall. The team can then be invited to read and cluster them into the most important themed areas.

4 *Highlights* – 'The participants start looking for situations in which the problem or the conflict either did not happen at all or was less severe' (Meier, 2005: 64). They find the enabling conditions and skills that allowed this to be different.

5 *Future Perfect* – 'the team designs a very precise picture of a future in which the problems have been solved' (Meier, 2005: 68).

6 *Scaling Dance* – scaling is the most significant contribution of solution-focused approaches to the coaching processes. It builds on AI and adds another dimension. The coach takes the topic under discussion and creates a visual scale from 1 to 10, where 10 represents the future perfect state and 1 its opposite. The coach then invites team members to write down where they are today and then consider the following questions:

   a How did you manage to get to this point? What is the difference between 1 and where you are now?

   b If you think about your best highlight, where was it on the scale? What is the difference here?

   c What did you personally contribute to get you to where you are now and to the highlight?

   d How would you know you have progressed just a small step towards 10?

   e Which resources did you use to be able to keep at X and not sink lower? (Questions taken from Meier, 2005: 73)

7 *Steps* – here the team, having explored the scaling questions, are asked to design measures that can be implemented immediately and that will create a sustainable shift on the scale from current state towards 'future perfect'.

8 *Personal Mission* – similar to the action phase in the CID-CLEAR model (Chapter 5) the team members are asked to make a small personal commitment to what they will do towards making this shift happen.

Team Sculpting

This is an approach taken from sociodrama which was originally developed by Jacob Moreno. In Chapter 11 I showed how team sculpting can be used in the supervision of team coaching. I have adapted and developed this approach for experientially exploring the underlying dynamics of teams:

Stage 1. The team are asked to find objects or symbols that represent what is at the heart or core of the team. These are placed in the centre of the room.

Stage 2. Without discussing it, the group members are asked to stand up and move around until they can find a place that symbolically represents where they are in the group, ie how far are they from the centre? Who are they close to and who are they distant from? Then they are asked to take up a statuesque pose that typifies how they are in the group. This often takes several minutes as each person's move is affected by the moves of the others.

Stage 3. One by one, each person is invited to make a statement beginning: 'In this position in the team I feel …'.

Stage 4. All the members are given the opportunity to explore how they would like to move to a different position in the team and what such a move would entail for them and for others. For example, one person who has sculpted herself on the outside of the team might say that she would ideally like to be right in the middle of the team.

Having stated this desire, she would be invited to find her own way of moving into the centre and seeing what that shift felt like for her and for the others in the middle.

Stage 5. Team members are asked to reframe the team by being asked: If this team were a family, what sort of family would it be? Who would be in what role? Or if this team were a television programme, which programme would it be? Who would be in what role and what would be the transactions? (It is possible for the teams to try out their own frames. There are countless possibilities – meals, animals, countries, modes of transport, myths, Shakespearean plays, etc).

Stage 6. The team members are given the opportunity individually to leave their position in the team sculpture and stand on a chair and view the whole matrix structure that has emerged. On this chair they are the creative coach to the team and can deliver a statement: 'If I was coach to this team I would ...'. I encourage people not to think what they will say until they stand on the chair, and to notice their first 'blink' response.

Picture Sculpts

Another way to help teams stand back and see the dynamic pattern of both the team and the wider system is to do a picture sculpt. These come in many forms.

The metaphorical progression

When working with teams in a large financial company we started the team off-site workshop by asking the team members to divide into three groups around three flipcharts. Each group had 10 minutes to create three metaphorical pictures or cartoons of the team and the wider company: a) three years ago, b) now, and c) three years from now. Every person had to be part of the drawing (whatever their artistic ability) and discussion kept to a minimum. As they finished the pictures they were encouraged to add voice bubbles to the representational figures and to come up with a title for each picture. The pictures were then displayed on the wall and presented by each group. This opened up a great deal of the feelings within the team and about the team's relationship to the organization, as well as how the way forward was conceived. It provided a metaphorical language to work with on the team event; for example one team had themselves as a train chuffing slowly through open countryside three years ago; currently hitting the buffers and being attacked from many sides; and then transforming into a plane in three years' time. Throughout the workshop the team would come back to these images and explore the 'buffers' and discuss how they were going to get off the rails and down the runway!

The inter-team dynamic

When working on a large-scale culture change with a large British manufacturing company I facilitated a number of leadership workshops with leaders from across the organization. At one point on the workshop they split into their divisional and departmental teams and drew a metaphorical picture of their team and the other parts of the organization they were connected to, illustrating the nature of the connection. One team drew themselves as a pirate ship, tattered and torn, the team leader as the only one on deck looking out through a telescope; the finance department as a shark, creating holes in their hull; the executive board as a hot air balloon dropping rocks on them; and other key linked departments as having run aground on different islands. This led to discussions of how to change the inter-team dynamics and organizational culture.

Individual representations

Here each team member is asked to draw their picture of the team and its wider system stakeholders and include where they see themselves within the picture. These pictures can be shared with the other team members and an exploration can ensue of how they would like the picture to change and what it would take to bring about that change.

Individual metaphors

A shorter usage of metaphorical inquiry techniques is to ask team members in the initial inquiry: If your team were a country, animal, meal, piece of music, etc, what would it be?

Each of these techniques is a way of bringing to the surface what may be half-felt but unarticulated dynamics within the team and between the team and the wider organization. Huffington (2008) develops Pierre Turquet's original idea of 'the organization in the mind'; how we each differently conceptualize the organization. These picture drawing and metaphor creating techniques are ways of surfacing how we hold 'the team, the inter-team, the organization and the wider system in mind'.

Team culture review

Elsewhere we have quoted the Chinese proverb about how the last one to know about the sea is the fish. To help a team access their taken for granted culture we have developed a series of exercises to help them become flying fish and more clearly see the sea they are swimming in. One of these is to divide the team into four small groups and ask them to prepare a presentation for the rest of the team. Each group has a different task:

1 *The unofficial induction process.* Everything you need to know to thrive in this team, but nobody tells you officially. The group are

asked to prepare and deliver this induction as though the other team members were new arrivals.

2 *The hero, villain and fools stories.* The stories, often about past members, that are handed down the generations. Hero stories tell you how to succeed, villain stories what to avoid, and fool stories show how people have tripped over the hidden boundaries or rules.

3 *The unwritten rule book.* This is similar to the first group, but this one lists the top four or five unwritten but generally accepted rules the team operates by.

4 *Passing on your wisdom.* The group imagine they are leaving the team and mentoring a new team member. They produce the best advice they would like to give that person about how to succeed in this team.

These presentations are often very entertaining, creative and funny as well as revealing about the deeper levels of the team's culture. Once they have been shared, the team coach can help the team analyse the emerging patterns that go across the presentations at the levels of team artefacts, team behaviours, team mindsets, the emotional ground of the team, and the fundamental motivations and values that drive the team functioning.

This can then lead to a 'three-way sort' of what the team want to hold on to, let go of and start doing differently in terms of their ways of being and relating (for a fuller description of carrying out a three-way sort see Chapter 5, page 78).

When to use which tools and methods

As well as the tools included in this chapter, there are many tools and methods for leadership team coaching scattered throughout this book. For ease of reference I include Table 12.2, which shows different tools and methods linked to the two core models of team coaching: the CID-CLEAR process model described in Chapter 5 and the five disciplines model described in Chapters 3 and 6.

Conclusion

We started this chapter with the quote: 'If the only tool you have is a hammer, you tend to treat everything as if it is a nail.' This can lead to some very bent bolts and screws and damaged or wounded pride!

I hope that this chapter has at least helped you, the reader, begin to widen your own sense of what might be useful when working with a team, whether you are an external or internal team coach, team leader, or a team member who would like their team to perform better.

This is only a very selective offering of possible team tools that I have found useful, while remembering that in team coaching the tool needs to be not only carefully chosen but also adapted to the needs of that particular team, their context and current needs. One of my criteria for a successful team coaching process is that the team and I have co-created a new model, tool or way of working that has arisen from the particular emergent needs of our work. So I owe an enormous debt of gratitude to the 100 or more teams in many parts of the world that I have had the privilege to coach and learn from.

TABLE 12.2

Team Discipline or Team Coaching Stage	Team Need	Possible Method	Where in this Book
Inquiry	Clarifying the nature of the team	What sort of team are we	Chapter 5
Inquiry and Diagnosis	Where the coaching should focus	High Performing team questionnaire	Chapter 12
Contracting with whole team	Team needs to collectively own the purpose and goals of the coaching	Mapping success criteria for the individuals, team and stakeholders	Chapter 5
Listening	Role clarity	Belbin Team Role Analysis	Chapter 12
Listening	Understanding each other's personality types	MBTI Other Personality Inventories	Chapter 12 Chapter 12
Explore	The team lacks confidence	Appreciative Inquiry Solution Focus	Chapter 12
Explore – Disciplines 1 and 2	Team needs to be clearer about its commission and mission	Mission exercise	Chapter 6

TABLE 12.2 continued

Team Discipline or Team Coaching Stage	Team Need	Possible Method	Where in this Book
Explore – Discipline 3	Teams need to explore its collective dynamic and the relation of that to the wider system	Team Sculpting Picture Sculpts	Chapter 12 Chapter 12
Explore – Discipline 3	Team needs to surface its hidden cultural norms	Team Culture Review	Chapter 12
Explore – Disciplines 2 and 3	Team needs to explore how it strategizes	Double loop strategizing exercise	Chapter 6
Explore – Discipline 4	Team needs to be clear about their critical stakeholders	Stakeholder mapping	Chapter 6 This chapter
	Team needs to understand their stakeholders' perceptions of them.	Team 360 feedback	This chapter
	Deciding what you want stakeholders to perceive	Descriptor Analysis Starting with the end in mind	This chapter
	Need to explore their individual and collective capacity to engage	Leadership Engagement Capacity questionnaire	Chapter 12
		Authority Presence and Impact	Chapter 11
Action – Discipline 3	Team needs to decide on how to develop going forward	Three Way Sort exercise	Chapter 5
Action – Discipline 4	Team needs to improve its stakeholder engagement	Pitch-side coaching	Chapter 6

TABLE 12.2 continued

Team Discipline or Team Coaching Stage	Team Need	Possible Method	Where in this Book
Review and Re-contracting	Need to review and upgrade the coaching relationships	Coaching feedback	This chapter
Discipline 5	Team needs to explore how it learns	Learning styles inventory	Chapter 6
		Domains of learning mapping	Chapter 6
	Team needs to review its five disciplines	Five Disciplines Review	Chapter 6
Evaluation	The need to evaluate the benefits of the work	Redoing: 360-degree feedback	This chapter
		Descriptor Analysis	This chapter
		High-performing Team Questionnaire Performance Data	This chapter

Conclusion

13

In 2010 John Leary Joyce of the Academy of Executive Coaching and I started the first UK one-year certificated course in team coaching. On the first module some of the participants were joking in the bar about banning the 'S' word – System. One of them explained to me that she experienced the word 'System' as a head word, whereas the other 'S' word, 'Self' was a 'heart word'. I turned to her and said: 'We will know this course has been successful when you experience "Self" as a head word and "System" as coming from the heart'. She reported the next day how this had not only fundamentally disturbed her thinking, but entered her dreams. Somehow she had begun to realize that training to be a team coach was not just about learning a string of tools, models and methods, nor about just acquiring new competencies and capabilities, but about a fundamental shift in the way we view the world.

Introduction

In this last chapter I draw together some of the themes that have permeated this book, but refrain from trying to conclude or end the explorations started in this book. This ending is a small contribution to a much bigger beginning. I hope these limited pages have made a small contribution to the formation of a relatively new field of endeavour: that of systemic team coaching. This field, as indicated in Chapter 3, has roots that spread back through organizational and team development, small group understanding, organizational learning, sports team coaching and individual executive coaching, and yet we are at the very beginning of developing an integrated approach where these strands are interwoven into a discernable and understandable method of working with a whole team in relation to its systemic context. So in this last chapter I will set out how I see the challenges and agendas for this field going forward.

Who or what does team coaching serve? Overcoming the Parsifal trap

The Parsifal trap is named after the legendary Knight of the Round Table Sir Percival or Parsifal, who left home very early in his life and went on his adventures in search of the Holy Grail. His courage and innocence served him well and, while still very young, he arrived at the Grail Castle, where he saw the awesome Grail Procession, carrying the much sought after Holy Grail. He was intoxicated with excitement and with the splendour and privilege of having got there. But the next morning he awoke on a damp, cold, open field and the whole castle, procession and grail had evaporated into the mist. He had failed to ask the question that would have allowed him to stay. Parsifal took many more years of travails and searching to find his way back to the Grail Castle but this time, with the wisdom of experience, he knew the question that must be asked: 'Whom does the Grail serve?'

Many teams fall into and stay in the Parsifal trap. They believe that getting on well together and having efficient meetings are the goal. A team only has a meaningful life if they are serving a need beyond themselves, and have stakeholders who require them to deliver something beyond what can be done by the separate individuals.

Team coaches too fall into the Parsifal trap of believing that team development or team coaching are an end in themselves and fail to ask: 'Team development in service of what?' When we fail to ask this question we, like the young Parsifal, may well find ourselves waking up in a cold misty barren field, wondering why our dream has evaporated and are condemned to many more long years of searching. If as a team coach I am going to create sustainable value, I must be clear about what and who my work is in service of. As a minimum I need to ensure that my coaching is in service of the team members, the team as a whole, their organization and the wider system that the organization serves. In addition I must be in service of the relationships that connect and weave between all these parties, for none of these entities can be successful by themselves and their value is intrinsically bound together. I need to be focused on the unrealized potential in all parties and the connections between them and assist in that potential being realized. However, in serving the individual team members it is important that I am not just serving their fragmented or egoistic self, but helping each person find their calling, their service, their purpose in doing what is necessary in the world. In serving the team, the team becoming high performing is not an end in itself, but merely a means to the team being better able to create value for their stakeholders.

In serving the organization I need to ensure that the work with the individual or team is not an end in itself, but is enabling that individual and team to more effectively lead and manage the organization through its next phase of development so the organization can fulfil its potential and make a better contribution to the wider world.

However, as I indicated in the opening chapter the current nature of world challenges demands that all human beings think and act in new ways. One of the earliest writers and thinkers to point this out was Gregory Bateson, the anthropologist, cyberneticist, systems thinker and epistemologist. In the 1960s and 70s Bateson was one of the first powerful voices to speak about the developing ecological crisis facing our planet. Some time before other commentators he showed how our current environmental crisis is rooted in our epistemological mindsets, that is how we generate knowledge of the world we inhabit.

If we look at how Bateson (1972) describes our collective human epistemological errors, you can reflect on how many of these are current in the behaviour and belief systems of the teams where you have been, or are, a member:

> The ideas that dominate our civilization at the present time date in their most virulent form from the industrial revolution ... may be summarized as:
>
> a It's us against the environment.
> b It's us against other men.
> c It's the individual (or the individual team or individual company, or the individual nation) that matters.
> d We can have unilateral control over the environment and must strive for that control.
> e We live in an infinitely expanding 'frontier'.
> f Economic determinism is common sense.
> g Technology will do it for us.
>
> (Bateson, 1972: 468)

Bateson also showed how these beliefs are rooted in a theology that separates God from Creation and creates a merely transcendent God separate from Nature:

> If you put God outside and set him vis-à-vis his creation and if you have the idea that you are created in his image, you will logically and naturally see yourself as outside and against the things around you. And as you arrogate all mind to yourself, you will see the world around you as mindless and therefore as not entitled to moral or ethical consideration. The environment will be yours to exploit ....
>
> If this is your estimate of your relation to nature and you have an advanced technology, your likelihood of survival will be that of a snowball in hell. You will die either of the toxic by-products of your own hate, or, simply, of over population and over-grazing.
>
> (Bateson, 1972)

To these can be added water shortage, climate change, famine and warfare.

If we now revisit each of these false and dangerous beliefs, we can look at what we could put alongside them as an antidote or cure that would help us overcome these ingrained and habituated dualistic beliefs. You might at this point like to write your own antidotes for each of the Bateson statements before comparing them with those I have written in Table 13.1.

Bateson (1972) writes very clearly of the problems we have created by choosing the wrong unit of survival:

> In accordance with the general climate of thinking in mid nineteenth century England, Darwin proposed a theory of natural selection and evolution, in which the unit of survival was either the family line or species of sub-species or something of that sort. But today it is quite obvious that this is not the unit of survival in the real biological world. The unit of survival is organism plus environment. We are learning by bitter experience that the organism that destroys its environment destroys itself.

Moving from individual coaching to team coaching will not be enough if all we do is move our individualistic self-centred thinking from the individual to the team or tribal level and compete to be the highest performing team on the block. As Bateson indicates we need to recognize that both the unit of survival and the unit of high performance is the team in relationship to their environment, ecological niche, their systemic context. This is why in this book I have throughout argued for team coaching being as much if not more focused on the external relationships of the whole team as on the internal relationships between the team members; and more focused on the contribution of the team to the wider system than on the team feeling good about themselves.

As a species we have a parallel but bigger challenge. We have to move from just fighting for saving this species or that, to working with the preservation and development of living ecologies; from thinking of the environment as a thing, to seeing that it is a complex web of connections; from seeing it as 'other' to experiencing it as part of us, and ourselves as an inextricable part of the environment. This is not an easy task and will require collective effort. To constantly serve the individual and team clients as well as their organizations is not an easy task, and to be effective all coaches constantly need to be reflecting on their work and expanding their coaching capacity. This requires the ability to stand back from the presenting issues and see the repeating patterns in the wider system. This continual need for process reflection and systemic awareness means that all coaches should undertake regular personal and professional development including quality supervision from those who are specifically trained in supervising team coaching.

TABLE 13. 1

	Bateson's (1972) Statements	Antidotes
a)	It's us *against* the environment	We and what we call environment are inter-dependent
b)	It's us *against* other men	Win-lose always becomes lose-lose. We need to create win-win relationships
c)	It's the individual (or the individual company, or the individual nation) that matters	The unit of survival is organism plus environment. We are learning by bitter experience that the organism that destroys its environment destroys itself
d)	We *can* have unilateral control over the environment and must strive for that control	Nature was before, will be after and is greater than that small part of it that is human beings
e)	We live in an infinitely expanding 'frontier'	There are limits to growth
f)	Economic determinism is common sense	90% of what is most important cannot be measured by economics. Money as the measure of all things actually serves to impoverish us all
g)	Technology will do it for us	Technology, on its own, will merely accentuate our own ability to destroy ourselves and our environment. You cannot solve a problem from within the thinking that created it

An agenda for moving forward

My hope is that in the next few years we will see the following:

- The best from organizational development, organizational consultancy and coaching being brought together to create a new and vibrant synthesis in team coaching.
- The development of a clearer language and generally accepted definitions on the complete continuum of team coaching activities, to enable client organizations and teams to better contract and re-contract the help they need.

- Organizations developing more effective coaching strategies that integrate all their different coaching endeavours, including team coaching, and align them to create a sustainable coaching culture, both within the organization and at its interfaces with its stakeholders, as outlined in Hawkins (2011).

- Professional coaching organizations beginning to accredit systemic team coaches and clarifying further the competencies and capacities needed to be effective and how to assess these.

- The further development of specific team coaching programmes that help individual coaches or organizational consultants develop the necessary re-education to work with all five disciplines of team coaching and become team coaching master practitioners.

- More evidence-based research on the practice and benefits of team coaching. The research on team performance is some way ahead of the research on how team coaching can most benefit a shift in team performance. This research needs to be linked to research on global best practice in leadership development as team coaching has an increasing role to play in providing leadership development able to help create the collective leadership necessary for tomorrow's challenges.

- More international exchange of practice, models, research and learning in this field, that bring together those with backgrounds in coaching, consultancy working with sports teams, leading teams, leadership learning and development and academics who teach and research these fields.

My hope is that this book has made a contribution to building the foundations of this important new craft and discipline, that many others will be able to build on.

GLOSSARY

account team   A multidisciplinary and/or a multi-regional team brought together from across a company to focus on the relationship with one key customer or client organization.

action learning   'Action learning couples the development of people in work organizations with action on their difficult problems ... (it) makes the task the vehicle for learning and has three main components – *people*, who accept the responsibility for action on a particular task or issue; *problems*, or the tasks which are acted on; and the *set* of six or so colleagues who meet regularly to support and challenge each other to take action and to learn' (Pedler, 1997).

appreciative inquiry   'Appreciative Inquiry seeks out the very best of "what is" to help ignite the imagination of "what might be". The aim is to generate new knowledge which expands "the realm of the possible" and helps the partners of an organization envision a collectively desired future and then to carry forth that vision in ways which successfully translate intention into reality' (Cooperrider and Srivastva, 1987).

coaching supervision   'The process by which a coach, with the help of a supervisor, can attend to understanding better both the client system and themselves as part of the client-coach system, and by so doing transform their work and develop their craft' (Hawkins and Smith, 2006). Supervision does this by also attending to transforming the relationship between the supervisor and coach and the relationship with the wider contexts in which the work is happening.

group coaching   Coaching of individuals carried out in a group setting, utilizing the resources of the rest of the group to support the coaching.

high-performing team   'A small number of people with complementary skills who are committed to a common purpose, set of performance goals, and approach for which they hold themselves collectively accountable. The common approach needs to include ways of effectively meeting and communicating that raise morale and alignment, effectively engaging with all the team's key stakeholder groups and ways that individuals and the team can continually learn and develop' (Chapter 2).

international team   'A group of people who come from different nationalities and work interdependently towards a common goal' (Canney Davison and Ward, 1999: 11).

leadership team coaching   Team coaching for any team, not just the most senior, where the focus is on how the teams give leadership to those who report to them and also how the team influences their key stakeholder groups.

learning team   A group of people with a common purpose who take active responsibility for developing each other, themselves, their team and the wider organization in which they operate, through both action learning and unlearning.

project team   A team, with members often drawn from different teams, brought together for a specific, defined and time-limited task.

systemic team coaching   A process by which a team coach works with a whole team, both when they are together and when they are apart, to help them improve their collective performance and how they work together, and also how they develop their collective leadership to more effectively engage with all their key stakeholder groups to jointly transform the wider business.

team building   Any process used to help a team in the early stages of team development.

team development   Any process carried out by a team, with or without assistance from outside, to develop their capability and capacity to work well together.

team facilitation   A process where a specific person (or persons) is asked to facilitate the team by managing the process for them so they are freed up to focus on the task.

team process consultancy   A form of team facilitation where the team consultant sits alongside the team carrying out their meetings or planning sessions and provides reflection and review on 'how' the team is going about its task.

transformational leadership team coaching   Where any team taking leadership at whatever level focuses on how they want to run their business and how they will transform their business.

virtual team   'A virtual team, like every team, is a group of people who interact through interdependent tasks guided by a common purpose. Unlike conventional teams, a virtual team works across space, time, cultures and organizational boundaries with links strengthened by webs of communication technologies' (Lipnack and Stamps, 1996).

RECOMMENDED READING

The literature and research on team coaching is still very thin, but for those wishing to read the best of what is available elsewhere, here is a short list of key texts.

Team coaching

Clutterbuck, D (2007) *Coaching the Team at Work,* London: Nicholas Brealey

Clutterbuck, D (2010) Team coaching, ch. 19 in (eds) E Cox, T Bachkirova and D Clutterbuck, *The Complete Handbook of Coaching,* London: Sage

Hackman, J R and Wageman, R (2005) A Theory of Team Coaching, *Academy of Management Review,* **30** (2), 269–87

Hawkins, P and Smith, N (2006) *Coaching, Mentoring and Organizational Consultancy: Supervision and development* (see in particular ch. 4), Maidenhead: Open University Press/McGraw Hill

Thornton, C (2010) *Group and Team Coaching,* Hove, East Sussex: Routledge

Research on teams

Hackman, J R (2002) *Leading Teams,* Harvard, MA: Harvard Business School Press

Katzenbach, J and Smith, D (1993) *The Wisdom of Teams. Creating the high-performance organization,* Harvard, MA: Harvard Business School Press

Wageman, R, Nunes, D A, Burruss, J A and Hackman, J R (2008) *Senior Leadership Teams,* Harvard, MA: Harvard Business School Press

Coaching strategy

Hawkins, P (2011) *Coaching Strategy in Organizations,* Maidenhead: Open University Press/McGraw Hill

General

Lencioni, P (2002) *The Five Dysfunctions of a Team. A leadership fable,* San Francisco, CA: Jossey-Bass

Senge, P, Jaworski, J, Scharmer, C and Flowers, B (2005) *Presence: Exploring profound change in people, organizations and society,* New York: Random House

RESOURCES FOR FINDING TEAM COACHES AND TEAM COACH TRAINING

Here is a short guide to the other sources of information about team coaching that you may find useful in developing your skills and experience.

As things are changing so rapidly, we offer basic details about the orientations and approach of each rather than evaluating them, which we leave to the cautious buyer.

Professional organizations

The following are organizations that have a contribution to make to the field and may provide readers with membership benefits:

Association for Coaching (**www.associationforcoaching.com**) sees itself as promoting excellence and ethics in coaching. It has individual, corporate and provider organization members. It has a code of ethics and good practice and a complaints procedure, and offers qualified members accreditation.

Association for Professional Executive Coaching & Supervision – APECS (**www.apecs.org**) is the top-level professional body for fully-qualified executive coaches and executive coaching supervisors. It is currently exploring accrediting team coaches.

Chartered Institute of Personnel and Development (**www.cipd.co.uk**) CIPD's commercial arm, CIPD Enterprises, offers a (200 learning hours) largely e-delivered Certificate in Coaching and Mentoring (Vocational Qualification level 3) which leads to Associate Membership of CIPD. It organizes an annual one-day coaching conference and it also carries out research and publishes in the field of coaching.

European Mentoring and Coaching Council (**www.emccouncil.org**) arose out of the European Mentoring Centre that was founded in 1992. It exists to promote good practice in mentoring and coaching across Europe. The EMCC is a unifying and inclusive body covering a wide spectrum of organizations from the voluntary and community, professional training and development, counselling at work, life coaching and academic psychology sectors. A key focus of EMCC is to develop European standards, ethics and a professional code with a view to assuring quality in the industry. By 2004 it had developed and applied a widely agreed code of ethics in coaching and mentoring and guidelines on supervision, a diversity policy and a complaints procedure. EMCC promotes the adoption of quality standards. It has established an electronic professional and academic journal, *The International Journal for Mentoring and Coaching,* and holds a major conference each year.

Institute of Business Consultancy (www.ibconsulting.org.uk) is the professional body for management consultants. It sets, maintains and raises the standards of professionalism and competence for the profession.

International Coach Federation (www.coachfederation.org) describes itself as the professional association of personal and business coaches that seeks to preserve the integrity of coaching around the globe. It is an international United States-based individual membership organization with more than 14,000 members. It has developed a code of ethics and of professional standards, offers a coach referral service and has a system for accrediting members. It holds an annual international conference.

Management Consultancies Association (www.mca.org.uk) The MCA was formed in 1956 to represent the consultancy industry to its clients, the media and government. Today the members represent around 70 per cent of the UK consulting sector.

Special Group in Coaching Psychology (www.sgcp.org.uk) was established to provide psychologists with a means of sharing research as well as practical experiences that relate to the psychology of coaching. SGCP was formed as a result of lobbying by the Coaching Psychology Forum (CPF). The SGCP is committed to fostering excellence in coaching practice through research, events, publications, discussion and professional development.

The Worshipful Company of Management Consultants (www.wcomc.org.uk) The Livery Company offers consultants membership and networks, a lecture series and seminar programme.

Team coaching training

Academy of Executive Coaching (www.academyofexecutivecoaching.com) along with **Bath Consultancy Group (www.bathconsultancygroup.com)** offers a one-year diploma in systemic team coaching.

Henley Business School
(**www.henley.com**) provides courses in team coaching and facilitation.

Oxford Brookes University (**www.brookes.ac.uk**) offers an optional module as part of its Masters in Coaching.

Team coaching supervision

Bath Consultancy Group (**www.bathconsultancygroup.com**) offers the Certificate in Supervision of Coaches, Mentors & Consultants. This training programme, run jointly with the Centre for Supervision & Team Development (CSTD), is aimed at experienced coaches, mentors and consultants and is taught by experts in this field. It consists of two three-day courses, an initial foundation course that is followed by the advanced course and two additional modules from the CSTD (**www.cstd.co.uk**). This includes a specialized three-day module on supervising work with teams and organizations.

Agencies that specialize in providing team coaching

Academy of Executive Coaching
(**www.academyofexecutivecoaching.com**).

Bath Consultancy Group (**www.bathconsultancygroup.com**) has provided top team coaching and board development internationally since 1986.

Clutterbuck Associates (**www.clutterbuckassociates.co.uk**) provides team coaching and board development.

Praesta (**www.praesta.co.uk**) provides team coaching and board development in many countries.

BIBLIOGRAPHY

Adair, J (1986) *Effective Teambuilding: How to make a winning team*, Gower Publishing Ltd

Ancona, D, Bresman, H and Kaeufer, K (2002) The comparative advantage of X teams, *MIT Sloane Management Review*, **43** (3), pp33–39

Argenti, J (1976) *Corporate Collapse: Causes and symptoms*, New York: McGraw Hill

Argyris, C (1993) *Knowledge in Action*, San Francisco, CA: Jossey-Bass

Argyris, C and Schön, D (1978) *Organizational Learning*, Reading MA: Addison-Wesley

Ashby, W R (1956) *Introduction to Cybernetics*, London: Wiley

Bateson, G (1972) *Steps to an Ecology of Mind*, New York: Ballantine Books

Beck, D and Cowan, C (1996) *Spiral Dynamics: Mastering values, leadership and change*, Oxford: Blackwell Business

Beckhard, R and Harris, R (1977) *Organizational Transitions: Managing complex change*, Reading, MA: Addison-Wesley

Belbin, M (2004) *Management Teams: Why they succeed or fail*, London: Heinemann

Bennis, W (1997) *Organizing Genius: The secrets of successful collaboration*. New York: Perseus Books Group

Berglas, S (2002) The very real dangers of executive coaching, *Harvard Business Review*, June, pp86–92

Beyerlein, M, Nemiro, J and Beyerlein, S (2008) *The Handbook of Virtual High Performing Teams: How to collaborate across boundaries*, San Francisco, CA: John Wiley

Binney, G, Wilke, G and Williams, C (2005) *Living Leadership: A practical guide for ordinary heroes*, London: Prentice Hall

Bion, W R (1961) *Experiences in Groups*, London: Tavistock

Block, P (1981; 2nd edn 2000) *Flawless Consulting: A guide to getting your expertise used*, New York: John Wiley

Bloisi, W, Cook, C W and Hunsaker, P L (2003) *Management and Organisational Behaviour*, Maidenhead: McGraw-Hill Education

Broussine, M (1998) *The Society of Local Authority Chief Executives and Senior Managers (SOLACE): A Scheme for Continuous Learning for SOLACE Members*, Bristol: University of the West of England

Burke, W (2002) *Organization Change: Theory and practice*, London: Sage Publications

Cadbury Committee, The (1992) *The Financial Aspects of Corporate Governance*, London: Gee and Co

Campbell, D and Huffington, C (2008) *Organisations Connected: A handbook of systemic consultation, systemic thinking and practice: work with organizations*, London: Karnac Books

Canney Davison, S and Ward, K (1999) *Leading International Teams*, Maidenhead: McGraw-Hill

Carroll, M (1996) *Counselling Supervision: Theory, skills and practice*, London: Cassells

Casey, D (1985) When is a team not a team?, *Personnel Management*, **9**, pp26–29

Caulat, G (2006) *Creating Trust and Intimacy in the Virtual World*, Ashridge Business School, www.ashridge.org.uk

Caulat, G (2006) Virtual leadership, *The Ashridge Journal*, 360, Autumn, pp6–11

Caulat, G and de Haan, E (2006), Virtual peer consultation: how virtual leaders learn, *Organisations & People*, November, **13** (4), pp24–32

Charkham, J (1994) *Keeping Good Company: A study of corporate governance in five countries*, Oxford: Oxford University Press

Clarkson, P (1995) *Change in Organisations*, London: Whurr Publishers

Clutterbuck, D (2007) *Coaching the Team at Work*, London: Nicholas Brealey

Clutterbuck, D (2010) Team Coaching, Chapter 19 in (eds) E Cox, T Bachkirova and D Clutterbuck, *The Complete Handbook of Coaching*, London: Sage

Clutterbuck, D and Megginson, D (2005) *Making Coaching Work: Creating a coaching culture*, London: CIPD

Collins, J (2001) *Good to Great*, London: Random House

Collins, J C (1999) Turning goals into results: the power of catalytic mechanisms, *Harvard Business Review*, July–August, pp71–82

Conference Board, The (1994) *Corporate Boards: Improving and evaluating performance*, New York: The Conference Board

Cooperrider, D and Srivastva, S (1987) Appreciative inquiry in organizational life, in (eds) Woodman and Passmore, *Research in Organizational Change and Development, Vol 1*, JAI Press, Greenwich, CT

Coulson-Thomas, C (1993) *Creating Excellence in the Boardroom*, Maidenhead: McGraw-Hill

Downey, M (2003) *Effective Coaching: Lessons from the coach's coach*, New York: Thomson, Texere

Dunne, P (1997) *Running Board Meetings*, London: Kogan Page

Dyer, W G (1977) *Team Building: Issues and alternatives*, Reading, MA: Addison-Wesley

Dyer, W G, Dyer, W Jr and Dyer, J H (2007) *Team Building. Proven strategies for improving team performance*, San Francisco, CA: Jossey-Bass

Dyke, G (2004) *Greg Dyke: Inside story*, London: HarperCollins

Edmondson, A, Bohmer, R and Pisano, G (2001) Speeding up team learning, *Harvard Business Review*, October, Reprint R0109, pp125–34

Eleftheriadou, Z (1994) *Transcultural Counselling*, London: Central Book Publishing

Gallwey, W T (1974) *The Inner Game of Tennis*, New York: Random House

Gallwey, W T (1976) *Inner Tennis: Playing the game*, New York: Random House

Gallwey, W T (1981) *The Inner Game of Golf*, New York: Random House

Gallwey, W T (1985) *Inner Game of Winning*, Listen USA, audio published, Riverside, CT

Gallwey, W T and Kriegel, R J (1977) *Inner Skiing*, New York: Random HouseGarratt, B (1987) *The Learning Organisation*, London: Fontana/Collins

Garratt, B (1995) *The Fish Rots from the Head: The crisis in our boardrooms*, London: HarperCollins Business

Garratt, B (2003) *Thin on Top*, London: Nicholas Brealey

Gersick, C J G (1988) Time and transition in work teams: towards a new model of group development, *Academy of Management Journal*, **31**: pp9–41

Golembiewski, R T (1976) *Learning and Change in Groups*, London: Penguin

Goodwin, D K (2005) *Team of Rivals: The political genius of Abraham Lincoln*, New York: Simon and Schuster

Gratton, L and Erickson, T J (2007) Eight ways to build collaborative teams, *Harvard Business Review* (online version: **http://hbrorg/2007/11/eight-ways-to-build-collaborative-teams/ar/pr, 05/02/2008**)

Greenbury, R (1995) *Director's Remuneration: A report of a study group*, London: Gee Publishing

Gregersen, H, Morrison, A and Black, S (1998) Developing leaders for the global frontier, *Sloan Management Review*, **40** (1), pp22–32

Hackman, J R (2002) *Leading Teams*, Harvard, MA: Harvard Business Press

Hackman, J R and Wageman, R (2005) A theory of team coaching, *Academy of Management Review*, **30** (2), pp269–87

Hammond, S and Royal, C (eds) (1998) *Lessons from the Field: Applying appreciative inquiry*, Plano, TX: Thin Books Publishing

Hargrove, R (2003) *Masterful Coaching*, San Francisco, CA: Jossey-Bass/Pfeiffer

Hawkins P (1986) Living the learning, PhD thesis, University of Bath Management School

Hawkins, P (1991) The spiritual dimension of the learning organisation, *Management Education and Development*, **22** (3) pp172–87

Hawkins, P (1993) *Shadow Consultancy*, Bath Consultancy Group working paper

Hawkins, P (1994) The changing view of learning, in (ed.) J Burgoyne, *Towards the Learning Company*, London: McGraw-Hill

Hawkins, P (1995) *Double-loop Strategic Decision Making*, Bath Consultancy Group working paper

Hawkins, P (1998) *Systemic Shadow Consultancy*, Bath Consultancy Group working paper

Hawkins, P (1999) Organisational unlearning, Keynote address at the Learning Company Conference, University of Warwick

Hawkins, P (2004) Gregory Bateson: his contribution to Action Research and Organisation Development, *The Journal of Action Research*, **2** (4), pp409–23

Hawkins, P (2005) *The Wise Fool's Guide to Leadership*, Winchester: O Books

Hawkins, P (2008) The coaching profession: key challenges, *Coaching*, **1** (1) pp28–38

Hawkins, P (2010) Coaching supervision, in (eds) E Cox, T Bachkirova and D Clutterbuck, *The Complete Handbook of Coaching*, London: Sage

Hawkins, P (2011) *Coaching Strategy: Creating a coaching culture*, Maidenhead: McGraw Hill/Open University Press

Hawkins, P and Schwenk, G (2006) *Coaching Supervision, CIPD Change Agenda*, London: CIPD

Hawkins, P and Schwenk, G (2010) The interpersonal relationship in the training and supervision of coaches, in (eds) S Palmer and A McDowell, *The Coaching Relationship: Putting people first*, Routledge: London

Hawkins, P and Shohet, R (1989, 2000, 2006) *Supervision in the Helping Professions*, Milton Keynes: Open University Press

Hawkins, P and Smith, N (2006) *Coaching, Mentoring and Organizational Consultancy: Supervision and development*, Maidenhead: Open University Press/ McGraw Hill

Hawkins, P and Smith, N (2010) Transformational coaching, in (eds) E Cox, T Bachkirova and D Clutterbuck, *The Complete Handbook of Coaching*, London: Sage

Hedberg, B (1981) How organizations learn and unlearn, in (eds) P Nystrom and W Starbuck, *Handbook of Organizational Design, Vol 1: Adapting organizations to their environments* (pp 3–27) Oxford: Oxford University Press

Helminski, K (1999) *The Knowing Heart*, Boston, MA: Shambhala

Hersey, P and Blanchard, K H (1977) *Management of Organizational Behavior: Utilizing human resources*, 3rd edn, Englewood Cliffs, NJ: Prentice-Hall

Holbeche, L (2005) *The High Performance Organization*, Oxford: Elsevier Butterworth-Heinemann

Holloway, E L and Carroll, M (eds) (1999) *Training Counselling Supervisors*, London: Sage

Honey, P and Mumford, A (1992) *The Manual of Learning Styles*, London: Peter Honey Publications

Hooper, R A and Potter, J R (2000) *Intelligent Leadership: Creating a passion for change*, London: Random House

Huffington, C (2008) The system in the room: the extent to which coaching can change the organization, in (eds) D Campbell and C Huffington, *Organisations Connected: A handbook of systemic consultation, systemic thinking and practice: work with organizations*, London: Karnac Books

Hunter, D, Bailey, A and Taylor, B (1996) *The Foundation of Groups*, Aldershot: Gower

Institute of Directors (1990) *Development of and for the Board*, London: IoD

Institute of Directors (1995) *Standards for the Board*, London: IoD

Jarvis, J (2004) *Coaching and Buying Coaching Services?*, London: CIPD

Katzenbach, J and Smith, D (1993a) The discipline of teams, *Harvard Business Review*, March/April, pp111–20

Katzenbach, J and Smith, D (1993b) *The Wisdom of Teams: Creating the high-performance organization*, Harvard, MA: Harvard Business School Press

Kempster, S (2009) *How Managers Have Learnt to Lead*, Basingstoke: Palgrave Macmillan:

Kets de Vries, M F R (2005) Leadership group coaching in action: The Zen of creating high performance teams, *Academy of Management Executive*, **19** (1), pp61–76

Kets de Vries, M F R (2006) *The Leader on the Couch: A clinical approach to changing people and organizations*, San Francisco, CA: Jossey-Bass

Kopp, S (1988) *If You Meet the Buddha on the Road, Kill Him*, New York: Bantam Books

Lencioni, P (2002) *The Five Dysfunctions of a Team. A leadership fable*, San Francisco, CA: Jossey-Bass

Lencioni, P (2004) *Death by Meeting. A leadership fable*, San Francisco, CA: Jossey-Bass

Lencioni, P (2005) *Overcoming the Five Dysfunctions of a Team. A field guide*, San Francisco, CA: Jossey-Bass

Lencioni, P (2006) *Silos, Politics and Turf Wars. A leadership fable*, San Francisco, CA: Jossey-Bass

Likert, R (1967) *The Human Organization*, New York: McGraw-Hill

Lipnack, J and Stamps, J (1996) *Virtual Teams: People working across boundaries with technology*, New York: John Wiley & Sons

Lojeski, K S, Lipnack, J and Ellis, J (2009) Boosting productivity through virtual collaboration, (Powerpoint slides reproduced by *Business Week*), Webcast

Lorsch, J W and MacIver, E (1989) *Pawns and Potentates: The realities of America's corporate boards,* Harvard, MA: Harvard Business School Press

Majchrzak, A, Malhotra, A, Stamps, J and Lipnack, J (2004) Can absence make a team grow stronger?, *Harvard Business Review,* May, pp131–37

March, J G and Olsen, J P (1976) *Ambiguity and Choice in Organizations,* Bergen Norway: Universitetsforlaget

McGregor, D (1960) *The Human Side of the Enterprise,* New York: McGraw-Hill

Megginson, D and Clutterbuck, D (2005) *Techniques for Coaching and Mentoring,* Oxford: Elsevier Butterworth-Heinemann

Meier, D (2005) *Team Coaching with the Solutioncircle: A practical guide to solutions focused team development,* Cheltenham: Solution Books

Meyer, C (1994) How the right measures help teams excel, *Harvard Business Review,* May–June, pp95–103

National Health Services Institute (2005) Lean 6 Sigma, Presentation to Lean Conference, Orlando, Florida

Obolensky, N (2010) *Complex Adaptive Leadership: Embracing paradox and uncertainty,* Aldershot: Gower

Okri, B (1997) *A Way of Being Free,* London: Phoenix House

O'Neill, M B (2000) *Executive Coaching with Backbone and Heart: A systems approach to engaging leaders with their challenges,* San Francisco, CA: Jossey-Bass Wiley

Oshry, B (1995) *Seeing Systems: Unlocking the mysteries of organizational life,* San Francisco, CA: Berrett-Koehler

Oshry, B (1999) *Leading Systems: Lessons from the power lab,* San Francisco, CA: Berrett-Koehler

Oshry, B (2007) *Seeing Systems: Unlocking the mysteries of organizational life,* 2nd edn, San Francisco, CA: Berrett-Koehler

Paige, H (2002) Examining the effect of executive coaching on executives, *International Education Journal,* **3** (2), pp61–70

Pedler, M (1996) *Action Learning for Managers,* London: Lemos & Crane

Pedler, M (1997) What do we mean by action learning?, in (ed.) M Pedler, *Action Learning in Practice,* Aldershot: Gower

Pedler, M, Burgoyne, J and Boydell, T (1991) *The Learning Company: A strategy for sustainable development,* London: McGraw-Hill

Pettigrew, A and McNulty, T (1995) Power and influence in and around the boardroom, *Human Relations,* **48** (8), pp845–73

Rogers, C (1967) *On Becoming a Person,* London: Constable and Company

RSA (1995) *Tomorrow's Company,* London: RSA

Ryde, J (2009) *Being White in the Helping Professions,* London: Jessica Kingsley

Sadler, P (2002) *Building Tomorrow's Company,* London: Kogan Page

Scharma, C O (2007) *Theory U: Leading from the future as it emerges. The social technology of presencing,* Cambridge, Mass: Society for Organisational Learning

Schein, E H (1969; 2nd edn 1988) *Process Consultation: Its role in organisational development,* London: Wesley

Schein, E H (1985) *Organizational Culture and Leadership,* San Francisco, CA: Jossey-Bass

Schein, E H (2003) On dialogue, culture, and organisational learning, *Reflections,* **4** (4), pp27–38

Schutz, W C (1973) *Elements of Encounter,* Big Sur, CA: Joy Press

Senge, P (1990) *The Fifth Discipline: The art and practice of the learning organization,* New York: Doubleday

Senge, P and Kofman, F (1993) *Communities of Commissions: The heart of learning organizations,* Organizational Dynamics (Autumn), pp5–23

Senge, P (2008) *The Necessary Revolution: How individuals and organizations are working together to create a sustainable world,* New York: Doubleday

Senge, P, Jaworski, J, Scharmer, C and Flowers, B (2005) *Presence: Exploring profound change in people, organizations and society,* New York: Doubleday

Senge, P, Kleiner, A, Ross, R, Roberts, C and Smith, B (1994) *The Fifth Discipline Fieldbook: Strategies and tools for building a learning organization,* New York: Doubleday

Surowiecki, J (2005) *The Wisdom of Crowds: Why the many are smarter than the few,* London: Abacus

Swords, D (2010) Leading Growth in, (eds) D Swords, C Bones and P Hawkins, *New World, New Organisations, New Leadership,* Henley: Henley Business School

Thomas, K W and Kilmann, R H (1974) *Conflict Mode Instrument,* California: Kilmann Diagnostics

Thornton, C (2010) *Group and Team Coaching,* Hove: Routledge

Tichy, N M and Devanna, M A (1986) *The Transformational Leader,* New York: John Wiley

Tricker, R I (1980) *Corporate Governance,* Aldershot: Gower

Tuckman, B (1965) Developmental sequence in small groups, *Psychological Bulletin,* **63** (6), pp384–99

Tyler, F B, Brome, D R and Williams, J E (1991) *Ethnic Validity, Ecology and Psychotherapy: A psychosocial competence model,* New York: Plenum Press

Wageman, R (2001) How Leaders Foster Self-Managing Team Effectiveness, *Organization Science,* September–October, **12** (5), pp559–77

Wageman, R, Nunes, D A, Burruss, J A and Hackman, J R (2008) *Senior Leadership Teams,* Harvard, MA: Harvard Business School Press

Ward, G (2008) Towards executive change: a psychodynamic group coaching model for short executive programs, *International Journal of Evidence Based Coaching and Mentoring,* **6** (1), pp67–78

Weinberg, R and McDermott, M (2002) A comparative analysis of sport and business organizations: factors perceived critical for organizational success, *Journal of Applied Sports Psychology,* 14, pp282–98

Whitmore, J (2002) *Coaching for Performance: Growing people, performance and purpose,* London: Nicholas Brealey

Womack, J P and Jones, D T (2003) *Lean Thinking: Banish waste and create wealth in your corporation,* London: Simon and Schuster

INDEX

NB: page numbers in *italic* indicate figures or tables

360-degree organizational feedback methods
144, 195,
descriptor analysis 134, 194–96, *196*

Academy of Executive Coaching 173, 207
account transformation model (and)
117–19, *118*
integrated trust/trusted adviser 117–18
performance partner 117–18, 119
solution supplier 117–18
strategic adviser 117–18
Adair, J 24, 48
Ancona, D 106
Argyris, C 35, 37, 48, 99

Bateson, G 99, 209–10
Bath Consultancy Group 24, 60, 91, 142,
189
website: www.bathconsultancygroup.
com 69
Beck, D 186
Beckhard, R 48
Belbin, M 24, 48
and Apollo syndrome/group 187
Belbin team role
and cultural differences 90
preferences 18
Bennis, W 8
Binney, G 87
Bion, W R 55
Bion study groups 48
Blair, T 9
Blanchard, K H 186
Block, P 56
board, the 121–37 (and) *see also* corporate
governance
clarifying the role of (disciplines 1 and 2)
124–32
director competencies 135–36
conceptual 135
personal 136
political 135–36
dynamics of (discipline 3) 124, 132–33

and record of potential conflicts of
interest 132–33
functions of 126–29, *127*
accountabilities/external
accountabilities 128–29
policy formulation 127, 128
strategic thinking 127, 128
supervising management 127, 128
growing challenges for 122
how it connects (discipline 4) 124,
133–35
using organizational feedback
methods 134
how it learns and develops (discipline 5)
135–37
individual board director development
for 135–36
stages in coaching relationship
(CID-CLEAR model) 123
structure of *see* board structure
board structure 129–32
advisory boards 131
board committees 131–32
executive board 130
non-executive board 130
two-tier/'senate' boards 130–31
unitary board 131
Boydell, 49
Broussine, M 155
Building Tomorrow's Company 10
Burgoyne, 49
Burke, W 48

Cable and Wireless 111
Cadbury Report (UK) on corporate
governance 124
Canney Davison, S 213
capabilities 156–57 *see also* capacities
systemic 157
capacities 157–66
encourages, motivates and carries
appropriate optimism 162–63
ethical maturity 164–65

humour and humility 165–66
relationship engagement 162, *163*
self-awareness 158, *159*
self-ease 158
staying in partnership zone 158
taking appropriate leadership (with)
    159–62, *161*
    authority 160–61
    impact 162
    presence 161–62
working across difference – transcultural
    engagement 163–64
Capespan (Outspan/Unifruco) 86–87, 89,
    133
Carroll, M 114, 115, 164
challenge for leadership teams 9–14
    increased capacity for working through
        systemic conflict 11
    in the interconnections/levels of
        relationships 13–14
    learning to live with multiple
        memberships and belonging
        11–12
    managing expectations of stakeholders
        10
    more complex and interconnected world
        12
    running and transforming the business in
        parallel 10–11
    virtual working 12–13
CID-CLEAR relationship process 67–82,
    199, 203 *see also* models
    action 78–80
        and six 'P' model 79
        three-way sort exercise for 78–80
    and CLEAR way of structuring an
        individual event 81
    and contracting outcomes/ways of
        working with whole team
        (contracting 2) 72–76
    boundaries/confidentiality 74–75
    contract with wider organization 76
    ethics 75
    practicalities 74
    working alliance 75–76
    diagnosis and design 70, 72, *71, 72*
    exploration and experimentation 77–
    initial exploratory discussions
        (contracting 1) 68
    inquiry 68–70
    listening 76–77, *78*
    review 80
    and team leader as team coach 81–82
Clarkson, P 70, 72
Clutterbuck, D 57–58, 60, 95, 104, 114

*Coaching, Mentoring and Organizational
    Consultancy: Supervision and
    Development* 58
coaching the board 121–37 *see also* board, the
coaching the five disciplines *see* systemic
    team coaching, five disciplines of
Coca-Cola 50
Collins, J 35, 98
compassion, fearless 160
confidentiality 74–75
Connolly, C 50
contracting inquiry and diagnosis (CID) 82
    look earlier
Cooperrider, D 197, 213
corporate governance *see also* board, the
    and the Cadbury Report (UK) 124
    and dilemmas for directors (Institute of
        Directors, UK) 125
Coulson-Thomas, C 121
Cowan, C 186

Darwin, C 210
Davison, C 112 Ward 112
Davos World Economic Forum (2008) 19
definition(s) of
    capabilities 155
    capacities 155
    effective team 24–25
    functions of team coaching 57
    international team 112
    learning team (Clutterbuck) 95
    organizational culture 118
    process consultation 56
    supervision 170
    systemic team coaching 60–61, 84
    team coaching 57–58
    team role (Belbin) 187
    unlearning (Hedberg) 97
    virtual teams 111
    a vision (Senge) 87–88
Devanna, M A 27
developing as team coach (and) 151–68
    core capabilities for 155–66
        capacities 157–66 *see also main entry*
        competences and capabilities 156
        systemic capabilities 157
    necessary demeanour *(adab)* for 154–55
    team coach dilemmas 166–68 *see also*
        main entry
    transition 152–53
        from individual coaching 152–53
        from organizational consultancy 153
discipline(s) *see also* board, the; coaching
    the five disciplines *and* five disciplines
    of successful team practice

clarifying (discipline 2) 36, 38–40, 77, 124–32
co-creating (discipline 3) 36–37, 39–41, 135–37
commissioning (discipline 1) 35, 38–39, 41, 77, 124–32
connecting (discipline 4) 37, 39–41, 24, 133–35
core learning (discipline 5) 37, 42–43, 132–33
Downey, M 50
Dyer, W G 24, 48

Edmondson, A 95
Einstein, A 9
Eleftheriadou, Z 115
emotional quotients (EQs) 17
ethics 75
and ethical dilemmas 164–65
exploring team dynamics/functioning, experiential methods for 196–202 *see also* models
appreciative inquiry (AI) – four Ds model 196–99
delivery 198–99
design/dialogue 198
discovery 197
dreaming 197–98
picture sculpts 201–02
individual metaphors 202
individual representations 202
inter-team dynamic 201–02
metaphorical progression 201
solution-focused team coaching 199–200
team sculpting 200–201

figures
account team transformation model *118*
action learning cycle *97*
authority, presence and impact *161*
coaching project teams *107*
continuum of team coaching *58*
descriptor analysis process *196*
elements of the mission *88*
five disciplines of high-performing teams *36*
five disciplines of team coaching with questionnaire scores *194*
five dysfunctions of a team *71*
four levels of engagement *78, 159*
four quadrants of systemic team coaching *85*
functions of the board *127*
learning cycle short circuits *97*
relationship engagement capacity *163*

scoring the four quadrants of systemic team coaching *85*
the team performance curve *27*
team presenting issues *72*
seven-eyed model of supervision *179, 180*
Financial Times 126
finding, selecting and working with a good team coach 141–49
and current stage of team coaching 142
seven-stage approach to 142–49
contracting 146–47
developing the relationship/regular reviews 147
ending and beyond 147–48
evaluation 147, *148*
finding suitable candidates 145
selecting coach 145–46
specifying/defining team need 143–44
and specification for team by defining 143–44
current state of team 143
specification for team coach 144
success criteria for team 143–44
Fish Rots from the Head 125
Fitzgerald, N 126
five disciplines of successful team practice 33–44, *36*, 149, 203 *see also* models
clarifying 36
co-creating 36–37
commissioning 35
connecting 37
connecting the disciplines 38–44
co-creating with stakeholders 40–41
commission-mission dialogue 38–39
policy into practice dialogue 39–40
stakeholder-commissioning body dialogue 41
core learning 37
connecting to the other disciplines 42–43
and role-playing stakeholders 34–35
and team mission 39
Freud, S 176

Gallwey, W T 50
Garratt, B 37, 39, 125, 126, 127
Gersick, C J G 55, 107
Goodwin, D K 9
Gregerson, H 113

Hackman, J R 55, 57, 60, 106, 107
Hammond, S 198
Harris, R 48
Hawken, P 8, 9

Hawkins, P 14, 16, 17, 19, 31, 37, 49, 51,
    57, 58, 60, 52, 67, 76, 79, 92, 93, 98,
    99, 114, 117, 154, 155, 157, 158,
    159, 162, 165, 166, 167, 169, 170,
    171, 172, 175, 178, 181, 189, 212 *see
    also* models
    and law of either-or 91
Hedberg, B 97
Henley Management College 48
Hersey, P 186
high-performing leadership teams 7–19
    and challenge to leadership development
        and coaching industry 16–19
    changing challenge for 9–14 *see also*
        challenge for leadership teams
    conditions for wisdom of 15–16
        aggregation 15
        decentralization 15
        diversity of opinion 15
        independence 15
    readiness of response of 14–16
high-performing teams (and) 21–31
    definitions of 24, 26
    effective 24–26, 27
        dimensions for 24
        ten aspects of 24–26
    inquiry questions for 22
    need for 22–23, 23
    transformational leadership teams 27–31
        see also main entry
Holloway, E L 114, 115
Honey, P 96
Hooper, R A 10
Huffington, C 202
Hussein, Z 114

Institute of Directors (UK) 125
intelligence quotients (IQs) 17
Iraq Inquiry (UK) 9

Jarvis, J 170
Jones, D T 108
Joyce, J L 173, 207
Jung, C 185

Karp, M 154
Katzenbach, J 21, 23, 24, 26, 27, 29, 38–39,
    55, 153, 165, 189
Kets de Vries, M 54, 111, 186
Kilmann, R H 186
Kopp, S 167
Kriegel, R J 50

leadership, collective 60–61
leadership development best practice (and)

behaviourally transformative
    development 17
involvement of real stakeholder
    perspectives 17
real time 17
relational development 17
unlearning 17
leadership style inventories 186–87
    Conflict Styles Inventory 186
    'Global Executive Leadership Inventory'
        186
    Situational Leadership 186
lean thinking (and) 108–09
    continuous improvement 108, 109
    respect for people 108, 109
learning
    action 96, 97
    core 95–98 *see also* limited learning styles
    double-loop 99
    and unlearning 17, 97–98
    zero 99
Lencioni, P 21, 33, 70, 71, 89, 92, 95
Lewin, 48
Likert, R 24, 48
limited learning styles 96–97, 97
    fire-fighting/compulsive pragmatist 96
    naval-gazing 96
    paralysis by analysis 97
    post-mortemizing 96
    totalitarian 97
Lincoln, A 9
Lipnack, J 12–13, 111

McDermott, M 50
McGregor, D 24, 48
March, J G 98
Maslow, A 183
Megginson, D 114
Meier, D 199
methodologies
    business process engineering 108
    lean manufacturing 108
    lean thinking 108–09
    Six Sigma 108
    total quality management 108
Michels, R 51
    and 'total football' 51
models
    account transformation 117–19, 118 *see
        also* account transformation model
    appreciative inquiry (AI) – four Ds model
        196–99
    CID-CLEAR 67, 81, 123, 149, 156, 199,
        203 *see also* CID-CLEAR
        relationship process

CLEAR 67, 78, 182
five disciplines 33–44, 69, 83–99, 149,
    189, *190–92, 193, 194,* 203
individual coaching 67
Lencioni's 92
organization mission 87, *88*
seven-eyed supervision 178–80, 182,
    179, 180
six 'Ps' – purpose, principles, parameters,
    programme, people, process 79
supervision 67
Moreno, J 176, 200
moving forward, agenda for 211–12
multiple double-loops of engagement in
    high-performing teams 40–41
Mumford, A 96
Myers-Briggs Typology Inventory (MBTI)
    184–86
and personality types 18, 69, 185–86
profiles 90

Nasrudin story 141, 147
National Health Service Institute (UK) 109
National Training Laboratories (US) 48
need for high-performing leadership teams
    see high-performing leadership teams
Nestlé 50
Nooyi, I 19 (President of PepsiCo)

Obama, B 9
Olsen, J P 98
Orange 50
organizational development 47
    and team development 47 *see also* team
        development stages
Organizational Learning, Society for 27
Oshry, B 12, 18, 94, 95

Parlett, M 158
Parsifal trap, overcoming the 208–11
    agenda for moving forward 211–12
    beliefs and antidotes 209–10, *211*
Pedler, M 49, 96, 213
PepsiCo 19
personality type inventories
    Myers-Briggs Typology Inventory
        (MBTI) 184–86
    Personality Audit (Manfred Kets de
        Vries) 186
    Spiral Dynamics (Beck and Cowan) 186
Potter, J R 10
project teams, phases of 106–10, *107 see
    also* lean thinking
    emergence: re-engaging 106, 109
    ending 106, 110

engaging 106, 107–08
exploitation 106, 110
exploration 106, 108–09
exportation 106, 110
psychometric instruments 184–89
    Belbin Team Role Analysis 187–88
        and nine team roles 187–88
    leadership engagement capacity 188–89
    leadership styles inventories 186–87 *see
        also main entry*
    Myers-Briggs Typology Inventory
        (MBTI) 184–86 *see also main
        entry*

questionnaires 69–70, *71, 72*
    Belgin team role analysis 69
    five disciplines self-scoring 69
    High Performing Team Questionnaire
        (Bath Consultancy Group) 69
    team 360-degree feedback 69
    team MBTI personality type 69
    what sort of team are you? 69

research (on/into)
    best practice in leadership development
        17
    effective learning of new procedures by
        surgical teams (Edmondson)
        95–96
    high-performing teams 189
    high-performing transformational
        leadership teams (Wageman *et al*)
        28–31, *29*
    performance of teams and Apollo
        syndrome/group 187
    team coaching 189
Reuters 126
Revans, R 96
Rogers, C 167
Royal, C 198
Royal Society of Arts, Manufacture and
    Commerce project: 'tomorrow's
    company' 133
Ryde, J 152, 164

Sadler, P 10
Scharma, C O 154
Schein, E H 48, 56, 153
Schön, D 35, 37, 48, 99
Schutz, W C 54, *55*
Schwenk, G 170
Senge, P 15, 18, 49, 87, 154, 162
seven-eyed supervision model 178–80, *179,
    180*
    coach 179–80

coach's interventions 179
coachee's system 179
relationship between coach and coachee 179
supervisor self-reflection 180
supervisory relationship 180
wider context 180
Shoher, R 178
SMART 79
Smit, T 8, 9
Smith, C 111
Smith, D 21, 23, 24, 26, 27, 29, 38–39, 55, 153, 165, 189
Smith, N 14, 16, 51, 57, 58, 60, 67, 76, 79, 91, 92, 114, 117, 154, 155, 157, 158, 159, 165, 166, 167, 170, 171, 172, 175, 178, 181
solution-focused team coaching 199–200
Sporting Bodymind 50
Srivastva, S 197, 213
Stamps, J 111
studies/surveys (on/of)
Fortune 500 companies in US on global leaders/global working (Gregerson) 113
qualities needed by effective global leader 114, *115*
supervising team coaching (and) 169–82
defining supervision 170–71
different contexts for 171–73
reflections on the six-step process 178–82, *179, 180*
seven-eyed supervision model 178–80, *179 see also* models and *main entry*
six-step team coaching supervision model 173–78
1: contracting 173
2: setting the scene 174
3: exploring the dynamics 174
4: clarification and decision 174
5: developing shift in team and team coach 175
6: review 175
example of 177–78
and variations on the process 175
team sculpting 176–77
three elements of supervision 170
Surowiecki, J 15
Swords, D 122
Syer, J 50
systemic team coaching, five disciplines of 83–99, *85*
and coaching the interconnections 98–99
see also learning

clarifying 87–89, *88*
and co-missioning 89
purpose, strategy, core values, vision 87–88, *88*
co-creation 89–93
areas of support to team meetings 90
away-day to explore team functioning 90–93 *see also* team functioning
and feedback 93
commissioning and re-commissioning 86–87
connecting 93–95
and organization splitting issues 95
core learning 95–98, *97 see also* limited learning styles
tables
Bateson statements and antidotes *211*
effective global leaders and global consultants *115*
evaluation *148*
five disciplines questionnaire *190–92*
international teams, advantages and disadvantages of *113*
limiting mind-sets and responses *53*
questionnaires *71*
tools and methods for team coaching *204–06*
working groups and teams *23*
Tavistock Institute (UK) 48
team, specification for 143–44
current state of team 143
specification for team coach/questions for team 144
success criteria for team 143–44
team, types of *see* types of team
team bonding 18
team coach *see also* developing as a team coach *and* finding, selecting and working with a good team coach
dilemmas *see* team coach dilemmas
finding and selecting a 145
role of 66
specification for a 144
team leader as 81–82
team coach dilemmas 166–68
advantages/disadvantages of coaching team/team members 166
balance of non-directiveness and focus on team performance 167
dealing with problem team leader 166–67
disagreement with team on disciplines 167–68

lack of commitment of team members
168
team coaching 47–63, *62 see also* team
coaching process
defining 52–61 *see also* definition(s) of
group coaching of team members/
action learning sets 54
leadership team coaching 59
systemic team coaching 59–61
team building 55
team coaching 57–58, 58
team development stages 54–55 *see
also main entry*
team facilitation 56
team process 56–57
transformational leadership team
coaching 59
extending team coaching continuum 61
history of 48–52
limiting assumptions concerning 52, 53
solution-focused 199–200
the who of 61–63
team coaching process (and) 65–82
CID-CLEAR relationship process 67–80
see also main entry
CLEAR way of structuring an individual
event 81
fast forward rehearsal 79
role of team coach 66
team leader as team coach 81–82
team development stages 54–55 *see also*
Schutz *and* Tuckman
forming 54, 55
norming 54, 55
performing 55
storming 55
team dynamics *see* exploring team dynamics
and functioning, experiential methods
for
team functioning 90–93, 117
barriers to 91–92
deciding way forward 91
and dysfunctions 92
exploring deeper team dynamic 91
interpersonal relationships and
understanding difference 90
team culture 90
team performance functioning 90–91
team roles 187–88
technological ingenuity vs wisdom gap 19
Thin on Top 125
Thomas, K W 186
Thornton, C 183, 184
Tichy, N M 27
'tomorrow's company' project (UK) 133–35

tools and techniques for team coaching
methods 183–206
exploring team dynamics/functioning,
experiential methods for *see main
entry*
principles for using 183–84
psychometric instruments 184–89 *see
also main entry*
team appraisal questionnaires and
instruments 189–96
descriptor analysis 194–96, *196*
Five Disciplines Questionnaire 189,
193, *190–92, 194*
team 360-degree feedback 193
team culture review 202–03
and when/which to use 203–04, *204–06*
Toyota 7–8, 108–09
transformational leaders, characteristics of
27
transformational leadership teams (and)
27–31
conditions for effectiveness of 29–31
compelling direction 30
competent team coaching 30–31
research on 28–31, *29*
the right people 30
solid team structure 30
supportive organizational context 30
interdependency, boundedness and
stability 29
Tricker, B 126, 127
Tuckman, B 54, 55
Turquet, P 202
Tyler, F B quoted 114
types of team 103–20
client or customer account 116–20
and account transformation model
117–19, *118*
international 112–16, *113, 115*
and cross-cultural/transcultural work
115
culture awareness exercise for 116
management 104–05
and leadership 105
project 106–10, *107 see also* project
teams, phases of
virtual 111–12 *see also* virtual teams

Unilever 126

virtual teams 111–12
conditions for success of 111–12
definition of 111
signs of trouble in 112
virtual working, growth of 12–13

Wageman, R 23, 28, 29, 29, 47, 55, 57, 60, 62, 65, 106, 107, 142, 153, 189
Ward, K 213
Watanabe, K 7–8
Weinberg, R 50
Whitmore, J 50
Wisdom of Crowds, The 15
wisdom of crowds 88

wisdom of teams, conditions for 15–16
   aggregation 15
   decentralization 15
   diversity of opinion 15
   independence 15
Wise Fool's Guide to Leadership, The 141, 165
Womack, J P 108

Zneimer, J 50, 51

The sharpest minds need the finest advice.
Kogan Page creates success.

www.koganpage.com